# The Rule of Law in America

PUBLISHING FOR THE WORLD
125 Years
THE JOHNS HOPKINS UNIVERSITY PRESS

# The
# Rule
# *of* Law
## in America

*Ronald A. Cass*

The Johns Hopkins University Press

BALTIMORE AND LONDON

© 2001 The Johns Hopkins University Press
All rights reserved. Published 2001
Printed in the United States of America on acid-free paper

Johns Hopkins Paperbacks edition, 2003
2 4 6 8 9 7 5 3 1

The Johns Hopkins University Press
2715 North Charles Street
Baltimore, Maryland 21218-4363
www.press.jhu.edu

A catalog record for this book is available from the British Library.


*The Library of Congress has cataloged the hardcover edition of this book as follows:*

Cass, Ronald A.
    The rule of law in America / Ronald A. Cass.
        p.    cm.
    Includes bibliographical references and index.
    ISBN 0-8018-6728-2 (alk. paper)
    1. Rule of law—United States.   2. Judicial process—United States.
    3. Executive power—United States.   I. Title.
    KF382 .C37 2001
    340′.11—dc21
    00-012494


ISBN 0-8018-7441-6 (pbk.)

*For my parents*

# Contents

# Acknowledgments

I owe thanks to many people who have helped start, shape, and support this project. The first thanks goes to Claudio Veliz, who initially suggested this subject as one for a seminar presentation to students and interested onlookers. As always, Claudio had a good eye for an interesting topic, one that extends well beyond what I can compass in this short volume. I had been thinking for some time about the rule of law in general and its implementation in America in particular—subjects that were brought into focus when I accepted the deanship of Boston University School of Law while serving as Vice-Chairman of the United States International Trade Commission. In my role as a dean-to-be, I was a constant recipient of bad lawyer jokes. In my role as a U.S. official, I saw the widespread approbation of the United States as a nation that people around the world sought to emulate. The disconnect between the information received in those roles lay exactly at the point Claudio identified to begin discussion of the American Legal system.

If Claudio's invitation prompted harder thinking about the topic, Justice Stephen Breyer of the Supreme Court of the United States bears responsibility for my beginning to put that thinking on paper. Justice Breyer had agreed to be the commentator on my presentation at Claudio's seminar and, understandably, asked if he could see a copy of my paper before the presentation. Rather than replying, "What paper?" I began writing.

During the long writing and rewriting and editing process, I have received helpful comments and guidance from many quarters. Among the notable contributors to the final shape of this work are Larry Alexander, Hugh Baxter, Jack Beermann, Bob Bone, Stephen Breyer, Ward Farnsworth, Mary Ann Glendon, John Haring, Keith Hylton, Fred Lawrence, Sai Prakash, Glen Robinson, Stephen Williams, and participants in the University Professors Seminar at Boston University. Many of these friends and colleagues contributed insights that kept me from going off track. Many were incredibly generous with their time and energy. All were extremely kind and helpful. Bob Bone deserves special thanks for his willingness to read and reread drafts, to comment and correct, to help think through knotty problems, and in many respects to serve more as coauthor than as reader. Ward Farnsworth, too, merits extra thanks for aid that went well beyond what is reasonable to expect of friends and colleagues.

I also owe debts of gratitude to Marlene Alderman, Caroline Hayday, Alissa Kaplan, Russell Sweet, and Courtney Worcester for unflagging energy and copious research assistance, and to Boston University and the International Center for Economic Research for research support. Thanks are due as well to Greg Alexander, Randy Barnett, Michael Boudin, Kurt Leube, Carol McGeehan, Jeffrey O'Connell, and Fred Schauer, who offered encouragement and advice. I also am grateful to the editorial staff of the Johns Hopkins University Press for their efficiency and understanding in the editing process.

Two final sets of acknowledgments are in order. I am indebted for this project as for so many others to Deborah Bertok and Susan Michals, my administrative assistants who put up with a too-full schedule, who keep track of manuscripts, including this one, and who generally keep my professional life in order. And I am grateful to my family—Valerie, Laura, and Alex—for their patience and understanding, which I have tried often but have never managed to exhaust. The standard apologia apply.

# Introduction

*Particular laws, we know, may fail to protect the freedom enjoyed in our society, and may even be destructive of some of that freedom; but we know also that the rule of law is the single greatest condition of our freedom, removing from us that great fear which has overshadowed so many communities, the fear of the power of our own government.*
—*Michael Oakeshott*

*In visiting the Americans and studying their laws, we perceive that the authority they have entrusted to members of the legal profession, and the influence that these individuals exercise in the government, are the most powerful existing security against the excesses of democracy.*
—*Alexis de Tocqueville*

A few fundamental choices set the pattern for a society. Among the most basic of these choices is the commitment to be governed by the rule of law. The depth and sustainability of that commitment affect societal prospects for wealth, for freedom, and for many other goods.

In a fundamentally just society, the rule of law serves to channel decision making in attractive ways, to make decisions more predictable, and to increase the prospects for fair administration of public power. In a society that lacks fundamental requisites of justice, the rule of law plays a more ambiguous role. Even there, it seems generally beneficial, as its tendency to limit official discretion is at odds with the most common sources of injustice.

The centrality of the rule of law to society was thrown into sharp relief at the end of the twentieth century. In the last dozen years of the century, a remarkable development—unthinkable only a few years before—took place as the organization of governments around the globe changed radically. As old regimes toppled, people almost universally proclaimed their desire for the freedom and prosperity they associate with governments operating under the rule of law. This was not a casual or incidental association in their eyes, the people of each newly democratic nation explained. The primary goal for a new government was not to achieve the lifestyle of Western nations, not to match their military might or their economic stability—although each of those figured among the benefits of governmental change. No, the most commonly invoked explanation was the people's ambition to attain the rule of law.

## America's Legal Rule

For most of the world, the prototype for that ambition—the nation most immediately associated with the rule of law—is the United States of America. The story of America, as Tocqueville observed more than a century and a half ago, is uniquely the story of law.[1]

The men who crafted the constitutional framework for the United States sought to design a system in which the legal order serves public interests, at once protecting individual freedom and promoting a stable polity. They saw law as an indispensable pillar of a well-functioning society and used law to channel human instincts in ways they hoped would achieve those ends. They saw constraining discretionary power of government officers—the central focus of the rule of law—as essential to the society they hoped to create. Thus, from America's founding, the legal order, and particularly the aspect known as the rule of law, has been considered central to our national self-definition.

That remains true today. Virtually any public argument features an appeal to the rule of law—should America support a world criminal court? should we demand changes to the World Trade Organization's mandate?—pundits and politicians, street demonstrators and academic theorists disagree over the answers but agree that the answer depends on what action best fits the rule of law.

Perhaps the most public examples of American appeal to the rule of law can be found in the discourse attending the impeachment of President William Clinton as the sands ran out on the twentieth century and the election of his successor, the first president of the twenty-first century. Americans who would impeach and remove a president from office styled their case as one compelled by fidelity to the rule of law.[2] The rule of law, they said, means that no one—not even the president—is above the law; others have been removed from office for crimes similar to the president's; the president should not be

judged by different rules. The president's supporters in opposing those arguments also claimed the mantle of the rule of law.[3] The rule of law, they said,
means that procedures and standards announced well beforehand must control decisions, and the efforts to remove President Clinton in their view did
not meet that test.

Both sides were confident that appeal to "the rule of law" associated them
with a concept that is both attractive and fundamental to all of our public proceedings—Americans of all political leanings would see this as an admirable
aspect of our history and of our government, and they would see it as relevant
to the decision at hand.[4] Discussion of the Clinton impeachment gave elo-
quent testimony that, whatever "the rule of law" means, it is good to have it
on your side.

So, too, following the closest presidential vote in more than one hundred
years, arguments over Florida's vote count routinely invoked the rule of law.
Democrats and Republicans alike claimed that the rules they favored were the
ones consistent with respect for the rule of law.[5] Both sides appealed to the
importance of established legal authority to the rule of law. Both sides declared
that the rule of law (not the correlation of one outcome to some other attractive norm) should determine who became our forty-third president.

The point is not merely that Americans respond to that rhetorical flour-
ish. Our affinity for legality extends well beyond sympathetic response to appeals to the rule of law. Americans turn to the legal order for guidance more
often than any other people on the planet and exhibit extraordinary faith in
our basic legal structures. That is why both presidential aspirants were prepared
to accept courts as the ultimate arbiters of matters crucial to their ambitions.
Complain as they might when decisions went against them, both candidates
credited the courts' legitimacy and bowed to their command. The politicians'
compliance reflected broad public deference to the legal decision makers. Our
Constitution has become a secular "Bible" to the American people. Law is the
touchstone for resolving the major issues of public life. Judges and lawyers
have become the priests and acolytes of our secular religious order—the order
of a constitution-based, law-based society.

It is an order that has worked well, certainly relative to other governance
systems, as far as we can judge from the results. America at the start of the
twenty-first century enjoys the highest standard of living among the world's
major nations along with an extraordinary level of personal freedom; has main-

tained stable, popularly supported governance for more than two centuries; and begins the century as the world's dominant power.[6]

## Paradox Laws: System under Fire

Paradoxically, Americans' cynicism about our legal system has increased sharply over the past decade or so, just as other nations have moved toward what our legal system represents to them.[7] Writing by American legal scholars reflects much of the cynicism visible in popular commentary, though the source of the cynicism and the solutions preferred by critics differ.[8] For most critics, however, the dismay over our legal system today links closely to concerns about the rule of law. Some critics who might not champion the rule of law expressly nonetheless discuss America's legal system in terms that look very much like complaints that it is incompatible with the rule of law.[9] Many more critics of our legal system directly assert that its failings are departures from the rule of law.[10]

How is this possible? How can a legal and political system so closely associated with the rule of law generate such widespread criticism for departing from the rule of law? Any attempt to solve this paradox quickly confronts the fact that what is meant by "the rule of law"—and, even more, what is desired by its advocates—varies greatly.[11] Most people understand intuitively that the concept is linked to limitations on the power of governments and of individual government officials, but views differ as to the contours of those limitations and the purposes they serve.

A particular problem is presented in understanding the limitations a rule of law imposes on judges. Of course judges should be limited by law; but just what does (should) that mean? And how is that limitation to be effected, consistent with the rule of law? Normative differences aside (easier said than done), views diverge sharply on the positive question, the degree to which judges are in fact constrained by law.[12]

Identifying what is wrong with our legal system and how it should be fixed requires understanding both of the normative goals to be pursued and of facts respecting the legal system's operation. Although there is disagreement on both counts, a focus on the rule of law and the American legal system's congruence with that concept is instructive—for what it says about America's legal system, for what it cannot say, and for what it suggests are fruitful avenues for legal scholarship.

## Organization

This book explores the place of the rule of law in America's legal system. Four questions are central to this inquiry: What is the rule of law? Why does it matter? How well does America conform to the rule of law? and What explains Americans' complaints about our legal system? These questions will be of immediate interest to Americans, but they should also engage others interested in the rule of law.

Chapter 1 begins this exploration by examining the meaning of the rule of law and its relation to democratic-representative government. Chapter 2 examines American implementation of the rule of law. It looks both at the general evidence of American commitment to the rule of law and at the ways in which the American system of governance promotes the rule of law. That chapter also adumbrates some concerns about American conformity to the rule of law.

Chapter 3 reviews the application of the rule of law in America in one particular context: application of legal strictures to the president of the United States. The cases discussed demonstrate strong American commitment to the precept that all government officials are subject to constraints enforced through the legal system. But this review also raises a question: the *degree* to which officials are constrained by law, specifically looking at the officials who have primacy within the legal system.

Chapters 4 and 5 turn to this problematic question. Chapter 4 begins by examining two alternative descriptions of American judging. One description supposes that judges generally operate as if they are subject to law's externally imposed constraints (the Agency Model). The other—the preferred model within the academy during the last quarter-century, especially among those who focus expressly on legal theory—supposes judges to be less rule-bound than rule-making. This description sees judges having sufficient discretion to defy a presumption of law's binding effects on judges (the Partnership Model).

The choice between these two models is critical. If the second model accurately describes judicial decision making, then the criticism of America's legal system has an obvious explanation: we have, indeed, strayed from the rule of law. But that is not the case. Continuing the inquiry begun in chapter 4, chapter 5 explains that American judges function largely in ways analogous to the work of translators. This description implies considerable limitation on judges' actions, despite the absence of substantial direct control over their decisions. American judging, then, does not fit the model of *fully* rule-bound judging (the Strong Agency Model) set forth as one polar model in chapter 4. But judging nonetheless *is* primarily a rule-constrained activity (best described by the Weak Agency Model). A fair view of American judging places it closer to the Agency pole than to the Partnership end of the descriptive spectrum.

The lesson of chapters 4 and 5 is that, though not fully governed by rule-of-law forces, American judging *does* predominantly fit the requisites of the rule of law. Leading legal scholars often miss this lesson, largely because they focus almost exclusively on a very narrow and peculiar set of judicial decisions. Those decisions come in cases that should be seen as comprising the tiny tip of an extraordinarily large pyramid—a tip composed of the cases least similar to the great bulk of cases below, least subject to rule-of-law constraints, and most closely bound up with considerations intensely debated in the political realm. This is the primary, but not the sole, reason that the most influential writings on judicial behavior in recent years have tended strongly toward the Partnership pole. There is another reason: beyond their focus on the pathological, scholars often are animated by their normative disagreement with prevailing legal rules. Looking at the ordinary case—and asking not whether the decision advances particular aspirations for society but whether it conforms to basic aspects of legal authority—produces a more law-governed view of American judging.

Given the congruence of the American legal system with rule-of-law values, Americans' expressed dissatisfaction with our legal system seems curious. It should not be. Chapter 6, which addresses possible explanations for such dissatisfaction, considers aspects of the American system that derogate from the rule-of-law ideal or from other concepts of a well-functioning system and notes changes in the system over time that may contribute to current criticisms. There is definite basis for concern that changes over time have weakened the rule of law in America. By and large, however, the criticisms that have the most force do not suggest a system ignoring the rule of law. Indeed, some of the most serious problems derive from *adherence* to the rule of law in a setting where the law that rules has gone awry.

The conclusion offers the view that some complaints about the American legal system are serious and that we should attend to them. In the main, these are not complaints about the *absence* of real constraints in our legal system but about the *nature* of the constraints. Changing the nature of these constraints depends primarily on political action—which is the source of the major problems, a clear signal that providing a reasoned explanation of what changes should be made leaves us a long way from actually making those changes. Aside from practical impediments to their implementation, identifying desirable changes is no mean feat (even if there is consensus on the goal against which "desirable" change will be assessed).

But it is the right task. Academic energies could be spent better by engaging the means of addressing serious complaints about our legal system than by emphasizing ways in which the system departs from perfectly constrained decision making. Complaints about our legal system's failure to constrain officials with the rule of law are part of the standard fare for academicians, whose brief largely is to critique inconsistencies in the law; but those complaints are too often overstated while more serious defects engage academic interests too seldom.

# CHAPTER ONE

# The Rule of Law

## Constraining Officials' Power

*Of all the dreams that drive men and women into the streets, from Buenos Aires to Budapest, the "rule of law" is the most puzzling. We have a pretty good idea what we mean by "free markets" and "democratic elections." But legality and the "rule of law" are ideals that present themselves as opaque even to legal philosophers.* —George Fletcher

The rule of law is an ancient concept, dating at least from Plato and Aristotle.[1] Its meaning has been the subject of innumerable scholarly discussions by great thinkers from that day to our own. But "the rule of law" still means very different things to different people.

At one extreme, a starkly positivist conception of the rule of law encompasses the notion of control to whatever extent and by whatever means the state chooses so long as certain formal requisites of laws' enactment and application are met.[2] It is a conception of *law-boundedness* irrespective of the ends served by the law.[3]

Critics of this conception at times refer to it as the *rechtsstaat* conception of the rule of law or as a conception not of the rule of law but of mere legality.[4] A principal objection to this conception is that because (in its polar form) it imposes no requirements concerning the substantive ends of state power, it could describe law-bound totalitarian regimes as well as more limited, benign governments as conforming to the rule of law.[5] Despite this possible construction, many of the most vigorous advocates of individual liberty and limited government favor positivist conceptions of the rule of law.[6]

At another extreme are conceptions of the rule of law that would make the concept synonymous with *justice*. These conceptions see the widespread appeal of the rule of law as dependent on the morality of the laws that rule.[7] Moral rule-of-law conceptions are criticized on two grounds. They conflate the rule of law—rightly understood as merely one component of justice— with other components; and in order to avoid the risk of allowing totalitarian power to fit within the rule of law, they run the greater risk of authorizing a despotism of judges.[8]

Moral rule-of-law conceptions are favored by many scholars whose predicate values seem quite distant from those of scholars in the positivist rule-of-law camp: moral rule-of-law advocates often take a more favorable view of government than positivists do, though even moralists who endorse broad government powers strongly object to specific uses of public power.[9] This general division among advocates of the different rule-of-law conceptions, however, does not explain very much; some scholars whose predicate values lie closest to those of the most avid positivists also embrace conceptions of the rule of law much nearer to the moralists' vision.[10]

In between the extreme views are numerous particular conceptions of the rule of law differing in the ends the concept serves and the requisites imposed in the concept's name. These various conceptions see the rule of law advancing goals of stability,[11] freedom,[12] efficiency,[13] utility,[14] formal justice,[15] and substantive morality,[16] and assign to the rule of law properties that conduce more or less directly to those ends. Given this array of disparate views, it is not surprising to find scholars declaring that the concept of the rule of law is opaque.

## Core Meaning: A Government of Laws

Despite the number and variety of these specific conceptions, the rule of law is not an entirely empty vessel into which any desired meaning can be poured. There is at least an understood core to the concept. The classic conception of the rule of law is captured in the now-familiar language found in David Hume's *Essays* and in the 1780 Constitution of Massachusetts, written by John Adams, both declaring the aspiration to "a government of laws and not of men."[17] That is the phrase invoked over and over to describe the rule of law, among philosophers, legal scholars, politicians, and ordinary citizens.[18]

It is a phrase that resonates with people in widely scattered lands and over long spans of time.[19] This is where we begin.

The essence of the Hume-Adams opposition of "government of laws" to "government of men"—the core conception of the rule of law—is that something other than the mere will of the individuals deputized to exercise government powers must have primacy. The reason for that is both obvious and subtle.

The obvious point is that freedom from control by the will of others is an enduring human value. Of itself, this is the basis for strong support given to the rule of law by Friedrich Hayek, Michael Oakeshott, and others who assign freedom paramount value.[20]

Something less obvious must be at work, however, because laws are inevitably produced by men (giving that word its old-fashioned, ungendered meaning); laws, no less than the commands of individual government officials, allow the wills of some people to control the fortunes of others.[21] Some quality of the law—of its source, its content, or both—must be present to explain why the commands of law are set apart from, and given primacy over, the will of governors.[22] As explained below, even a conception of the rule of law that is relatively parsimonious—sticking close by the core marked out by Hume and Adams—must impose some requirements on both the source and content of law.

One more thought also is implicit in the Hume-Adams formula: that laws *can* govern, that they *can* control "men" (people). It would be fatuous to suggest that we can distinguish a government of laws from a government of men unless laws can constrain. After all, we will not do away with human beings; they will still be occupying positions of power; they will still be the means of carrying on government's functions. Absent action *by* laws *on* humans (on men, in Hume's and Adams's terms), apart from the mere will of those who purport to act for the government, there can be no such thing as a government of laws.[23]

## Elements of the Rule of Law

The phrase handed down from Hume and Adams has broad appeal because it suggests values central to nearly all conceptions of a well-functioning government. More is needed, however, to flesh out the rule-of-law conception associated with their formulation.

It is easier to examine that conception of the rule of law by considering its four constitutive elements. These elements are (1) fidelity to rules (2) of principled predictability (3) embodied in valid authority (4) that is external to individual government decision makers. These elements are common to many conceptions of the rule of law, positivist and moralist alike, though different scholars give different divisions to the component parts or add further requirements.[24]

### 1. Fidelity to Rules

The first element states the central thesis of the classic conception of the rule of law: in a government of laws, not of men, individuals—including individuals exercising governmental power—must obey laws. This is the sine qua non of the rule of law: government power limited not by opposing force but by legal rules. The rules represent choices among potential courses of action; they embody certain values. The rules tell officials how, to what ends, and within what limits they may exercise power of the sort that is the government's peculiar domain in an ordered society: power backed by threat of force. And the officials must conform their behavior to the rules. When they do not, they act in derogation of the values expressed in those rules. Obvious as this requirement is, it is easier to state it in the abstract than to give it more concrete meaning. And even the abstract statement becomes problematic to a degree—we need to clarify what is meant by fidelity and by rules.

*Fidelity.* *Fidelity* is a term that might strike nonlawyers as odd. It suggests *faithfulness* rather than *obedience*.[25] Surely, as stated above, if we are to have a government of laws, laws must rule and men must obey the laws. That is true, but it also is somewhat misleading. *Obedience* presupposes laws that are both clear and directive—that they command or prohibit specific behavior. Many laws are of this nature, but many are not. Laws that are less clear or less directive, however, also have binding authority—at least they have that authority up to the point at which we cannot understand them as providing the sort of principled predictability required by the rule of law.[26] On this score Professors Lon Fuller and Ronald Dworkin are right to disparage H. L. A. Hart's distinction between a central core of directive, determinate law and the surrounding penumbra in which decision makers have discretion, as it were, outside the law.[27]

The requirement of fidelity is one mandating systemic allegiance to all laws, giving both more and less clear, more and less directive laws binding effect. This formulation is necessarily vague because the nature and degree of law's binding cannot be characterized in a meaningful way independent of the particular, authoritative instruction. Argument over these qualities—over the exact sort of binding effects laws have or should have—is endemic to discussion of legal systems.[28] That argument recurs throughout this book.[29] What can be said at the outset is simply that, as the term *fidelity* connotes, adherence to law—not merely a token acquiescence to legal forms, but faithful adherence to a sincere understanding of what law instructs—is vital to the rule of law.

*Rules.* Rendering the first requirement as fidelity to *rules* as opposed to the broader term *law* brings us back a shade—but only a shade—toward the meaning associated with *obedience*. The term *rules* is used here to suggest that law's instructions, to merit fidelity, must be given in a form that does instruct, even if not in so plainly directive a way as to make clear in all cases what would constitute obedience.

The use of this terminology is not, however, intended to limit the form of instructions to one particular type. Confusion over that point is possible in light of the linguistic distinctions often drawn in scholarly discourse. Scholars frequently distinguish *rules* from *standards* and from *principles* as separate forms of instruction to decision makers.[30]

Here is a more or less (and, for reasons that follow shortly, the truth is *less*) accepted distinction among these categories.[31] *Rules* are canonical (given by higher authority) and generally conclusive instructions (if they apply, they are decisive); an example is "No liquor sales on Sundays."[32] *Standards* are instructions that on their face require judgment in application; for instance, "A manufacturer is liable for injury caused by products that are unreasonably dangerous when used in a reasonably foreseeable manner." Note that this standard also can be a rule as defined for this purpose; it can be both canonical and conclusive—*if* a product is found unreasonably dangerous, and so forth, *then* the manufacturer must be deemed liable—even though the standard is not susceptible of mechanical application. When distinguished from standards, rules are commonly described as not requiring a similar degree of judgment in their application.[33]

*Principles* are considerations that, although relevant to a decision, are not visible on the face of an authoritative, conclusive instruction. Consider, for example, the claim, "The constitutional guarantee of freedom of speech should, in light of the structure of the Constitution, be understood to protect only speech integral to the political process." This claim has been made by First Amendment theorists,[34] but the First Amendment to the U.S. Constitution *says* nothing about politically important speech, referring only to "the freedom of speech." What makes this proposed political-speech construction a principle is its *inference* from sources of guidance to decision makers, rather than its *statement* in instructions to them. This example should not be viewed as exhausting the sources from which principles are derived; they may be deemed to inhere in a rule or may be drawn from other sources.

Unfortunately, these distinctions are not helpful to most analysis. The distinctions between rules and standards or between rules and principles—at least along the dimensions normally marked out as constituting the important differences—are not sustainable across an array of cases.[35] That is why so many well-respected scholars use the terms in inconsistent ways.[36] Even if it is useful at times to differentiate among instructions by reference to the characteristics of specificity, conclusiveness, and authoritativeness commonly associated with rules, attention to these linguistic divisions should generally be put to one side in considering the operation of the rule of law.[37] The roles played by these characteristics in a legal system will command attention in any event. They will affect the degree to which legal rules will have the quality of principled predictability (the rule-of-law element discussed next) and the degree to which the rules can induce fidelity. But these characteristics will not produce the effects we are concerned with in a way that can be specified axiomatically.

For that reason, casting the first element of the rule of law as fidelity to "rules" is not designed to specify a single mode of authoritative legal instruction. Fidelity to *rules* does not mean fidelity only to narrowly drawn, canonically inscribed, conclusive instructions, even though those instructions may be *most* conducive to rule-of-law values in many circumstances. But the use of the term does connote a quality that should be associated with the law for the rule of law to operate. It should be sufficiently clear and sufficiently directive to provide meaningful instruction.[38] That is the sole limitation associated with the term *rules* in this element.

## 2. Rules of Principled Predictability

The second element associated with the Hume-Adams conception of the rule of law is that legal rules have the quality of principled predictability. This element picks up from the notion of fidelity to rules. Many scholars and jurists have emphasized that legal rules should be predictable.[39] But to have a government of laws, not of men, the laws must of themselves provide the keys to their effectuation. That requires both a degree and a type of predictability.

Professor Hayek, for example, declares that the rule of law "means that government in all its actions is bound by rules fixed and announced beforehand—rules which make it possible to foresee with fair certainty how the authority will use its coercive powers in given circumstances and to plan one's individual affairs on the basis of this knowledge."[40] Hayek's statement makes a stronger claim for the degree of predictability than most other rule-of-law theorists, but his statement is instructive in two respects. His linkage of content, process, and effect as joint venturers in creating the rule of law—the rules, the timing of their adoption and mode of imposition, and the ability of individuals to predict their implementation—accurately reflects the classic conception. Hayek's demand that the rules themselves play the central role in enabling those affected by rules to predict their deployment also is faithful to the classic conception of the rule of law.

*Rule-Based Predictability.* The type of predictability required by this conception is associated first of all with rules that carry with them a particular sort of guidance about their meaning.[41] It is not enough that the rules announce a mechanism for their application. That limited requirement—which is all that would be imposed by a conception of mere legality—could be met by specifically conferring authority for decision at the will of an official, even if the decision turns on caprice. Imagine, for example, a rule declaring that in property disputes, judgment will be rendered for whichever party the judge deems most attractive or a tax law that allows the individual auditor virtually unlimited scope to set each taxpayer's assessment based on the auditor's feelings about that taxpayer. If any system can be legally established and yet be classified as a "government of men" rather than a "government of laws," this surely is it.

*Clarity.* The rule of law requires that legal rules instruct those affected by them in a way that allows a knowledgeable party to anticipate the manner in which a rule will be applied without knowing particulars about the individuals who will interpret and enforce the law.[42] This means that the legal rules are sufficiently clear to be understood.

That is true not just for a single rule but for the *set* of potentially applicable legal rules. It is not enough that Rule *A* gives a clear indication what legal rights and duties attach in particular circumstances if Rule *B* also applies in those circumstances but with different results. A legal system's rules can meet the test for principled predictability in such settings only when there is a Rule *C* that provides guidance for resolving conflicts among other rules—and that gives a reasonably clear directive which rule (*A* or *B*) has priority.

*Accessibility.* The requirement of principled predictability also implies that, insofar as a legal rule is directed to particular individuals, it is reasonably accessible to those persons.[43] Both facets of principled predictability—clarity and accessibility—increase the odds that citizens subject to a rule will be able to minimize the costs of rule compliance; if you can predict how the rule will work, you can anticipate and (within limits) moderate its impact.[44]

*Reasonableness and Cost.* The connection between principled predictability and the cost of rule compliance explains why neither the clarity nor the accessibility component is framed in a more didactic fashion. Both clarity and accessibility come at a cost. Try making any complex rule clear and you find that out in a hurry. Casual perusal of the U.S. Code of Federal Regulations will persuade almost anyone that the authors of federal regulations do not speak English, that they have the intelligence of plankton, or that they specifically intend to write incomprehensibly. Yet diligent efforts by other officials and expert consultants to put federal regulations into "plain English" have made little progress and often have misstated the applicable rule in the process.

For the same reasons that other rules attempting to specify the right amount of costly goods so often incorporate balancing tests and escape hatches, clarity and accessibility cannot be absolute requirements of the rule of law. How much we as a society want to invest in clarity and accessibility must depend on the cost associated with less clear or less accessible rules in a given context. The less predictable a legal rule is from the ordinary expectations of those subject to it and the greater the penalty for failure to comply with the rule's commands, the higher the requisites for clarity and accessibility must be set to assure the principled predictability necessary to the rule of law.

*Generality.* Requirements of generality (that each rule cover a sufficiently large class of cases not to be tailored to individual cases) and of neutrality (that each rule reflect principles that are transferable to other settings) often are attached to the rule of law and would fit a requirement of principled predictability.[45] Rules that are general and rest on neutral principles are less likely to reflect judgments of specific individuals about other specific individuals, and for that reason the requirements of generality and neutrality advance the prospect for a government of laws, not of men. Neither requirement, however, is quite so unequivocal as typically conceived.

Take generality first. A rule that says "John Jones must pay half his annual income to the government" looks more like the rule of men (notably, of men who do not particularly like Mr. Jones) than a rule that says "Individuals with annual incomes in excess of $10 million will be taxed on their income for that year at the rate of 50 percent." At least that is so if there are many people in the same fortunate position as Mr. Jones.[46]

That said, there may be good reasons for a rule that effectively treats one or a few individuals as a separate class.[47] Imagine that in 1970 you are asked to write rules governing long-distance telephone service in the United States. At that time, the American Telephone & Telegraph Company (AT&T) had a virtual monopoly in the long-distance market.[48] Any rule plainly would be, for all intents and purposes, a rule for AT&T.

In this setting there would still be a virtue to a rule written in general language, even if it applied only to AT&T. The same rule would cover others if and when market conditions changed, providing some assurance that the rule reflected considerations apart from officials' personal views of that one firm. This would be an especially modest virtue unless there were a strong likelihood of additional firms entering this market and also some constraint on the frequency with which the general rule could be changed. Indeed, in this market, as additional firms entered and became significant competitors to AT&T, the rules *were* changed, and separate rules were adopted for the competitors and for AT&T.[49] It is not easy to fashion constraints on the amendment of rules that are at once meaningful (effective) and desirable, and the less durable the conditions that inform a rule's adoption, the more difficult it is to fashion appropriate constraints.[50]

*Neutrality.* The limited assistance gained from a requirement of generality provides the primary reason for a requirement of neutrality. If the generality requirement cannot be imposed effectively by requiring that the rule itself must be framed in generic terms, a requirement that the rule be supported by neutral principles could supply the missing ingredient. It may be proper to have a rule that applies only to AT&T or only to John Jones, but we cannot draw that conclusion without knowing *why* a rule should apply only to that firm or that person. If the rule rests on a principle that is applied to other people in other contexts—a rate-setting principle that applies not only to telecommunications but also to power generation and to other regulated utilities or a taxation principle, such as the principle of progressivity, applied in a transparent (or at least translucent) way across taxpayers—we can have a fair degree of confidence that the rule represents more than the personal reaction of the individual decision makers to the particular objects of decision. That is the argument powerfully advanced by Professor Herbert Wechsler.[51]

Neutrality is a more widely applicable criterion than generality, and it is an important guideline for decision makers,[52] but it also is a notoriously slippery guide.[53] Anywhere this requirement is necessary, there will surely be difficulty sorting through the competing principles that might govern. In such settings, identifying the right neutral principles is likely to be considerably more difficult than framing a tolerably good rule. This point lies at the heart of claims that law is quintessentially a *pragmatic* discipline.[54] Ultimately, the additional requisites of generality and neutrality must be seen as part of the rule of law so far as necessary to limit official power from the sort of rule manipulation that would move toward a government by individual will—but only that far.

*Fuller's Approach.* The attributes of principled predictability identified above are the other side of several items on Lon Fuller's list of eight ways in which a legal system could fail. His list includes five possible failures that, turned around, point to considerations that influence the extent to which the system is composed of rules that have the principled predictability required for the rule of law. Though Hayek and Fuller disagree on many points about the rule of law, Fuller's list is in the same spirit as Hayek's call for rules of "fair cer-

tainty" to be "fixed and announced beforehand." Thus, Fuller lists as contra-
dictions to the rule of law: "(2) a failure to publicize, or at least make available
to the affected party, the rules he is expected to observe; (3) the abuse of retroactive legislation . . . ; (4) a failure to make rules understandable; (5) the enactment of contradictory rules or . . . (7) introducing such frequent changes in
the rules that the subject cannot orient his actions by them."[55]

Even more than Hayek's statement, Fuller's list emphasizes that the fair certainty fixed in the rules depends on the rules themselves and also on circumstances surrounding their adoption and application. Fuller frames the point as
part of the reciprocal understanding between governors and governed: the governed have a duty to obey the law, and those who govern have a duty to provide laws of a sort that can be obeyed.[56] But laws cannot be obeyed unless their
terms can be understood by those who must obey. For Fuller, governors should
aspire to a legal system that produces the reciprocity that is more than mere
avoidance of his modes of failure; even though we should not expect governors to satisfy those aspirations—to implement the rule of law fully—they
should behave in ways that approach this end.[57]

*"Principled."* As with the requirement of fidelity to rules, a caveat on language
is necessary to prevent confusion. Despite the distinctions often drawn between "principles" and "rules," the word *principled* in the term *principled predictability* is not meant to specify a single form of reasoned guidance for legal
instructions. The requirement of "principled predictability" insists not on the
form of instruction but only that the instructions to which fidelity is given
within the legal system—whether they give small *or* large scope for reasoned
interpretation and whatever their source—guide decision making in ways
meaningfully inferred from the instructions.[58]

*"Predictability."* Just as the word *principled* should not be read to narrow the
ambit of covered instructions too sharply, the word *predictability* should not be
stretched too far. It should not be taken to command a caricatured certainty—
*perfect* predictability cannot be the test for the rule of law.[59] The goal for rules
of *principled* predictability is predictability that is adequate to allow individuals
to plan their lives, but for reasons already given there is no obvious quantum
of certainty that meets that standard.[60] Nor should readers see a requirement
for rules of principled predictability as implicitly claiming to be the only source

of predictability for rules. As indicated in discussion that follows shortly, it is not.

Rules that conform to the requirements of principled predictability, however, are likely to provide, over time and across an array of decisions and decision makers, both greater predictability than other rules and the only sort of (rule-based) predictability that is associated with rule-of-law norms.[61]

### 3. Rules from Valid Authority

The third element of the rule of law is that the rules that govern must be products of valid authority. A government of *laws* is not merely a government of *instructions*. The source of the instructions matters.

*Hart's Rule of Recognition.* A great deal has been written about the sources of authoritative instructions acceptable to the rule of law. One of the best known is H. L. A. Hart's discussion. Hart found that valid instructions could not be defined by any determinate set of criteria but rather were best described as those directives that satisfy a "rule of recognition"—which is whatever signals the community's recognition that a particular rule comes from a valid source of law for the given setting.[62]

Most established legal systems have well-developed guidelines for determining the validity of a legal rule. Hart's rule of recognition distinguishes among sources of instruction readily in better-developed systems, as opposed to those in which the order of rule validity is less structured. Systems that formally define (and therefore impose substantial constraints on) the legitimate sources of government authority generally find the formal rules strongly congruent with public acceptance of legitimate authority. But those are not the settings in which the rule of recognition is needed to identify valid sources of law.[63]

As discussed below, the problematic cases are those that arise in governance systems that blend democratic trappings with an extreme concentration of power in relatively few hands, often only two. The typical example follows the breakdown of democratic governance structures, even if those structures initially facilitate a leader's access to lawmaking power. The concentration of power, which is inimical to the rule of law, then undermines the legitimacy of the governing authority.[64] The plain conflict between the concentration of power and the essential understanding of the rule of law is a clearer basis for the invalidity of instructions derived from that authority than is Hart's rule of recognition.

*Secondary Rules.* Questions about the limits to sources of legal instructions tend to be harder to resolve than questions about the underlying validity of formal directives. Instances in which these questions arise typically are those in which guidance strictly derived from formally announced rules would leave issues unresolved. Positivist conceptions purport to limit sources of guidance to a definitely circumscribed set of valid rules and their derivatives, and for most purposes this is a fair account of how the legal system should work. But it is nearly impossible to work out all the details of a rule system in advance, and the rule of law does not command the impossible. Thus, as both Hans Kelsen and Fred Schauer have observed, Hart's approach to rule validity does not preclude advertence in the operation of a legal system to rules derived from sources other than those responsible for establishing the system's principal substantive rules.[65] For example, common law adjudication might, consistent with this element of the rule of law, provide scope for decision-rules rooted in pragmatic or prudential concerns.[66]

Such decision-rules are common means of effectuating substantive legal rules. Consider, for example, two related rules. One, formally promulgated by means readily cognizable as valid, directs automobile drivers to obey posted speed limits and identifies the range of penalties that can be imposed on speeders. The second rule, not legislated or formally inscribed, directs police officers not to ticket drivers whose speed is less than five miles per hour in excess of the posted limit. The second rule is a prudential rule, drawing boundaries around official action in a way that is intended to balance resource constraints, concerns about official discretion, and concerns about the harms from speeding. To be credited within the rule of law as rules that command fidelity, both rules must be valid; both must have the qualities of principled predictability; but the rule of law does not require that both rules be formally promulgated and publicly available in the same way.[67]

*Validation of Secondary Rules.* In this context, validity comes from the relationship of the rules to reasonable expectations associated with decision structures. Formally enacted rules authorized through processes that are themselves seen as valid—as, for instance, the underlying structural governance processes of constitutional democracies—do not require such second-order validation. But there is seldom a well-defined validation process for the pragmatic and prudential rules deployed to effectuate primary responsibilities. The only test for such rules is their consistency with reasonable expectations. Professor Fuller captures this point in saying, "There is no doubt that a legal system derives its ultimate support from a sense of its being 'right.' However, this sense, deriving as it does from tacit expectations and acceptances, simply cannot be expressed in such terms as obligations and capacities."[68]

That is why the pragmatic-prudential rule on enforcement of speed regulations passes muster. The interplay of several factors—the means available to law-enforcement officials for measuring speed; the risks attending excessive speed; the difficulty for vehicle operators of *their* constantly monitoring speed (notably the risks created by that activity); and the existence of substantial benefits to speed as well as costs—makes it reasonable to leave some leeway, but not enormous leeway, between the rule as written and as enforced. One might see the intuitive appeal of the pragmatic rule arising from the imperative of the extant—police commonly use rules that look like this, so of course they seem reasonable. This explanation cannot be discounted entirely. It is more probable, however, that causality runs the other way: police use rules like this *because* they strike a reasonable balance, one that fits common expectations.

*Relation to Principled Predictability.* As this example illustrates, second-order rules will generally be deemed valid—within the ambit of authority for the government decision maker—when they meet requirements that look very much like the requisites of principled predictability. But validity and principled predictability are directed to different ends.

Look again at the primary rule commanding obedience to posted speed limits and an alternative secondary rule issued by a police captain instructing his or her officers to allow different variance between posted limits and arrests for different vehicles or on different days. The primary rule, if adopted by a competent legislative body in accordance with its prescribed procedures, meets the test for valid authority; the secondary rule may or may not meet the test. If it is not expressly authorized or expressly prohibited, its validity will turn in some fashion on its fit with reasonable expectations. If the difference specified in the secondary rule allows rescue vehicles greater leeway or allows more leeway on days when traffic is especially light and higher speeds are less likely to be problematic, the rule would seem reasonable. A different result would obtain if the rule allowed red vehicles to go faster and provided for, say, no variance on the first Tuesday of the month and a twenty-mile-an-hour variance on the third Thursday.

The unreasonable secondary rule *could* satisfy the test for principled predictability if it were sufficiently well publicized and clearly written. But that would not bring it within the ambit of valid authority for the police captain without express authorization. It is not a reasonably expected choice of the sort we assume is implicitly authorized when we are given the power to enforce the speeding rule.

*Morality and Validity.* Some theorists would qualify the validity element by requiring that primary conduct-regulating rules meet not merely formal requisites for public acceptance but also moral requisites. That is the thrust of arguments for anchoring the rule of law in concepts of justice or natural law.[69] These arguments serve a different conception of the rule of law than that associated with Hume and Adams. Moralist arguments urge a conception of a government of *good* laws, as the alternative to a "government of men."

Beyond its departure from the most widely accepted conception of the rule of law, there is a pragmatic reason for rejecting the moralists' approach. The rule of law—of fidelity to rule-based decisions that constrain government power—is complex enough without subsuming it in a broader concept of justice.[70] Whatever the merits of greater congruence between law and morality—a centuries-old debate[71]—there is need for a separate concept of power-constraining rule-fidelity. That concept is the rule of law. It can be cast as a subordinate component of a broader moralist vision of the law; but if we refer to that broader vision as "the rule of law," we risk losing the narrower concept as a separable goal worthy of independent attention.

The common source of the imperative to make the rule of law cohere fully with conceptions of morality is readily seen. The concept of the rule of law is an attractive concept, a concept with strong and broad appeal. If the concept can be extended to cover fidelity to immoral laws, it can be made to serve unattractive ends. The inherent attractiveness of the rule-of-law concept can provide additional force to arguments for acceptance of immoral laws. In some settings, it could undermine resistance to immoral laws. This is the fear of those loath to give the term its more limited and more natural meaning.[72]

This fear is only partly justified. The cases of greatest concern fall outside the ambit of the rule of law on other grounds.

The most frequent rule-of-law problem in settings of concern to moralists will be validity. Consider the case of Hitlerian Germany. Hitler's rise to power was accomplished in part through the democratic processes of the Weimar Republic. Although force and intimidation played a role even then, Hitler's critical first steps to national power were taken largely through legitimate means, giving his rule the patina of legitimacy.[73] The essence of Hitler's rule, however, was the concentration of power in one person, power not limited by defined rules but changeable as the Führer's will changed.[74] Wholly apart from the degree of acceptance such dictatorial control can generate, only the narrowest formalistic conception of the rule of law could deem such an authority as consistent with the rule of law. At base, the dictates of Hitlerian Germany failed the requirement of validity inherent in the Hume-Adams conception of the rule of law.

Governments that lack the legitimacy essential to rule-of-law values are those most likely to adopt laws at odds with widely shared notions of morality. But any government can adopt a law that is immoral. Certainly, any government can adopt a law that fails to meet well-conceived standards of morality or that fails to accord with moral standards to which large portions of the populace are committed. America's acceptance of slavery for many years is one example. More recently, controversy over laws regulating abortion show a divide between legal rules and at least some strongly held conceptions of morality. Yet American laws on slavery or abortion do not fail the test of validity. They were not products of concentrations of uncabined personal power; though slavery gave such power to slave owners, the *laws* permitting and regulating slavery and abortion were products of a political system that meets standards of democratic legitimacy despite allowing some individuals and some interests greater scope than others.[75] Philosophers can debate the proper posture to be taken by one who believes those laws to be immoral,[76] but they command the respect of those who are committed to the rule of law.

Thus, a divide between morality and the rule of law does admit the possibility that devotion to the latter concept can diminish adherence to the former. That risk, however, is not so great as often supposed. The language of rule-fidelity, like abstract concepts more generally, probably is less persuasive to ordinary folk than academic commentators typically assume[77]—so allowing fidelity to immoral laws within the concept of the rule of law will have scant practical effect. And as shown above, many of the most worrisome laws already fall outside the circle of those to which the rule of law would command fidelity. All in all, concerns about its impact on morality do not justify pulling the meaning of the rule of law away from its accustomed shape.

*Authority and Interpretation.* Issues of validity recur frequently in academic argument over interpretation, focusing on core sources of law that tend to be the least directive.[78] Questions of interpretation are explored further in chapters 4 and 5. The most important aspects of validity in practice, however, revolve less around accreditation of the validity of particular rules than around application of the next element of the rule of law, constraining decision makers through external authority.

## 4. Rules from External Authority

The final element of the rule of law, constraint from external authority, like its other elements, helps assure that the processes of government, rather than the predilections of the individual decision maker, govern. The issue here is both legitimacy and predictability.

*External Authority and Predictability.* Look first at predictability. Acceptance of external authority as the basis for decision is useful to, but not always essential to, predictability. It is possible to understand the preferences of particular officials sufficiently to predict their decisions over a significant range of issues; and many individual actions that are likely to be examined by a government official will be taken with knowledge of the person who will render that official judgment. Think of the baseball pitcher who knows that one umpire will call knee-high pitches just at the corner of home plate strikes whereas another umpire will call the same pitches balls; the pitcher has a profile of each umpire and knows he must adjust his targets to the particular umpire officiating each game; and, of course, the pitcher knows the umpire's identity (despite the mask) before he pitches.

However, many actions that could engender legal consequences will not be taken with such knowledge. The assurance that *any* official decision maker will comply with externally generated authority should tend to increase predictability in those circumstances. If decision makers follow instructions that are knowable in advance, as external rules tend to be, the resulting decisions should be predictable without need for greater information about the decision makers.[79]

*External Authority and Legitimacy.* More important, external authority is inescapably part of the limitation of official power, without which the exercise of official power is illegitimate.[80] Whatever the determinants of rule validity, the recognized sources of constraining rules must share one feature: they must be embodied in authority outside the control of (external to) the individual exercising legal power. If the same individual can at the same time, without constraint, define the scope of the power to be exercised and the terms on which it is being exercised, that power exists outside the strictures imposed by the rule of law. In a legal order operating in accord with the rule of law, officials are granted power—backed ultimately by coercive force that is the state's legal monopoly—only insofar as its exercise is predicted to advance public interests.[81] Conformity to that structure necessarily means conformity to limiting instructions external to the individual official.[82]

As with other elements, specifying the contours of this requirement is difficult. It is far easier to state the broad parameters that align allegiance to external authority with legitimacy than to explain the boundaries around legitimate exercise of government power, how tightly external authority must constrain decisions. Considerable effort has been expended, particularly in the heyday first of Legal Realism and later of the Critical Legal Studies movement, on showing that external authority cannot fully constrain government decisions.[83] Those efforts, however, have limited import for the questions relevant to the rule of law, because less than full constraint can still be very far from insufficient constraint. The latter term defines the relevant issue for the rule of law.

Certainly, at some level the scope of discretion allowed to individual officials is a problem for definition of the rule of law.[84] Although at times scholars have suggested that discretion is at odds with the rule of law, conflating discretion to arbitrary action or to action uncabined by rules,[85] some discretion is inevitable and broad discretion may at times be desirable.[86] Discretion within limits must be compatible with the rule of law, even if broad grants of discretionary authority are in tension with rule-of-law values.[87] Just how confining external authority can be in particular circumstances, and when it is acceptable to leave scope for decision making less structured by clear external authority, are matters taken up later in this book.[88]

## What the Rule of Law Does—and Does Not Do

Together, these four elements define the classic conception of the rule of law. Insofar as we can make these elements operational, they should constrain unpredictable, undirected, or unauthorized official action and, by doing so, promote freedom and stability.[89] A system characterized by fidelity to rules of principled predictability derived from valid authority external to individual government decision makers will have a strong tendency toward limited official power, toward the exercise of power in ways that accord with reasonable expectations, toward gradual (not precipitous) change in law that fits with other changes in society.

The rule of law acts in society much as a large body of water acts on weather patterns. The ocean does not guarantee warm or constant temperatures, but it dramatically moderates the changes brought on by other forces. The larger the body of water, the more pronounced this moderating effect. At times this can make all the difference between a comfortable environment and an oppressive, even unbearable, one. Annual migrations to the seashore in summer began not as a pilgrimage to the sun but as an escape from inland heat.

The rule of law performs the same function with respect to government and with a similarly universal attraction. That is its enduring appeal. It pulls society in the direction of knowable, predictable, rule-based decision making, toward limitations on the power entrusted to government officials, toward alignment of power with legitimacy. Insofar as rule-of-law values become ingrained in the social order, they bring society closer to conformity with broadly embraced goals.

Just as the water can only moderate the weather, not change arctic climates into temperate ones, however, the rule of law can only moderate societal forces that shape the operation of the law. It can promote values attractive to a nation's citizens only to the degree that the interests of citizens *expressed through legal processes* admit.[90] The rule of law is neither a protection for freedom in all instances nor a guarantor of stability in all instances.[91] Legal processes for making rules—to which rule-of-law values demand deference—can produce outcomes that impinge on freedom and on stability.[92] The rule of law is part of a set of processes that serve to restrain such tendencies, though not to prevent them entirely.

## The Norms of Constitutional Democracy

The conception of the rule of law described above does not deduce the essential qualities of the rule of law from a well-defined norm. Given the complexity of the values served by legal systems, it would be surprising if any single, normative precept could provide an adequate basis for the rule of law.[93]

Nonetheless, the absence of a defined normative basis such as those proposed by various philosophers and legal scholars leaves the attractiveness of societal conformity to the rule of law dependent on the attractiveness of the underlying social order. Perhaps that is why Thomas Hobbes, John Locke, and Jeremy Bentham, writing against the background of governance systems whose basic legitimacy was seriously contested, perceived the need to describe a normative basis for their particular conceptions of the rule of law.

Those who write about the rule of law for democratic republics, such as those governing most nations in the economically developed world today, arguably stand on different footing.[94] These societies do not enjoy any theoretical exemption from scrutiny for congruence with attractive normative predicates, but they are widely seen as grounded in normative precepts that provide attractive underpinnings for government action.[95] Democratic republics are built primarily on norms of individual autonomy and its derivative, consent.[96] These societies are broadly credited as promoting the welfare of the citizenry. Even if the society's proximity to optimum social welfare inevitably is open to question and each government's definition of social welfare varies, democratic republics are less prone to charges of dramatic departures from social welfare than are nations organized under other forms of government.[97] Ideally, a democratic republic will be structured to take account of the individual interests of all the nation's citizens.[98]

This expressly was the vision animating the American Constitution: the nation's founders endeavored to stitch together the various interests of the citizenry, cognizant of the differences among citizens at that time and of the inevitability that those interests would change over time.[99] The founders embraced the notion of "the general welfare" as a goal for government action, but they did not expressly announce a more definite normative standard for social choices, nor would they have agreed on one.[100] Some of the founders were strong believers that certain rights of citizens were *natural* rights, deriving from God or from an innate order not of our making.[101] Other founders saw rights in narrower, positivistic terms.[102] The system that emerged was not grounded cleanly on an agreed normative construct of any sort; instead, differences among the founders were compromised in a system that allows most substantive choices to be made as we go, with very few side constraints.[103]

These choices, as a formal matter, are accepted as defining the *public interest*.[104] Any given choice will not necessarily be accepted in fact as promoting the public interest (witness widespread expressions of dissatisfaction with specific public programs at particular times), but even choices that generate substantial complaint are very broadly accepted by the citizenry as products of a *system* that serves the public interest.[105]

As already acknowledged, acceptance does not speak to the congruence of the system to any theoretically attractive norm. American government—and, more generally, American society—is regularly criticized for its inconstancy with regard to particular norms.[106] Broad acceptance of the system's legitimacy does, however, make it more likely that specifying normative predicates will not substantially increase government's alignment with public interest. If government is broadly acceptable to the populace, whatever normative predicates are implicit in the government's organization are likely to be fairly reflective of the public interest.

In these circumstances, "negative" approaches to instructing government will be likely to be more effective than identification of underlying norms in further aligning official action with public interest.[107] Negative approaches to government seek to *prevent* actions we fear will be inimical to public interest, in contrast to positive approaches composed of specific commands to *promote* particular values. Although the preamble speaks of a set of positive values as the goals of the U.S. Constitution, the document itself—along with discussions that surrounded its creation and ratification, and the history of its interpretation—relies almost entirely on negative approaches, constraining the allocations of power and the incentives of officials.[108]

The rule of law serves constitutional democratic republics such as America's as one such negative instrument for improving the likelihood that government actions will be consistent with the public interest. Its object is to constrain public agents from behavior expected to be at odds with public interest and to induce behavior expected to serve public interest. And its focus is the use of law to accomplish this constraint. If the governmental structure is broadly congruent with the advancement of public interest, the rule of law—the features that constrain officials to exercise power only within the limited framework allowed by constitutional processes—should be particularly felicitous. The question, then, is how well particular nations do at implementing that constraint.

# CHAPTER TWO

# Limited Government
## Implementing the Rule of Law in America

*Scarcely any political question arises in the United States that is not resolved, sooner or later, into a judicial question. . . . [T]he spirit of the law, which is produced in the schools and courts of justice, gradually penetrates . . . into the bosom of society . . . so that at last the whole people contract the habits and tastes of the judicial magistrate. The lawyers of the United States form a party which . . . acts upon the country imperceptibly, but finally fashions it to suit its own purposes.*
*—Alexis de Tocqueville*

## Popular Sovereignty, Official Constraint

Just as implementation of the rule of law should yield especially attractive results for democratic republics such as the United States, the history of America's founding is encouraging for implementation of the rule of law. From its inception, American government has been constructed with an eye toward limiting official power.

Constraining the individuals who would hold governmental power was the foremost concern animating the framers of the American Constitution. The framers hoped to create a system that would assure the use of that power for the public good; but their first commitment was to prevent tyranny.[1] The basic design of American government—limiting the authority of any government official and creating divergent, and to some degree competing, competencies among government officials—was intended to prevent officials from turning public power to personal ends, a use of power that, to the framers, led

23

to or was equated with tyranny.[2] That same design was intended to prevent groups within the larger population from gaining control over government powers and using them to advance group interests at the expense of the more general public interest; in the framers' view, that use of government powers, too, would lead to tyranny.[3]

It was not thought sufficient simply to construct a system that prevented government from being "hijacked" by individuals or smallish groups. Although that was a prominent goal, constructing the system around that concern alone would not prevent one sort of tyranny that concerned the framers. Recognizing that majorities, as well as minorities, might essay to use government power to their own private advantage, the framers constructed a system that was not fully congenial to majority control.[4] The system has been changed to facilitate majority rule—through the direct election of senators, the expansion of the franchise, and increased restraints on size and composition of electoral districts. But important countermajoritarian features remain, such as the staggered terms for senators, equal senatorial representation for each state (regardless of population), the electoral college for presidential elections, the life-tenured judiciary, and constitutional limits on government power.

Concern about majoritarian abuses has been criticized as misplaced. Robert Dahl stressed the elusiveness of the "tyranny of the majority"—indeed, of any evidence of effective rule by a majority, as opposed to a series of conveniently connected minorities—in asserting that the Madisonian definition of tyranny was either empty or false.[5] In general, Dahl is correct that our majoritarian-representative processes are not driven by clear majority-shared preferences.

Professor Dahl's argument overreaches, however. Elections may not convincingly indicate majority views on particular issues, and minority views may gain added weight in our governance processes, as Dahl contends;[6] but that does not disprove the proposition that majority interests *do* prevail on important issues or the proposition that majority interests pose a threat to minority interests. Those propositions—accepted by Madison and other founders of the United States and critically important to aspects of our constitutional system—seem intuitively compelling.

Accepting those propositions does not compel us to make tyranny of the majority our sole or even our primary concern. John Hart Ely no doubt overreaches in his endeavor to make an argument that is the mirror image of Dahl's (inflating the famous Footnote 4 from *Carolene Products* to the size of the Constitution).[7] Nevertheless, Ely surely is right that a majority can threaten a minority and that the threat can be inimical to the public good—and that must be so whether the public good is defined by aggregating current, individual interests, by reference to norms congruent with long-term success of polities, or by natural rights. McCarthyism may at heart have been tyranny by a minority, but it drew on widespread support, probably from a substantial majority of Americans, for some of its fears and for the enforcement of its solutions. Many writers and actors in the 1950s devoutly wished that only a minority of private employers in their industries would blacklist suspected Communists, a wish that went for nought. The same was no doubt true of Jim Crow legislation at many times and in many places in the southern states—legislation which depended on extremely broad support for its effectiveness. Had a significant minority of those with voting rights and economic power opposed these laws' implementation, their impact on southern life would have been far less pronounced.[8] Likewise, anti-Semitism has not always been a minority taste or the preserve of antidemocratic societies.

At the time the Constitution was written, many of the framers worried that one or another group would gain control of the government—generally by virtue of representing a majority—and use that control to advantage themselves at the expense of others. Northerners and southerners saw their interests divided, as did representatives of large and small states.[9] The compromises they struck were intended to frustrate any group, large or small, from oppressing others. If Madison and the other framers did not have a precise definition of tyranny in mind that would withstand critical examination, they were rightly concerned that concentration of government power could lead to actions inimical to individual freedom and public welfare.

## Nation of Lawyers, Nation of Laws

The constitutional structure provided a system of limited powers, of divided authority, and of competing governmental competencies. American society in the early days of the republic did not reveal the sort of harmony often portrayed in reconstruction of the founding era, but it did evidence a penchant for resolving differences through law.

This penchant was striking to Tocqueville, who saw the legal orientation of American society as a positive aspect of the new democracy. In the epigraph to this chapter, Tocqueville decidedly was not making the argument advanced by modern critics of the legal profession that lawyer-dominated legislatures pass laws that serve the profession's selfish purposes, creating new work for lawyers to the detriment of society.[10] To the contrary, Tocqueville surmised that lawyers and judges generally were the instruments of society, rather than the other way around, and that they were instruments generally used to good purpose.

For Tocqueville, this did not mean that the interests of lawyers and judges were entirely aligned with social interests. Indeed, one particular aspect of lawyers' and judges' own interests lies at the heart of the passage quoted above. In Tocqueville's view, the legal profession has a peculiarly strong interest in restraining facile changes of policy, in assuring that the power of government is exercised in accord with prescribed rules, and in protecting individuals against application of that power beyond the ambit predictable from previously exercised authority. Those interests may be outweighed at times by other societal interests (for individual lawyers and judges and, even more likely according to Tocqueville, for the society overall), but the legal profession's interests should be recognized as aligned with the primary elements of the rule of law, as elaborated above.

Tocqueville's observation in essence was that America seemed peculiarly bound by—indeed, devoted to—the rule of law. As Tocqueville phrases the role played by judges and lawyers in America, they induce in the general population the *habit* of accepting legal constraints on the exercise of power, even if they do not especially influence the *ends* to which power is devoted.[11] Tocqueville did not find the interest of American judges and lawyers in sustaining the rule of law exceptional, but he was struck by their success in spreading that attitude broadly among the populace. He was particularly impressed that in a society without a distinct class invested in preserving the social order (the role of the aristocracy elsewhere), there was such widespread deference to law.

From one perspective, the deference to law Tocqueville observed might be expected (rather than noteworthy) in light of the desuetude of institutions that have encouraged social cohesion in other nations. America has no single, dominant religious order whose hierarchy can resolve disputes. As Tocqueville noted, we lack as well the degree of class structure that characterizes many societies and that can both suppress some types of disputes and assist in the

solution of others. Moreover, greater geographic mobility in America undermines the order imposed elsewhere by extended families or by local networks
of other kinds. These networks do exist, of course, and can supply dispute-
resolving norms in some circumstances.[12] But an American spirit of independence and adventure, often noted in the nation's formative years, shortens the
reach of such networks and reduces their stability over time.[13] The institutional
characteristics that make these efficient dispute-resolution mechanisms for
broader groups in other nations typically are atrophied or absent in America.

What Tocqueville saw in America was the absence of institutions that frequently are associated with fidelity to law. This does not necessarily signify a
less important role for law, because those institutions also can be seen as alternatives to law: they can be means of dispute resolution, of social cohesion, and
of social control. When those institutions disappear or dwindle, law is the obvious mechanism to fill the vacuum. But that does not answer how much or
how well law fills that void. It does not tell us how well America conforms to
the rule of law.

## The Rule of Law Today: Common Ground

There is a common assumption (among Americans at least) that we are
still the nation Tocqueville saw more than a century and a half ago—that the
rule of law is well entrenched in America and not so well established in many
other nations. Consider, for example, the following (probably apocryphal) story.
In the mid-1980s, President Ronald Reagan is said to have told Mikhail Gorbachev, then leader of the Union of Soviet Socialist Republics (a then-nation),
that the greatness of the United States—what would inevitably lead to the triumph of our system over the Communist system—lay in our respect for law,
not power; in our belief that no individual is above the law. To illustrate, Reagan observed that anyone in the United States could stand directly in front of
the White House, the very seat of government power, and criticize the American president and his policies, in the harshest terms imaginable, without fear
of punishment. Gorbachev replied that the same was true in the Soviet Union:
there, too, anyone could stand directly in front of the very seat of government
power, the Kremlin, and criticize the American president and his policies without fear of punishment.

The Reagan-Gorbachev story embodies assumptions that government officials in the United States are limited by laws that cannot be defined to suit an official's whims and that provide a fair degree of predictability. Surface evidence, at a minimum, supports those assumptions.

Look first at the setting referenced by that story. In fact, protesters outside the White House can know well before they get to Lafayette Park the general contours of (very substantial) constitutional constraints on the president's power to punish critics. Freedom to criticize the president is not a function of judges' and law enforcers' hostility to the president or their sympathy for the critics but of accepted free speech doctrine.[14] All of the following were safe bets: police officers who idolized Ronald Reagan would not arrest critics condemning him in the vilest terms; if arrests were made, prosecutors whose sympathies were strongly with Reagan would not take such cases to court; and if the cases got to court, judges, including those who owed their appointment to Reagan, would not allow his critics to be punished. As the story suggests, and scholars have underscored, the rules we follow permit the same criticism of our most revered and most reviled leaders.[15]

This is the point of a rule of law, that extrinsic rules of principled predictability constrain official power (including the power to resolve individual disputes as well as power deployed on the state's behalf directly against individuals).[16] The proof of America's acceptance of the rule of law in the setting referenced by the Reagan–Gorbachev exchange is our expectation that we can predict in advance what is within and without the law: you do not need to know who is on duty in Lafayette Park or who might be in charge of prosecutions or who might be assigned your case in court to know (with a fair degree of certainty) what you can say about the president of the United States.[17]

Even though most Americans (and outside observers) seem to believe that America is strongly ruled by law,[18] establishing that proposition in a rigorous way is problematic. Yet surface indications that we are a nation living by the rule of law abound. At the most obvious level, America has not experienced a violent change of government—the use of force to alter the constitutional order for succession to government power—in its more-than-two-century history. Fewer than a dozen sovereign nations have gone through the past century without a government transition through force. Further, in the United States, few officials within government wield real power except insofar as they can persuade other officials that what they are doing is proper; government officers are subject to a variety of checks on their authority, and the authority most threatening to individual liberties is safeguarded by officials whose conduct is substantially guided by rules, conforming to the requirements of principled predictability, articulated in advance by other decision makers.[19]

To be sure, government in America (at virtually all levels) is far larger than the framers' most expansive imaginings, and government officials often enjoy substantial discretion to take actions that have significant consequences for particular citizens. Prosecutors are the archetypical administrative officials: their discretionary decisions whether to proceed with cases and on what bases are not directly reviewable and can have enormous effects on individuals.[20] In some measure, that discretion pulls our practice away from the rule of law, a point taken up below.[21]

Nonetheless, the most serious potential consequences of prosecutorial decisions are metered through a substantially constrained judicial process, and the same is generally true for other administrative decisions.[22] Courts have curbed official decisions that are authorized by rules that lack qualities essential to principled predictability and also have restricted categories of official decision making that seem unchanneled by external rules. Thus, courts have prevented the imposition of penalties against individuals when the rules assertedly authorizing the imposition were overly ambiguous or not reasonably knowable in advance.[23] Courts have rejected such penalties as well when the rules granted broad discretion to officials whose judgments predictably would be self-interested in ways that derogate from societal interests (or where the risk of such derogations presented a high cost and the prospects of effectively limiting that cost through individual, ex post supervision were poor).[24] And, albeit fitfully, courts have demanded that delegations of authority to administrative officers be governed by "intelligible standards" and have struck down or narrowly construed statutes to that end.[25]

These steps have not eliminated discretion from American government, nor have they constrained discretion sufficiently to guarantee full conformity to rule-of-law values. That tension is explored below. For the immediate point, however, what is most important is this: notwithstanding the growth of government, including substantial grants of discretionary authority, the American system has not produced the sort of unchecked government power that has been, and still is, so common around the globe.

By way of contrast, consider the comment of the Russian-émigré comedian, Yakov Smirnoff, who observed on the difference between the United

States and the Soviet Union, "What I like most about America is the little things—like warning shots; in Soviet Union was different concept; police don't like what I do, shoot me; is *warning* to you!"[26] Or look at three incidents that occurred in China in the 1990s. In January 1999, following a trial that was closed to the public and to the defendant's family, a Chinese court sentenced a man to two years in jail for providing E-mail addresses of other Chinese citizens to a U.S.-based electronic, Internet publisher.[27] The publication was critical of the Chinese government. In 1997 the Chinese government banned distribution of a novel, *The Wrath of Heaven,* because it portrayed fictional—but perhaps not fictional enough—government officials as corrupt.[28] A few years earlier, China sentenced a journalist to life imprisonment for revealing to a Hong Kong newspaper the text of a speech Chinese Party Chairman Jiang Zemin delivered at a Party Congress.[29] The refusal of the Supreme Court of the United States in "The Pentagon Papers Case" to allow government to block publication of a confidential Department of Defense report that had been turned over illegally to two news organizations reveals a sharply different governmental authority over speech.[30] The difference looks very much like the caricature of the Reagan-Gorbachev story.

Our conformity to the rule of law extends beyond such central matters to more quotidian fare. Not only do officials typically follow the rules; ordinary citizens do as well. For example, in many developed nations (not to mention developing nations), tax cheating is rampant,[31] but in the United States tax compliance is the norm—an estimated 80 to 90 percent of Americans file income tax returns that conform to the applicable law, which is frequently difficult to understand and almost never pleasant to follow.[32]

## American Factions and Factotums

The success of the American system rests not simply on having frustrated tyranny but on achieving a balance among interests, a balance that makes the important policy choices for governance difficult without making governance impossible. Though it may seem a guarantee against tyranny, the latter route—requiring a balance of interests so difficult that government is dramatically constrained—is an invitation to anarchy or to the substitution of private force for public force as the source of social control. Colombia or southern Italy at times have been modern exemplars of this problem. In the United States, too, on some matters the impossibility of harmonizing intense opposing interests has led to episodic breakdown of social order. The Civil War is the most notable episode, but the Prohibition era also fits this category as do periodic riots arising from unresolved racial tensions. For the past century and a quarter, however, these episodes have been relatively confined and short-lived.

Although America's constitutional structure has avoided such extremes, the route it followed—making governance difficult by dispersing power—is not without costs. The downside of this structure has been noted often by public-choice theorists among others: it increases the capacity of smaller interests to hold up larger ones.[33] The common focus for this point is the ability of smallish groups of intensely interested individuals to benefit at the expense of more diffuse, general interests.[34]

Critical to the topic at hand is that the capacity to secure private gains from democratic-representative government is not confined to those who are outside the government. With dispersed power, competing constituencies, and ill-defined measures of success in government operation, those who work within the government often are able to extract personal benefits, including higher pay, better pensions, reduced work hours, and the ability to turn government decision making more in a direction the government functionary would approve.[35]

Many of these benefits derive from formal actions (legislation, union contracts, etc.). Assignment of discretionary authority to administrative officers is one form of benefit, often serving the interests both of the government officer and of nongovernment parties.[36] Overly broad discretionary authority poses problems for rule-of-law values even if it is formally authorized, and the factors that create such authorizations are not readily distinguished from those that permit exercise of discretion where not formally sanctioned.

Discretion that is not expressly conferred—that is not conferred in a formal manner—more often has been cited for conflicts with rule-of-law values. Much that occurs in large bureaucracies, government most of all, takes the form of relatively invisible behavior. Such behavior is notoriously resistant to supervision, especially since the outputs of government seldom are well defined and readily assessed.[37] This point—the difficulty of supervising personnel in a bureaucracy—was the basis for the long-running British television series *Yes, Minister*, satirizing the uneven contest between a political boss and his entrenched agency staff.[38] Professor Glen Robinson, former member of the

Federal Communications Commission, offered a more serious thought in the same vein; commenting on the "agency capture" thesis, he said that if agencies are captured by anyone, it is by their staffs.[39]

Some scholars have drawn a more alarming conclusion, seeing the prospect for relatively invisible influence on government conduct, especially conduct of lower-level functionaries, as a source of serious threats to public order. Professor Peter Schuck, for example, after confessing that "we know little about the amount or character of official wrongdoing in America," nonetheless speculated that the expansion of government activity in the modern bureaucratic state has multiplied opportunities for official misbehavior. He added, "Activist government breeds official misconduct on a large scale."[40] The same sentiment is voiced in popular complaints about rogue agents of the Internal Revenue Service wielding government power to confiscate citizens' property or otherwise to disrupt their lives.[41] Accounts of excessive zeal in law enforcement or insufficient attention to legal constraints in other government activity also make news from time to time.[42]

Even if these complaints are seen as focused on the tail of the distribution of government actions, the problem of official exercise of discretion is substantial and deserves attention. The problem has complex roots, deriving from choices made in framing legal rules, from the nebulous quality of some legal constraints on official action, and from the inherent difficulty of devising efficacious means to govern official behavior.[43]

The problem is not the existence of administrative discretion. The very fact that administrators are subject both to ex ante limitations specifying the bounds of their authority and to ex post review (commonly from more than one source) to assure that actions stay within those bounds is what makes the concept of administrative discretion sensible. Professor Ronald Dworkin makes that point effectively: "The concept of discretion is at home in only one sort of context; when someone is in general charged with making decisions subject to standards set by a particular authority. It makes sense to speak of the discretion of a sergeant who is subject to orders of superiors, or the discretion of a sports official or contest judge who is governed by a rule book or the terms of the contest. Discretion, like the hole in a doughnut, does not exist except as an area left open by a surrounding belt of restriction."[44]

The serious problem is that, if not sufficiently circumscribed beforehand and sufficiently well monitored after, discretion is incompatible with the rule of law. The contentions Professor Schuck and others advance are that the current scope of American government has increased the occasions that allow such effectively unconstrained action and, perhaps more important, that the significance of such action has risen with the rise of government power. Yet, other critics have made exactly the opposite claim, that American government is increasingly—and unduly—constrained by rules and practices that have removed discretion from government officials.[45]

The conflict between these claims is important to understanding current views of the American legal system, as discussed in chapter 6. But whichever claim is more on target—whether government in America is characterized by too much discretion or too little, whether discretion in government action is increasing or diminishing—it is difficult to brand the system as one that is substantially out of control, ungoverned by law. As chapter 3 argues, the evidence from cases of greatest pressure to relax rule-of-law strictures offer strong support for the proposition that America exemplifies the rule of law.

# CHAPTER THREE

# Judges' Rule

## Presidents in the Dock

*For generations, Americans prided themselves that ours was a nation of laws, not of men, and that no one, not even the president of the United States, was above the law. —Sol Linowitz*

One key to officials' constraint in the United States, and what is particularly striking to many outsiders from Tocqueville on, is the degree to which judges have the power to stop other officials—including those who fund and direct our armed forces—from carrying out plans and policies in which those officials are deeply invested. On paper, judges would not seem likely to wield such power. They are, after all, a small set of officials with extraordinarily limited resources at their immediate command—a personal staff of one or two or a handful of people armed with law books and computer terminals—far less than the resources immediately within the control of many other officials. The power of "the least dangerous branch" (as Alexander Bickel aptly paraphrased Alexander Hamilton)[1] rests solely on the respect it is accorded by those who occupy the coordinate branches and by the populace at large. Yet it has sufficed to change the way America deals with some of the most politically sensitive issues: abortion, race relations, criminal responsibility, education, apportionment—the list is long and growing.

In addition to the broad sweep of subjects that have come within judges' purview, as Sol Linowitz stresses, no person in America is beyond their reach. The power of the courts has extended to personal commands to the president of the United States, notably in cases involving Richard Nixon and, twenty-three years later, Bill Clinton. Those cases are instructive about the strength of the rule of law in America and also about the claims we can make about the rule of law.

## The Nixon Tapes Case

On July 25, 1974, the Supreme Court announced its decision in *United States v. Nixon*.[2] The very title of the case is extraordinary: the government of the United States against the president of the United States. The setting also was extraordinary. Investigations into wrongdoing in President Nixon's administration in connection with the June 17, 1972, break-in at the Watergate Hotel headquarters of Senator George McGovern, President Nixon's opponent in his bid for reelection, had been commenced by a Select Committee of the Senate and separately through the appointment of a special prosecutor, Archibald Cox. The president resisted Cox's demands for access to information and, when Cox pressed, insisted that officials in the Justice Department fire Cox. Under intense public pressure, a successor to Professor Cox, Leon Jaworski, was appointed to continue investigation and prosecution of Watergate-related criminal misconduct.

During the course of hearings before the Senate committee, two revelations had transformed the proceedings; what had begun as a general inquiry on wrongdoing by administration officials and associates had become an investigation of possible criminal behavior by the president. The first revelation was by John Dean, an assistant to the president, who accused the president of direct involvement in obstructing investigation of the Watergate break-in. The second was the disclosure by Alexander Butterfield, an assistant to presidential chief of staff H. R. Haldeman, that a voice-activated tape-recording system in the White House preserved records of all conversations in the Oval Office.

In February 1974, the House of Representatives authorized the Judiciary Committee to commence proceedings to determine whether the president should be impeached, only the second time in the nation's history that this step had been taken. In March, a grand jury in Washington, D.C., under the guidance of the special prosecutor, indicted seven individuals in connection with the break-in and its aftermath and named the president among the unindicted co-conspirators. In April, responding to a subpoena of White House tapes and other materials issued by the House Judiciary Committee, the president released twelve hundred pages of edited transcripts of the taped conversations sought by the committee, withholding other material on the basis that it was covered by executive privilege, a doctrine that in some circumstances protects from disclosure information sensitive to the deliberation of the president and his advisers.

Much of the same material was sought in a subpoena from the District Court of the District of Columbia at the request of the special prosecutor, who stated that the material could be relevant to the government's case against John Mitchell, Nixon's former attorney general and election campaign manager. In May the president's lawyers moved to quash that subpoena, the motion that was directly at issue in *United States v. Nixon*. But everyone knew that much more was at stake. Two days after the Supreme Court's decision—rejecting the president's arguments against compelled disclosure by a vote of 8–0— the House committee voted to adopt an article of impeachment charging the president with obstruction of justice. Less than two weeks later, Richard Nixon became the first president of the United States to resign his office.

President Nixon's lawyers asserted (1) that the case presented only a dispute internal to the executive branch, not a matter justiciable in an Article III court, (2) that the president enjoys an absolute right to protect all sensitive communications with his subordinates, (3) that determining the scope of that right is within the president's, not the courts', domain, and (4) that in all events executive privilege was properly invoked with respect to the materials withheld in the instant case. The Supreme Court, in an opinion by Chief Justice Warren Burger, one of three Nixon-appointed justices participating in the decision,[3] rejected the first three of these assertions outright. The fourth contention was rejected insofar as the Court held that invocation of executive privilege based only on a generalized claim of the need for confidentiality conferred a presumptive privilege, but not one strong enough to preclude *in camera* inspection by a judge to determine whether the contribution of the evidence to a particular prosecution made it necessary to override the asserted privilege. If Nixon wanted to withhold evidence that bore directly on the trial—and he did not claim that the evidence would reveal diplomatic or military secrets—he could neither prevent its inspection by a judge nor, ultimately, its introduction at trial.

The Court approached these issues in two different ways. The first and third issues were disposed of on the basis of fairly formalist analysis. The analysis of justiciability was as follows. The formal delegation of prosecutorial authority in federal criminal matters to the attorney general of the United States was followed by a delegation to the special prosecutor under terms expressly allowing the special prosecutor "to contest the invocation of executive privilege in the process of seeking evidence deemed relevant to the performance of [his] specially delegated duties."[4] Further, the attorney general had expressly forsworn any authority to interfere with Mr. Jaworski's actions except under extraordinary circumstances not applicable here. The statute governing the appointment and functions of the special prosecutor authorized litigation on the matter, and the Court was not prepared to look behind that.

Similarly, the claim that the president was the final arbiter of executive privilege was rejected because the constitutional text grants the courts "the judicial power"—and cases back to *Marbury v. Madison* have interpreted that grant as conferring on the courts responsibility "to say what the law is."[5] Burger cited several judicial precedents interpreting immunities claimed by members of Congress, another coordinate branch. These left no doubt that acceding to the president's claim would break with prior law.[6]

When dealing with the second and fourth issues, the Court deployed a more functional analysis. The special prosecutor had argued that the president's claim must fail given the absence of an express constitutional grant of immunity for executive branch communications, in distinction to the Constitution's Speech or Debate Clause for legislators' communications. The chief justice's opinion brushed this argument aside in a footnote, stating that, notwithstanding constitutional silence, the Court would find a privilege for executive branch communications if it were "reasonably appropriate and relevant to the exercise of a granted power."[7] The Court recognized that the privilege claimed by the president would serve the interest of the president and the public in candid communication between the nation's chief executive and his advisers, but an absolute privilege "would interfere with attempts to do justice in criminal prosecutions [and] would plainly conflict with the function of the courts under Art. III."[8]

In rejecting an absolute privilege, however, the Court almost offhandedly accepted the president's contention that an executive privilege of some dimension was implicit in the Constitution's devolution of executive powers to the president. "Nowhere in the Constitution . . . is there any explicit reference to a privilege of confidentiality, yet to the extent this interest relates to the effective discharge of a President's powers, it is constitutionally based."[9] But, Chief Justice Burger cautioned, this constitutional interest must be balanced against the rights to a fair trial expressly recognized in the Fifth and Sixth Amendments to the Constitution. Judicial balancing of opposed constitutional interests requires finding that one constitutional interest has greater weight than the other—presumably because it is either more important or more seriously implicated in the particular case. Here, the Court said, the balance tilts in favor of disclosure:

> [T]his presumptive privilege must be considered in light of our historic commitment to the rule of law. . . . We have elected to employ an adversary system of criminal justice in which the parties contest all issues before a court of law. The need to develop all relevant facts in the adversary system is both fundamental and comprehensive. . . . exceptions to the demand for every man's evidence are not lightly created nor expansively construed . . . no case of the Court . . . has extended [a] high degree of deference to a President's generalized interest in confidentiality.[10]

The rule of law here meant a presumption in favor of the established evidence-gathering process for criminal trials. The presumption was buttressed by the Court's finding that the claimed privilege was less important to the constitutional interests it advanced than to those it impaired. On the one hand, the Court said, a remote risk of disclosure will not chill advisers' candor. On the other hand, nondisclosure of "evidence that is demonstrably relevant in a criminal trial would cut deeply into the guarantee of due process and gravely impair the basic function of the courts."[11]

## Clinton v. Jones

The Supreme Court again heard argument in a suit against a sitting president in 1997. Paula Corbin Jones sued President William Clinton in federal court (on both federal and state law claims) for alleged improper sexual advances when he was governor of the state of Arkansas eighteen months before he was elected president and for statements about that incident by Clinton and "persons authorized to speak for" him after he had assumed the presidency. The suit asked for compensatory and punitive damages against Clinton.

The president's lawyers moved to dismiss the case on the ground that civil suits could not be brought against the president during his term in office and also asked the district court judge to bar discovery while the president held office. The district judge rejected those motions but granted a stay of trial until the end of Clinton's presidency. The U.S. Court of Appeals for the Eighth Circuit affirmed her decision on Clinton's motions but reversed the temporary stay.

The Supreme Court's decision of *Clinton v. Jones*,[12] in May 1997, was free from the drama that surrounded the "Nixon Tapes Case." No one foresaw at the time exactly how the decision would alter history or just how profound the decision's affect on President Clinton would be. Nonetheless, this was viewed as an important decision with potentially far-reaching implications for the presidency. As in Nixon's case, the president lost. As in Nixon's case, there was no dissent.

Justice John Paul Stevens delivered the opinion of the Court, joined by all but one justice. The opinion begins with precedent. Civil suits against three sitting presidents had been heard previously. Suits against Theodore Roosevelt and Harry Truman had been filed and dismissed prior to their taking office, and the affirmance of those dismissals during their presidencies offered little guidance. A motion to stay suits against John Kennedy, concerning an automobile accident that occurred prior to his presidency, was denied in district court and not appealed—but the motion was based on a statute not invoked by Clinton, and the Kennedy cases settled without further court proceedings. Again, there was nothing of use as precedent.[13]

Stevens next turned to precedents concerning official immunity. In all cases, he found that the immunity was tied to the nature of the acts performed by the official rather than the official's identity. Officials are immune from all damage actions for certain types of conduct taken in their official capacities—principally legislative, judicial, and prosecutorial conduct. Officials also are immune from damage actions for other conduct provided that the actions do "not violate clearly established constitutional or statutory rights of which a reasonable person would have known."[14] Reviewing the cases that led to this standard, Justice Stevens declared, "[President Clinton's] effort to construct an immunity from suit for unofficial acts grounded purely in the identity of his office is unsupported by precedent."[15]

Clinton's lawyers had argued that the historical record showed that those who participated in framing the Constitution had intended to protect the president from being answerable to judicial process, save for impeachment proceedings in the House and subsequent trial in the Senate. Though they framed their argument for exemption from judicial process differently, Clinton's lawyers had no more success than Nixon's. Stevens crisply disposed of the historical argument, stating that history has left no clear dictates on the matter.

Finally, the Court reached Clinton's functional argument—that being accountable to civil suits would undermine the president's ability to carry out the uniquely burdensome duties of his office and therefore was at odds with the constitutional plan.[16] The justices clearly had sympathy for this argument, a point driven home more emphatically in Justice Stephen Breyer's concurrence.[17] Indeed, that point is stressed in the Court's discussion of the ways in which judicial discretion in the conduct of a suit against the president should be exercised. But it was not enough to sustain Clinton's argument for an absolute, or at least presumptive, immunity: "[The President] errs by presuming that interactions between the Judicial Branch and the Executive, even quite burdensome interactions, necessarily rise to the level of constitutionally forbidden impairment of the Executive's ability to perform its constitutionally mandated functions."[18] Nor was it enough—without more information on the costs to the president of moving forward with trial and the costs to the plaintiff, Ms. Jones, from delay—to sustain the district court's stay.

## Reading Cases for Consonance with the Rule of Law

At one level, the *Nixon* and *Clinton* cases offer unambiguous proof of the vitality of the rule of law in America. First, each president formally obeyed the decision of the Court. This is the most important point about the health of the rule of law in America. President Nixon turned over the subpoenaed materials. President Clinton contested the *Jones* suit in the court, submitted to a deposition, and otherwise followed the ordinary forms of civil litigation. Regrettably, his obedience fell short of what we should expect of litigants, both in his responses to deposition questions and in other actions that arguably influenced evidence available in this case. But President Clinton did not declare the Supreme Court's decision illegitimate; he did not directly confront the Court's authority; he did not simply ignore the civil suit.

Even though President Clinton's behavior departed from the ideal liti-

gant's, the two presidents' formal acquiescence to the Supreme Court's decisions is a critical datum in evaluating the rule of law in America. These cases
were important to the presidents. Clinton dearly wanted to avoid the potential embarrassment of a trial publicly airing accusations of his sexual wander-
ing, which (as subsequent events made eminently clear) was fraught with opportunities for further troubles. Nixon had even more at stake: he was fighting
immediately for his political life. Both presidents lost their cases, and in any
nation without a robust rule of law, they would have been sorely tempted to
resist efforts to enforce the decisions. Despite a suggestion that Nixon might
not comply with a less than "definitive" decision and despite the painful medicine that each decision handed out, the presidents felt constrained by the decisions, surely a reflection of popular sentiment. Two presidents with little
respect for the law in so many ways had no doubt that the public (and other
political leaders, friends as well as foes) would rebel at any overt attack on the
authority of the Court.[19]

Further, the decisions themselves reaffirm core precepts of the rule of law.
In each case, the Court declared that the president is not "above the law"—
and each time, over the president's objection, the Court subjected the president to the same judicial process to which all other Americans are subject. The
decisions should put to rest any question about the independence of the federal judiciary. Given what was at stake, if either president could have influenced the outcome, he would gladly have done so. Neither president could.
Together, the presidents had personally appointed six justices to the Supreme
Court—and together the presidents received zero votes for their legal claims.
It is hard to imagine clearer proof that ours is, indeed, a government of laws
and not of men.

There is, however, a but. *Nixon* and *Clinton* are evidence that the officials
who seem most powerful do not control—and, instead, are controlled by—
judges' interpretation of the law in America. But the rule of law means more
than just freedom from control by the most powerful officials. It also means
that the judges are constrained by external authority, by governing law (constitutional, statutory, and judicial precedent). Under the rule of law, judges are
not dictators in their own right, free to make up the rules as they go.[20] It is
considerably more difficult to establish that proposition from the presidents'
experience before the Supreme Court than to show that American judges are
independent from the presidents.

Look at the evidence of the decisions themselves. In *Nixon,* the Court's disposition of the issues easily could have been different. For example, the president's claim of authority to interpret the scope of executive privilege was rejected as incompatible with judicial authority. As Professor Gerald Gunther has argued, that conclusion rests entirely on the justices' presumption that the courts' authority to interpret the law precludes strong deference to a competing claim of constitutional authority.[21] Gunther rightly suggests that, as a matter of logic, the justices could have construed the Constitution's grant of executive power to the president as encompassing the determination of the necessary extent of confidentiality. Had they done so, the president's claim would have been fully compatible with the justices' primacy in interpreting constitutional commands, just as deference to administrative determinations on a variety of statutory matters is thought to be compatible with the courts' primacy in law interpretation more generally.[22]

In addition, the Court's exposition of fair trial rights in its balancing of conflicting constitutional interests plays a bit fast and loose. The defendant's right to confront opposing witnesses, though referenced by the Court as a basis for rejecting the claim of executive privilege, was not implicated in *Nixon.* The prosecution, not the defense, wanted the subpoenaed material to use as evidence *against* a defendant. The justices may have meant that if the shoe were on the other foot, the defendant would have a right that would overcome executive privilege; and if it is constitutionally impermissible to have different executive privilege rules for prosecution and defense claims to the evidence, then the president's claim must give way. But the *ifs,* though reasonable, are not self-evident propositions.

Perhaps the justices did not mean to invoke the Confrontation Clause as a basis for decision and instead referenced it only as exemplary of concerns that create judges' obligation to assure the integrity of the judicial—and particularly the criminal—process, an integrity essential to protection of the public as well as of the accused. That might have been the gravamen of the Court's references to the tension between executive privilege and "attempts to do justice in criminal prosecutions" and "the function of the Courts under Art. III."[23] But the Court appears to have used these more general concerns only to support the proposition that an absolute privilege would be unlikely, not to identify the limits around the privilege. That is where the weighing of executive interests against defendants' constitutional safeguards takes over. Further, the opinion does not articulate the scope or precise source of the general interest in judicial process or how it would be weighed if deployed to bound executive privilege. Whichever analysis moves the Court, there is no evidence in the Court's opinion that the legal arguments necessary to the decision have been worked through rigorously.

The same can be said of Justice Stevens's opinion for the Court in *Clinton*. Justice Breyer's concurring opinion painstakingly examines the historical sources relied on by the Court in its *Clinton* opinion and in earlier cases cited as support for the *Clinton* decision. Although he ultimately agrees with the Court's disposition of the case, his reading gives a very different account of the precedents, historical and judicial. Breyer sums up the latter: "Case law . . . strongly supports the principle that judges hearing a private civil damages action against a sitting President may not issue orders that could significantly distract a President from his official duties."[24]

Although Justice Stevens had found immunity law triggered by the nature of official conduct, not by the office held, the Supreme Court's 1982 decision in the *Fitzgerald* case held that the president is absolutely immune from damage suits for *all* actions taken in his official capacity as president.[25] That decision was predicated on the Court's finding that the president's unique status within the constitutional order supported insulating him, in distinction to other executive officers, against the distractions of potential litigation.[26] *Clinton* presented a different issue from *Fitzgerald,* as the Clinton suit did not arise from the president's official actions while in office (and *Fitzgerald* did not reach the Court until long after the president whose actions were at issue had left office). *Fitzgerald* did not assert a blanket presidential immunity to suit, grounding its limited immunity in a functional argument over the effect of litigation concerns on presidential decision making. Nonetheless, *Fitzgerald* suggested considerably greater concern for presidential tranquility than the *Clinton* majority acknowledged.

Even the threshold issue in *Clinton*—which implicitly was resolved in *Nixon* and on which Breyer concurred with the other justices—is not, in modern parlance, "a slam dunk." This is the issue of presidential subjection to judicial process during his term of office. The Court rightly says that the Constitution does not expressly preclude subjection of the president to ordinary civil process. But that does not dispose of the issue. The Constitution does not expressly authorize subjecting a sitting president to ordinary civil process. The president's counsel was correct in arguing that the Constitution mentions only one means of proceeding against the president while in office: impeachment by the House of Representatives and conviction by the Senate are specified as the only means for removing a president from office, and the Constitution further specifies that, if convicted, the president would be "subject to indictment, trial, judgment, and punishment, according to law."[27] The justices could have interpreted the silence about use of civil judicial process directed against the president while in office—together with the implication that the president is *not* subject to criminal prosecution *prior* to impeachment, conviction, and removal from office[28]—as an implicit denial of authority to use such process.

The Court's starting point, in both *Nixon* and *Clinton,* evidently is that, in the absence of explicit instruction to the contrary, ordinary civil process applies. But why is that the right baseline? It is the justices' job to articulate reasons for their decisions that connect principles inherent in governing authority to the result. Here, the Court chose a shortcut; its unexplained assumption of the president's burden to resist the assertion of jurisdiction essentially was dispositive.

That assumption can be explained, and the Court probably adopted a construction of the Constitution more faithful to text and precedent than if it had concluded that presidents are not subject to ordinary civil process. Consider what we know from the text of the document: the Constitution does not say in express terms—or even in terms from which fairly direct inference is possible—that no civil process can be served on the president; the process of impeachment and conviction is solely a process for removal from office; judicial process can serve a broad array of interests unconnected with the president's continuation in office; and the same constitutional provisions that apply to presidential removal from office also apply to the vice president "and all civil officers of the United States."[29] As far as the constitutional text goes, if the inclusion of the removal clause was thought to signal that only the constitutional impeachment-conviction process could be used to reach a sitting president, the text logically would extend the same immunity to all other officers of the United States. That would work a far more blatant departure from both historical and judicial precedent than would permitting civil suit against the president.[30]

Moreover, the baseline chosen in *Nixon* and *Clinton* coheres with an understanding of the rule of law rooted in the precept, articulated by Oakeshott, that law safeguards our liberty by restricting the power of government. That position implies that political power is not to be presumed the source of privilege against ordinary rules of law—it is, after all, the power most in need of constraint. That understanding, as explained above, can be seen as animating the Constitution in its entirety.

The Court's construction of the Constitution, thus, certainly was sound. It was compatible with, and helped reinforce, the rule of law—it followed a principled path from constitutional rule to decision and was the more predictable outcome based on external authority. However, it was not inevitable; it did not follow ineluctably from prior legal authority.

# CHAPTER FOUR

# Ruling Judges

## Partners in Lawmaking or Agents in Application

*The theory is that each decision follows syllogistically from its precedents.*
*But . . . the law is administered by able and experienced men who*
*know too much to sacrifice good sense to a syllogism.*
*—Oliver Wendell Holmes, Jr.*

## Two Models of Judging

The story of the *Nixon* and *Clinton* cases is that judges' decisions constrain even the president and that those decisions conform to reasoned constructions of external commands. But those cases also show that there is space between what we observe in judicial decisions and a description of judges' decisions as fully and unquestionably rule-governed. "Sound" and "reasoned" are not the same as "fully bound."

The space between real-world judging and fully rule-bound (or fully external-authority-bound) decision making raises a question. If the easy route when confronting a president is accommodation and if the justices had arguments that could have led them to conclusions more congenial to the presidents, why then did the justices unanimously reach unfriendly results in those cases?

The absence of perfect constraint over judicial decisions from reference to prior legal authority has fueled twin debates over what judges in fact *do* in deciding cases and over what judges *should* do. These debates are conflated in much of the literature; both the positive question and the normative question are difficult enough that commentary has often imported evidence or argument from one field in support of assertion in the cognate field. Both sets of debates will be referenced, but the focus of this chapter and of chapter 5 will be the positive question.

Arguments on both positive and normative aspects of judicial decision making cover many diverse positions. The primary divisions have been along lines describing the degree of judicial autonomy and the source of judicial guidance. Accurate description of the various stances taken in the literature on judicial decision making would require, at the least, presentation of a spectrum, with commentators taking positions all along the continuum. That approach, however, risks losing the flavor of the principal arguments about judges and judging. To better capture the main points of controversy—though necessarily overstating the claims of individuals who are cast as protagonists of polar positions—this chapter begins by fashioning the writings about judicial decision making into two opposed models (using the term *model* in its colloquial sense, a stylized description rather than a set of propositions that produce testable hypotheses).

The first set of writings can be characterized as subscribing to the Partnership Model of judging. On the positive side, these writings describe judges as substantially unconstrained, motivated by a complex set of instincts, interests, and incentives.[1] Judge Richard Posner, adverting to a distinction common in economics, captures an aspect of this when declaiming that judges should be seen as "principals" rather than "agents."[2] Political scientists Ken Shepsle and Mark Bonchek express the thought more pithily, referring to judges as "legislators in robes."[3]

Political scientists often treat legislators as if they were constrained only by their desire to gain reelection. Though this approach undoubtedly conveys a distorted impression of legislators' motivations, it provides extremely useful— and fairly robust—descriptions of the political process.

Identifying the incentives that govern "legislators in robes" has proved more difficult. Some authors in the Partnership school see judicial decisions (and law more generally) as inseparable from "politics," with each judge motivated by his or her own personal preferences and affinities.[4] At times, these authors offer more particular descriptions of the politics and affinities that must have moved specific judges in specific cases.[5] Other writers find the inquiry into judicial motivation fruitless beyond the abstract depiction of general tendencies.[6]

The normative analog to this positive commentary treats judges as partners with other branches of government in the lawmaking process, rightly granted substantial room to choose among several legitimate, alternative decisional paths.[7] The law for these authors cannot be given shape other than through its articulation in particular instances—it is only what judges and legislators say it is—and legal scholars should be absorbed in preaching good values to judges rather than in ascribing determinate content to legal texts.[8]

The opposed set of positive and normative arguments can be characterized as framing the Agency Model of judging. This model stresses constraints on judicial action.

On the positive side, the Agency Model finds judges' decisions primarily governed by external legal authority. The judges' backgrounds, politics, and personal preferences do not disappear entirely, but they are treated as incidental, not dominant, factors.[9] External constraints on judges are not fully divorced from politics—and indeed are, in the main, derived from political processes—but judges operate at a remove from active, current politics, constrained instead by forces that can be characterized as belonging to a relatively autonomous domain of law.[10]

Related normative writings support the image of the judge as more agent in law application than partner in lawmaking. Typically the judge is not enjoined to do what the judge thinks is best or what the writer deems best according to some principle divorced from positive law, but instead the judge is directed to find the right meaning for a particular law.[11] Some writers make judges agents of authority not strictly derived from the commands of positive law inscribed by other branches of government,[12] but all within the Agency school emphasize that the judge's goal is fixed irrespective of her or his own individual preferences. Even within the Agency school, one may question how fixed and impersonal some goals cast in Agency form are (especially in the arena of constitutional interpretation). Nevertheless, for at least the paradigmatic proponents of this model, there is strong appeal to external constraints for nearly all legal issues, and some assert that the real point of much positive law is to constrain the judge.[13]

The contest between ideas associated with the Partnership Model and those assimilated to the Agency Model is both important and long-standing.[14]

The positive evidence leads to the conclusion that judging in America does not conform fully to either model but that on the whole our judging is much closer to the Agency Model than to the Partnership Model, conforming closely to the Weak Agency Model elaborated further in chapter 5.

## What American Judges Do: Arguments for Partnership

*Incentives along the Partnership Track*

The first conclusion—that judging conforms fully to neither polar model— is the more readily supported. Because the second conclusion is that American judging has greater congruence with the Agency Model, it is best to start with positive evidence that is more consistent with the Partnership Model. The strongest evidence emerges from observing something that the American legal system does *not* have: binding constraints that would prevent judges from injecting personal beliefs into decisions.

Federal judges enjoy life tenure, and their pay cannot be reduced. In inflationary times, we might expect interest in pay *raises* to play a constraining role. But judicial pay is set by class, not individually, and there are enough federal judges (825 Article III judges) that free rider problems should overwhelm this constraint.[15]

Most state judges must stand periodically for election. This may check tendencies to follow personal predilections that are far from the current political midpoint. And that may have notable consequences for a few issues that come before the courts.[16] But judicial elections are even more of a blunt instrument than most elections—typically less frequent than other official elections (hence, more remote in time from acts to be constrained) and more restricted (limiting who can contest for a judgeship, sometimes to those certified by some screening body and at times even reducing to a vote solely on retention of the incumbent).[17]

Further, elections for state judges do not move us off the partnership track, since these are political, not legal, checks on judicial decisions. It is consistent with the Partnership Model that judges have substantial freedom to make law even if subjection to the electorate still places bounds around that freedom. Unless those bounds induce judicial fidelity to a relatively autonomous domain of law, they do not fit the Agency Model. Of course, blatant disregard of legal authority could be the basis for removing judges from office—through

impeachment and conviction in the federal system or recall in state systems—
but only if the dominant view in the political process strongly values adherence to legal authority and the requisite political actors agree on when it is
and is not followed. If those conditions are not met, the constraint looks more
like ordinary politics again.

The prospect of reversal by a higher court is often thought of as a check on
judges' conformity to law. This too, however, proves little, for several reasons.

First, few decisions in fact can be reviewed by higher courts. Whether at
the state or federal level, the winnowing process between one level of court
and another is quite severe. Annual case filings in courts of initial jurisdiction
are roughly three hundred times as numerous as filings in courts of intermediate appellate jurisdiction and are nearly one thousand times the number of
filings in courts of last resort (the highest court in the state system or, for federal cases, the Supreme Court).[18] Even this may overstate the prospect that a
decision will receive serious attention on appeal. For example, although more
than eight thousand cases were filed in the Supreme Court during the 1998
term, only ninety were argued and decided with opinions by the justices.[19]

Second, the *in terrorem* effect that review is said to occasion in lower courts—
which should reach a broader spectrum of decisions than those actually reviewed, as judges hew closer to the line expected to be favored by higher-
court judges in order to reduce the risk of review and reversal—generally is
overstated. Judges who respect the decisions of the higher court will endeavor
to decide cases similarly even without the prospect of review, whereas those
who believe that their reviewing court's judges are in error will generally not
be shamed by review. The intersection of this fact with the winnowing effect
is illustrated by the reaction of one judge of the U.S. Court of Appeals for the
Ninth Circuit after a term in which the Supreme Court reviewed twenty-nine
decisions from the circuit, reversing twenty-eight. The judge's reported comments evidenced little interest in following Supreme Court precedent, declaring in effect, "They can't catch *all* my decisions."[20]

Third, and related to the last point, stronger constraints from reversal and
reversal aversion support the Agency Model only if the basis for reversal is
rooted in failure properly to follow the apposite sources of law. Unless we accept that model of judging as generally applicable, there is no obvious reason
to accept it for higher-court judges.[21]

Some scholars in the Partnership school treat judges as more constrained than this discussion suggests, but constrained by strictures indistinguishable from those operating in the realm of ordinary politics. For example, McNollgast (the corporate nom de plume of Mathew McCubbins, Roger Noll, and Barry Weingast) urge that judicial decision making can be modeled best by treating each judge as endeavoring to promote his or her own preferences subject to the preferences of other relevant actors, notably higher-ranking judges and lawmakers. In their model, the decision of higher-ranking judges to review a given lower-court decision is a function of the distance between the lower court's decision and the appellate judges' preferences (ranked on a linear preference scale for expositional ease).[22] Lower-court judges then alter their behavior to maximize the proximity of expected outcomes (including those pursuant to appellate review) to their own preferences. Appellate judges do the same, treating the lawmakers as an appellate court.

If judges are moved by outcome preferences, as this model supposes,[23] it is rational for judges to take account of the effects of subsequent decision makers, inside the legal system and out. But this seems to exaggerate the influence of subsequent decision makers just as other versions of the reversal-aversion story (generally associated with the Agency Model) do. On average, judges probably attach a negative value to reversal, but it is highly unlikely that this is a strong input to their decisions.[24] Certainly, the recent evidence from the Ninth Circuit would not corroborate a significant role for reversal aversion.

An alternative incentive is the carrot, rather than the stick: judges may aspire to higher office and tailor their behavior to curry favor with those who select or approve higher-court judges. This carrot may be withheld if judges depart from the Agency Model. Judges who ignore precedent, who disregard the textual commands of statutes or of the Constitution—who do not, in short, conform to the accepted standards of the profession—may be at a substantial disadvantage in gaining higher office.[25] More than a few judicial nominees have been challenged on the ground that they did not seem suitably judicial—that they did not show the proper respect for external legal authority in their writings or in their actions (as academicians, government officials, or lower-court judges).[26]

This incentive, like reversal aversion, probably exercises some constraining influence on judges, but it, too, is likely to be a weak reed for the Agency Model. First, the prospect of higher office, even more than the prospect of reversal, is remote. There are more than 25,000 trial court judges in the state courts, but fewer than 950 judges sit on intermediate state appellate courts and only 357 on state courts of last resort.[27] In the federal court system, there are roughly 650 district court judgeships, 167 positions on the U.S. Court of Appeals, and 9 on the Supreme Court of the United States.[28] Because judges tend to have substantial longevity in office, the number of openings at any level is far smaller than the number of positions. On average fewer than 5 percent of federal judges resign or retire each year.[29]

Looking only at these numbers—and not at the broader pool of lawyers, law professors, and public officials outside the judiciary who may contend for judicial appointments—the possibility of moving up the judicial ladder seems fairly small except for judges on intermediate state appellate courts who are interested in moving to their state's court of last resort. Of course, even a very small probability may yield behavioral changes if the payoff is great enough.

If this hurdle is cleared, the Agency Model's argument on judicial incentives for advancement quickly encounters a second, higher hurdle. Though judges should expect that great departures from the norms of the legal profession regarding obeisance to governing authority will impede chances of advancement, they should also see the relationship as something other than a monotonic function. Departures from professional norms can raise a judge's profile, bringing the judge to the attention of those who help select the next candidate for the desired position. Justices like Oliver Wendell Holmes and Benjamin Cardozo were not known for their performance as state court judges simply because they knew proper citation form—both judges broke new ground and did so with flair.[30]

It is not clear which factor—breaking new ground or writing with flair—contributes more to raising a judge's visibility to critical audiences. Our two immediate exemplars of the unusual judge split on this score. Especially in their state-court incarnations, Cardozo was more noted for what his judicial opinions accomplished, Holmes for his epigrammatic style. Nor is it plain that increased visibility to critical audiences necessarily results in increased appeal. Either a significant departure from precedent or a notable-and-quotable remark carries the prospect for pleasing or for irritating those whose views matter most.

Pushing the limits of fidelity to governing authority probably raises the individual judge's notoriety within the profession, but straying significantly from the norm does not seem to have been the path for judicial advancement.

Holmes and Cardozo are exceptional, having been better known and more identified with changes in the law (as judge or author) than other justices of the past century at the time they were elevated to the Supreme Court. Most judges who have been elevated to higher courts have been less willing to break new ground, sticking closer to traditional practice. And even Holmes and Cardozo fit safely within the profession's norms.[31]

Even if political actors (whose judgment counts in elevating lower court judges to higher courts) value adherence to legal rules, it is plain that other values count as much or more. Politicians seldom evince the same concern for fidelity to statutory or constitutional text and precedent that they show for results. Popular commentary on "hot" issues in the courts—issues respecting abortion rights, the death penalty, race relations, assisted suicide, or even presidential susceptibility to suit—characteristically displays scant interest in the technical and professional debates over interpretive niceties. Judicial decisions are assigned to bipolar positions: for or against abortion rights, for or against the death penalty, and so on. Politicians ask potential judges questions about the weight they would give to precedent or text, but the questions frequently are attempts to get a promise or a confession—senators want the nominee to take a stand publicly on abortion, not to give a lecture on the abstract issue of precedent's role in constitutional interpretation, as hearings on Robert Bork's nomination to the Supreme Court made abundantly clear. That lesson is not lost on judges who would be justices.

At the end of the day, the serious question is not whether judges have strong incentives from external monitoring by higher courts and by politicians to hew to predictable rules and principles, predictably applied. Instead, it is whether the externally supplied incentives have any appreciable effect and, if so, whether the net result is positive or negative insofar as principled predictability is concerned.

*Partnership's Tracks: Novel Decisions*

If the absence of evident, binding constraints on judging seems more consistent with the Partnership Model, what is the evidence from judges' outputs? Can more be said than that judges' decisions, as evidenced by *Nixon* and *Clinton,* are not fully determined by prior authority?

The answer must be yes. Sort of. Some judicial decisions are merely open to argument, as in *Nixon* and *Clinton,* turning on matters as to which there is a predictable if arguable disposition.[32] But other decisions are sufficiently novel that they affect a corner of the law the way El Niño affects weather patterns—changing the climate and altering settled expectations based on prior experience. Such decisions are not frequent, but they are not unknown. As we see from examining some of them, they also do not take us far toward the Partnership Model even if they cast doubt on very strong versions of the Agency Model. The settled expectations these decisions upset generally have been unsettled to some significant degree beforehand, and the issues they present can be distinguished from the general run of issues that come before the courts.

A famous example of a decision that breaks new ground is *Brown v. Board of Education of Topeka, Kansas.*[33] The Supreme Court in *Brown* and its companion cases affirmed one lower court decision and reversed four others. The decision that was upheld, *Belton v. Gebhart,*[34] came from a court of chancery in a state system that still divided law from equity. The chancellor, Collins J. Seitz of Delaware, declared that as a lower-court judge, he was bound to follow the then-governing law, the separate-but-equal doctrine announced by the Supreme Court of the United States in *Plessy v. Ferguson.*[35] Seitz announced that the *Plessy* rule was both morally wrong and fundamentally at odds with the constitutionally protected principle of equality under the law. In his judgment, separate-but-equal was inevitably an oxymoron: at least where state-provided education was at issue, *separate* was simply incompatible with *equal.* But, he said, it was up to the Supreme Court to overrule *Plessy*—he could not. His decision for the plaintiffs in *Belton* was based on the incomparability of the white and black high schools for residents of Delaware. In making that finding, however, Seitz applied a test that stretched the contours of *Plessy's* rule to the extreme, declaring that any significant inequality in any aspect of the educational experience sufficed to make education unequal. Even if the education in white and black schools was roughly equivalent—one school better in some respects, the other in different respects—that would not meet Seitz's interpretation of the *Plessy* test. Plaintiffs, he said, had a right to *full* equality. Seitz also departed from precedents regarding remediation of the inequality, ordering immediate admission of the black plaintiffs to the superior, white schools.[36]

In affirming, the Supreme Court, buttressed by social scientists' assertions, adopted essentially the same view of the constitutional guarantee of equality that Seitz articulated but could not directly follow. That reading of the Constitution marked a significant departure from the approach of prior cases.

The *Brown* decision, now universally (and rightly) acclaimed for its contribution to social justice, is debatable as a proper *legal* decision.[37] The *Brown* decision's reading of the constitutional guarantee of equality under the law seems to follow a track given by the justices' personal conceptions of justice far more than externally generated authority. No one today would argue against the *moral* claim recognized by Chancellor Seitz in *Belton* and by the Supreme Court in *Brown*, but scholars who see the Agency Model as providing the proper norm for judging would place the moral claim outside the realm of considerations appropriate for a court.[38] That is why Seitz in *Belton* and Chief Justice Earl Warren in *Brown* were careful not to rest on that ground.

What, then, is the legal basis for *Belton* and *Brown?* To begin, the cases deal with a specific but open-textured constitutional guarantee against state action denying individuals equality under the law. In interpreting that provision, judges must advert to an understanding of the meaning of equality. A commonsense rendering of the phrase would seem at odds with state provision of one education to white citizens and another to black citizens. Nothing in the text of the constitutional guarantee suggests a basis for permitting that. And no one today would dissent from the assertion that the concept of equality under the law is squarely incompatible with state-mandated racial segregation of educational facilities, especially given the manifest evidence that segregation produced gross disparities in resources and opportunities available to white Americans (who played the leading roles in segregating American society and in allocating resources to our educational systems) and to black Americans (who seldom had much voice in those decisions).

The problem for *Brown* and *Belton*, however, was that judicial precedents had made the guarantee turn on the particulars of the disparate treatment— on the *degree* of difference rather than on the *fact* of race-based separation. The social science assertions cited in *Brown* are not hard evidence that the *Plessy* doctrine could never be satisfied, and their contingency on time and method has been a source of criticism of the *Brown* decision for years.[39]

In the absence of a solid factual basis for rejecting *Plessy*, what the courts needed to satisfy critics of *Brown*'s and *Belton*'s legal merit was grounding for the decision in a principle of general applicability found in the law. The challenge laid down by Professor Herbert Wechsler was whether such a principle could be found.[40] The state is allowed to make any number of distinctions among citizens, a point *Brown* did not contradict. The text the Court interpreted in *Brown* did not by its terms outlaw all discrimination by the state nor even all discrimination on racial grounds. What serious contemporary critics of the reasoning in *Brown* found missing, hence, was an explanation of the source and scope of the legal principle that required a finding that *this* discrimination violated the Constitution—an explanation of why the rule announced in *Plessy* was at odds with a more important principle that must govern decision of such cases.[41] Was any racial discrimination by government anathema? any separation of students in state-provided education? including separation by sex? by age? by geography? Where in the law was there a set of decisions that provided a rule for the Court that would answer such questions?

Professor Wechsler's famous critique of the *Brown* decision exposes the difficulty of casting the Court's opinion as anchored squarely in external legal authority. Racial discrimination is today generally seen as repugnant and education as of fundamental importance. But those understandings cannot be invoked as support for *Brown*—they owe their origin in no small measure to *Brown,* which changed the law and, in time, helped change American attitudes. The values we hold today, which make *Brown* appear a straightforward construction of the equal-protection right, may mirror values held by those who framed the constitutional right; and *Brown* may be entirely consistent with the initial understanding of the provision.[42] But those values, and the reasons why those values require a construction of the equal-protection clause outlawing state-sponsored segregated education, cannot readily be said to have *derived from* the legal authorities that had elaborated the provision's meaning up to that time. It is, in other words, hard to square *Brown*—and, likewise, *Belton*—with a very strong version of the Agency Model.[43]

For those who find the Partnership Model a better description of reality, several facts about *Brown* and *Belton* offer support. Among them are that the Delaware chancellor who decided *Belton* was a devout Catholic who grew up in poverty and experienced discrimination firsthand; that when *Brown* was decided, the Supreme Court was led by a new chief justice who understood the immense political implications of the case and who had been tarred by his role in removing Japanese-Americans from the West Coast during World War II (perhaps making him more sensitive to a history that would link his name either to racial and ethnic segregation or to its extirpation); and that the roles played by black Americans during World War II, on the battlefield and the home front as well, had helped to reduce the support for segregation among many white Americans. These facts are consistent with a conclusion that the decisions in *Belton* to deploy a new remedy (plainly reflecting dissatisfaction with the *Plessy* framework even while formally employing it) and in *Brown* to jettison *Plessy*, however justified, responded to personal and political preferences rather than to the claims of an autonomous legal order.

Of course, these facts may not illuminate the actual bases for the decisions. At least arguably, despite Professor Wechsler's appraisal, the decisions could have been based strictly on readings of standard legal sources with the judges' personal views or experience or the judges' perceptions of popular sentiment playing no role. Principles at odds with the *Plessy* doctrine can be extracted from constitutional text and judicial precedent. Though *Plessy* remained the governing law, a line of cases stretching over thirty years preceding *Brown*—finding state-provided services unequal, typically in the context of graduate and professional education—had sapped much of its vitality.[44] These cases were cast as applications of the *Plessy* doctrine, but they were understood at the time to be raising the equality bar, making it harder for states to clear that hurdle when segregating black and white Americans. The *Brown* Court drew from those cases a new sense of what equality was constitutionally guaranteed. The movement through incremental, judicial decision making—from *Plessy*, through the refinements of what could be called equal while separate, to *Brown*'s conclusion that state-mandated separation is incompatible with equality—could be consistent with versions of the Agency Model that find room for principles embodied in the Constitution's text to trump a more narrowly directed and seemingly apposite rule.[45]

Yet making that argument requires a new element to explain how the court was applying well-formed external authority or a version of the Agency Model weaker than its standard representation. All of the background change in legal authority leading up to *Brown* makes it more predictable, to be sure, than if the decision had been rendered three decades earlier. But the Agency Model requires something more than that decisions be predictable. It looks to predictability that derives from fidelity to a system of legal rules—authoritative, external guides to decision—that is autonomous within some domain. That is the point of decisions constrained by external rules. That is the basis for claims that the law's instructions are not merely (reasonably) *predictable* but also (reasonably) *determinate.*[46] To bring the *Brown* judgment within the ambit of such a legal regime requires a rule of decision that specifies how and when broader principles govern over more "local" ones.[47] And it requires articulation of the source and shape of the broader principle that supported the Supreme Court's *Brown* decision (and the Delaware court's *Belton* decision as well).

The more natural reading of *Brown* and *Belton* is not as simple and direct applications of external authority but rather as fitting the description of judges as "legislators in robes." As social mores changed—or as the identity of judges changed to put cases before jurists with stronger concerns for the poor, the powerless, the outcast or with greater courage to stake out unpopular positions—judges' interpretations of constitutional text changed, much the way legislators' votes on the same issues changed over time.

Other, less famous decisions make an even stronger case for seeing judges as "legislators in robes." Consider, for example, a decision by Judge (later California Supreme Court Justice) Armand Arabian during the trial of Leonardo Rincon-Pineda on rape charges.[48] Judge Arabian refused to give a legally required jury instruction cautioning jurors against accepting the testimony of the prosecutrix. Judge Arabian decided that, though the law in California clearly required him to give the requested instruction, the instruction was morally indefensible. It rested on factual assumptions that Arabian thought untrue. And it was the residue of prejudices born of social circumstances long since changed. Arabian declared that because the required instruction was judicially mandated—not statutorily required—judges could alter the rule. The court of appeals said, in effect, "Maybe so, but not a trial judge." The rule had been confirmed repeatedly by the state supreme court, and judges of the intermediate appellate court did not believe that any lower court could change the rule. The Supreme Court of California (long before Judge Arabian's elevation) reversed the appellate court along with its own prior decisions.[49]

It is difficult to read *Rincon-Pineda* as consistent with the Agency Model. Judge Arabian's decision was the product of his own sense of fairness and justice, not of his construction of external governing authority. We can speculate about the source of his sense of the injustice that adhering to the law would have wrought—did it come from his Armenian heritage (encompassing both personal exposure to discrimination and familiarity with stories of the "Armenian genocide" at the turn of the century), from his education, or from other sources? Whatever the answer to that question, the answer cannot be that it came from a simple reading of legal authority. Judge Arabian saw his role in *Rincon-Pineda* as helping to *correct* the law, not simply to *apply* it. In his own words:

> The legislative process offers an appropriate vehicle for abolishing the cautionary instruction. An overwhelming majority of states have not had legislative involvement on this issue, however, and the task of educating these jurisdictions in order to obtain an enlightened response looms as an immediate stumbling block.
>
> . . . A viable alternative to the legislative process is judicial refusal to give the instruction. By this method, on appeal of a conviction, the appellate court would be afforded an opportunity to render a present-day view.[50]

That evinces the same sense of judicial role as the statement by another thoughtful judge that it is better for the legislature and agencies to make the law right, "but when they don't, *we* have to."[51] Undoubtedly, that statement and Judge Arabian's are not proclamations that judges are not—or should not be—limited by external command. Judge Arabian might well have acted differently if the rule he disputed was legislated or had been recently adopted by the state supreme court or had been specifically reconsidered in the recent past. Such comments are, however, at the least evidence that some judges consciously allow considerations outside the immediate ambit of external authority to affect some decisions.[52]

## What Judges Do: Arguments for Agency

### Evidence of Predictability and Limitation

Discussion of positive evidence thus far has established two propositions: (1) that judges lack strong external incentives—from monitoring by other officials or by the public, acting collectively through electoral processes—to conform to a set of externally generated rules, and (2) that judicial decisions can take different paths and reach different ends, depending on the weight judges give to external authority and the particular reading of such authority the judges adopt. This second point encompasses a recognition that some decisions not only do not derive strictly from the most immediately applicable pre-existing law; they plainly depart enough to mark a clear change in the law.

These propositions do not prove that judging in America conforms to the Partnership Model more closely than to the Agency Model. In fact, both propositions are consistent with either the Partnership Model or most versions of the Agency Model.

The propositions are not consistent with an extreme, mechanical version of the Agency Model, what might be called the Strong Agency Model, which so often is the straw man fought by Partnership advocates. Some formalist writings have portrayed the legal system as a highly determinate, almost mechanistic, regime in which the judge essentially plays the role of transmission belt, taking the facts in each case before him and running it through the rules provided by the political branches of government.[53] These writings long have been regarded as painting an unduly crabbed picture of what judges do, one that gives too little scope for judges to be anything but ciphers.[54]

The Strong Agency Model cannot be reconciled easily with the variations observed in the rules suggested by judicial decisions or with the intensity of some contests over the selection of judges. If judges were not exercising some discretion, there would be little reason to care who held the gavel and wore the robes. Thus, as has been observed often, the highly formalist writings fail to explain important real-world events.[55] And, though this is less often observed, these writings also fail to identify a mechanism for inducing judges to play their assigned role. Some judges—perhaps all judges—may play that role nevertheless, but the Strong Agency Model does not articulate *why* all or nearly all or the majority of judges would do so.

That said, there is ample reason why, in less extremely rule-bound forms, the Agency Model still provides the dominant conception of the American legal system. (These forms generically will be termed the Weak Agency Model, a model more fully described in chapter 5.) Like the evidence presented above, the information supporting the Agency Model is not ironclad—its meaning can be debated. But the most obvious and natural inferences from that evidence are closer to the Agency Model than to the Partnership Model.

The most important evidence is that when all is said and done, judicial decisions are relatively predictable and are predictable on the basis of the material being interpreted rather than the identity of the interpreter.[56] Judicial decisions do at times break new ground and can surprise even knowledgeable observers, but the vast majority are straightforward applications of understood legal precepts.

This point is evident, first, from statistics on litigation and appeal rates. Litigation is most likely when parties' predictions of success diverge.[57] That is not the only variable accounting for litigation.[58] If it was, we would not see vastly differing success rates for plaintiffs across various classes of litigation—ranging from roughly a 10 percent chance of success in defamation actions (less than 5% against media defendants)[59] to a 60–70 percent chance of success in contract and other business-related suits.[60] But the decision to proceed with litigation at each stage (rather than to resolve matters before a suit is filed, to settle a suit without trial, or to accept a decision without taking an appeal) correlates positively with differing assessments of success.[61]

The very strong tendency to resolve lawsuits through settlement and to accept first-level decisions without appeal, hence, is consistent with a narrow range of predicted outcomes. According to those who keep the statistics, in 1995 more than 87 million lawsuits were filed in American courts, 1.2 million in federal courts and the remainder (85.8 million) in state courts.[62] Appellate filings in 1995, however, totaled only 335,000 (counting separately appeals to successive levels in the judicial hierarchy), including approximately 90,000 filings in courts of last resort (the highest court in each state and the Supreme Court of the United States).[63] Less than .4 percent of total case filings, thus, resulted in appeals to higher courts, and only .1 percent to courts of last resort. If our focus is narrowed to civil cases (excluding traffic cases, criminal cases, domestic relations cases, juvenile offense cases, and bankruptcy proceedings), there were 15 million case filings in 1995. In civil cases, more than 90 percent settle without trial, only 3 percent are appealed following a first-level determination, and just over 1 percent are appealed to a court of last resort.[64]

This statistical evidence, though most consistent with a high degree of predictability, is only mildly probative of the sort of principled predictability the Agency Model posits. The congruence between the evidence and principled predictability rests, first, on the observation that generally, as parties' expectations for the outcome of litigation converge, settlement is increasingly likely (assuming that settlement is less costly than trial).[65] High settlement rates and low appeal rates, therefore, both support the Agency Model as a positive description of American law.

Qualification of the declaration that these observed rates are probative of the Agency Model's claims is necessary because the relationship between predictability and settlement does not always hold. If each party projects a wide dispersion of potential outcomes—one party expecting that the result, for instance, could be anything from no liability to a $50 million judgment, the other party anticipating judgments between $100,000 and $100 million—they might reach a settlement despite the gap in expectations. Indeed, with widely dispersed expected outcomes, risk-averse litigants may be *more* likely to settle than they would in a regime that generated a narrower range of predicted outcomes (a more predictable legal regime).[66] This tendency toward settlement in cases with *less* predictable outcomes may be exaggerated by factors that are common in much civil litigation today: the costs of settlement are not borne directly by the individuals making litigation judgments, but those individuals would be more directly harmed by a bad litigated outcome, one that falls toward the lower-valued end of their predictions. This might be true in litigation by large business enterprises, where the costs are dispersed among shareholders but highly visible events create pressure to replace senior managers.[67]

Nonetheless, the typical litigant—who is not a Fortune 500 company—is more likely to fit the prototype modeled by Professors George Priest and Benjamin Klein, which holds that greater predictability decreases the prospect that a case will be litigated to judgment or appealed.[68] On this view, high settlement rates and low appeal rates are consistent with—and inferentially may be probative of—substantial, principled predictability.

*Judicial Output and Judges' Domain*

The picture suggested by evidence of litigants' judgments—of predictable court decisions resulting from a judicial role limited to application of relatively well-defined principles—also fits the set of issues that courts most often are called upon to resolve. The vast majority of judges' work—what in other contexts we would call the bread and butter of their profession—is made of disputes among small numbers of known individuals (generally two) over the obligations owed in respect of a contractual arrangement (e.g., purchase and sale, insurance, finance), a quasi-contractual relationship (e.g., employment, marriage), or an accident (e.g., involving automobiles). The rest of the typical judge's work is a collection of probate-related issues, minor crimes, and regulatory offenses (including traffic offenses, but also including violations of an array of other statutory and administrative directives).[69] These cases—the *ordinary* cases—share three features: they involve only a few, known parties; the issues they present are limited, not open-ended (not, in Lon Fuller's term, polycentric);[70] and they are retrospective.[71]

Concerns over social welfare and individual freedom support a very limited role for judges in ordinary cases,[72] and the focus of dispute is conducive to a limited judicial role.[73] The arguments in ordinary cases commonly center on factual questions. Legal issues do, of course, provoke argument as well. But parties typically agree on the meaning of the vast corpus of legal rules that govern the interactions that gave rise to the dispute. Disputes over interpretation of law, in other words, are a small part of ordinary cases and also focus on a small part of the system of legal rules that in one way or another affected (or at least could apply to) the parties' conduct. Judges' resolutions of law-interpretation disputes commonly go uncontested in some measure because, even though the resolution is not incontestable, it is a thoroughly reasonable interpretation of the law, well grounded in the externally generated authorities.[74] Typically, the answer given is more than merely reasonable; it is the obvious answer to a question that would not be debated seriously if there were not money or joy in the debate.[75]

Discourse about judging rarely addresses ordinary cases. Commentary by American legal scholars tends to focus on appellate decisions, especially Supreme Court decisions, despite (or perhaps because of) the fact that the Supreme Court decides only one hundred or so cases a year, just .0001 percent of the total annual U.S. judicial caseload. Needless to say, the Supreme Court generally addresses the most controversial, least predictable cases. These cases disproportionately involve less tractable issues, less cabined interests, and more forward-looking judgments—features that move decisions closer to those commonly found in the legislative arena and further from the typical judicial case.

Even if Supreme Court justices endeavor to decide cases in the same manner as other judges (a matter taken up again below), the difference in the nature of the issues before them—especially the far greater difficulty of extracting clear resolution from external authority—necessarily brings the individual justices' personal views of the world into play far more than in ordinary cases. Examining the workings of the Supreme Court can offer insights into the way our judges and our legal system function, but assessing the degree to which

American judges exercise discretionary lawmaking power based on what happens in the Supreme Court would be akin to assessing Americans' health by focusing on patients in the Dana-Farber Cancer Institute.[76]

There is one aspect of the work of other courts that may require qualification as well. A unique feature of U.S. law that is striking to foreign observers is that all courts of general jurisdiction, and all Article III federal courts (courts exercising judicial power conferred by Article III of the Constitution), have the power to declare legislative and administrative actions void as unconstitutional. This broadly shared power of judicial review makes all U.S. courts seem more similar to the Supreme Court than would be the case in other nations where a single court (or tightly limited group of courts) has such power.

The point is not simply that the power to declare acts of other branches unconstitutional is a substantial weapon in the arsenal of judicial powers; equally important, the basis for declaring acts unconstitutional could be more subject to judicial discretion than the basis for declaring rights among competing private parties. This is true insofar as constitutional doctrine is less directive than statutory interpretations. There is at least a plausible case that constitutional text tends to be less confining, its background considerations and initial understanding less clear, and the judicial decisions interpreting it less readily made consistent than typically is the case with statutes.[77]

The power to declare acts unconstitutional historically has been deployed quite sparingly, however,[78] because numerous doctrines—some plainly mandated by formally inscribed law binding on judges, others prudential precepts developed by the judges themselves—grant deference to the political branches, including unelected administrative officers who are only indirectly under the control of elected officials. Although these doctrines operate on all U.S. courts, they should especially constrain lower courts, which are less likely than the Supreme Court to see cases in which an assessment of unconstitutionality is difficult to avoid. Having the power of judicial review may move other courts in the direction of the Supreme Court, but there remains a dramatic difference between the cases decided by that court and the ordinary cases that are typically before lower courts.

As the Supreme Court's cases diverge from other courts' dockets, so appellate cases in general diverge from ordinary cases in at least one respect. Appellate cases typically present more difficult judgment calls on questions of law. Although the economic value of the case critically affects decisions to appeal, those decisions also turn on the existence of a dispute on a question of law.[79] These issues typically are less fully governed by clear, controlling external authority than issues presented in the general run of lower-court cases. For that reason, appellate judges might be less constrained by external authority, and their decisions should be less predictable.

Even so, the evidence suggests that judging in these cases, as in ordinary cases, resembles the Weak Agency Model. Appellate cases present closer questions of law more often, but decision of these cases seldom divides judges as should be expected if decision making conformed to the Partnership Model (with individual judges' personal views playing a greater role and "neutral" efforts to interpret legal directives a lesser role). For example, in the U.S. Court of Appeals, roughly 80 percent of the cases that are submitted for decision on the merits are disposed of without a published opinion, even though any judge could move them out of the "table" category.[80] These cases seem to the judges so clear as not to call for explanation. Further, many more cases decided by appellate courts represent the unanimous vote of the participating judges, and the great majority represent a very strong consensus.

The picture of consensus extends even to the Supreme Court. In the Court's 1999 term, for example, close to half of all of the cases set for argument and submitted for decision by the Court on signed opinions—32 out of 73 cases—were decided without dissent.[81] Another 15 cases were decided with two or fewer justices in dissent.[82] This is typical for the Court. The figures for the 1995 term were 38 of 85 cases without dissent and another 26 with two or fewer dissenting votes.[83] Hence, even for the set of cases that, by far, present the most difficult, controversial issues—for which legal authority provides the least certain directives—two-thirds to three-quarters of the time the justices overwhelmingly agreed on the outcome.

### The Selection and Motivation of Judges: Sources of Consensus

That sort of agreement on outcomes is not, strictly speaking, proof of judicial adherence to external authority or even of judicial predictability. It is possible that case outcomes are products of personal determinations that are tied closely neither to legal reasoning from accepted authority nor to circumstances that are discernable ex ante (at least not before identification of the deciding judges). Judge Posner suggests this possibility (if not probability) in his discussion of judges' incentives, opining that agreement on outcomes is a product of judicial indifference and self-interest (the judge's interest in collegial relations).[84] Scholars associated with the Critical Legal Studies movement, such as Professor Joe Singer, also attribute predictability to judges' sameness: people with similar personal characteristics and biases will reach similar decisions.[85]

Explanations that do not take into account the strong pull of externally generated legal rules and principles, however, can only explain behavior that is marginal, not central, to judicial decision making. Judge Posner's assertions about judicial incentives—that judges want to have good relations with other judges and that judges typically have less strong commitments to specific outcomes than might be expected—can be accepted as plausible descriptions of considerations that, among others, shape judicial behavior. These incentives are compatible with frequent consensus among members of a multijudge court and might provide a basis for consensus even if judges do not reason from existing legal rules to a conclusion respecting particular case outcomes. But these incentives, even if they explain some instances of accord among judges who sit together in multijudge panels, do not provide the most plausible explanation for the degree of consensus we observe, nor are they convincing explanations for the degree of consensus that appears in disposition of similar legal questions by judges on different courts.

Consider the question why judges on different courts so often reach similar outcomes in similar cases, a question that points to stronger dissonance with Judge Posner's assertions than emerges from analysis of behavior among judicial colleagues on a multijudge court. The worlds of legal education and law practice are replete with evidence that those who are most familiar with the law believe that common principles dictate outcomes for cases that share certain identifiable features respecting issues and circumstances—not tied to the identity of specific parties. Those who deal regularly with the law also manifest their conviction that these principles apply to many different courts and are relatively stable over significant periods of time. Bar review courses and treatise writers compress a wide array of decisions across many American jurisdictions into sets of legal principles that are accepted bases of decision of similar cases. Legal commentators in one field after another fill law review volumes with descriptions of the precepts guiding decisions of various courts. And lawyers dispense advice drawing on their predictions about the way principles will dictate outcomes, typically finding similar principles embodied in

the law of most U.S. jurisdictions. None of these commonalities across jurisdictions is explicable as the product of collegial relations in the ordinary sense.

That is not to say that no explanation more in line with the Partnership
Model than with the Agency Model can be imagined. Cross-jurisdictional
commonalities in legal rules and judicial decisions might be explained as products of judicial laziness—with judges merely aping the decisions of other jurists
in order to limit the effort involved in deciding matters before them—or of a
desire for collegial relations writ large, within the broad community of judges.[86]

They might be explained, as Professor Singer and other Critical Legal Studies proponents urge, on the ground merely of judges' similar backgrounds and
attitudes.[87] The strong version of this argument—that judges decide cases as
they wish, looking to their own preferences regardless of the legal authorities[88]—seems manifestly at odds with reality unless one posits a sameness of
views, *other than views respecting the force of legal authority,* that is wildly implau-
sible. The weaker version of the CLS critique—that judges are not truly constrained by law but only seem to be because they share certain linguistic conventions, perspectives on morality, and commitments to artifices of the legal
system—adds little to the discussion of how the legal system works.

A final alternative to a rule-of-law-friendly explanation of the commonalities we find in the American legal system is that the commonalities might
not truly exist, at least not in such significant measure as suggested here. We
might see them even though they are not there because we want to believe
that judges make decisions on the basis of principles that we associate with
"legal reasoning."[89] This is the law-as-theology explanation.

Notwithstanding the possibility that each of these alternatives has some
validity, the most obvious explanation for the high degree of consensus and
predictability in the law is that judges in fact act for the most part as agents
rather than as principals: they seek to determine what the law dictates by looking at controlling legal authority and then seek to apply those dictates reasonably to the facts before them. This description provides only the broadest parameters for judicial decision making—more details are given below. But the
description stresses what is most critical: that judges neither see themselves
as unconstrained by external authority nor behave as if they were unconstrained.[90]

The key question, as Judge Posner recognized, is Why? Why do judges act
this way? The answer seems to be largely that judges act this way because they

think they should, and one judge's constrained conception of the judicial role tends to be reinforced by feedback from professional peers holding similar views.[91] If judges' views vary on some particulars of the judicial role, they vary within quite a narrow compass.

To say that judges act constrained because they feel constrained—and feel constrained because their peers feel constrained—though true, does not advance our understanding much. We need to know why American judges have this rule-bound (or at least law-bound) conception of judging. Writing emphasizing judicial constraint asserts the congruence of constraint with public interest.[92] But congruence with public interest does not provide a basis for belief that judges will think constraint appropriate. Ultimately, this is the strongest argument for those on the positive side of Partnership, for there is no robust response to the question why judges believe themselves constrained that holds up under examination.

There is, however, a basis for the Agency Model's assertion of judicial self-constraint. Wholly apart from the professional values imparted in legal training,[93] this conception tracks a bias built into the judicial selection process. The selection process screens judicial candidates to assure as far as possible that they are disposed to see themselves as morally bound to follow the rules of law. Politicians want judges to feel bound, not because politicians are invested in legal process but because judicial adherence to legal rules increases politicians' power.[94] Politicians' first preference is for particular outcomes on specific issues—outcomes that advance their own interests. They do not want controversial issues dumped in their laps; they do not want outcomes opposed by their constituencies (which may blame politicians if they do not reverse those outcomes, often a difficult and costly process).[95] Judicial fidelity to external authority will not guarantee outcomes favored by politicians, who may seek specific commitments on those issues from candidates for judgeships. But a rule of fidelity to external authority generally minimizes risks to politicians from future judicial decisions.[96]

The selection process, then, commonly screens out lawyers with strong intuitions about just outcomes, especially those whose intuitions are significantly at odds with current law. Occasionally such a lawyer may be given a seat on a higher appellate court, but that almost exclusively happens only after the consensus among public and politicians has swung strongly in the direction of the judicial aspirant's views, with the law changing apace.[97] With those rare exceptions, lawyers with strong views on justice instead spend their careers urging judges to shade the interpretation of law in a particular direction or lobbying legislators to change the rules that judges apply.

The lawyers who become judges, then, seek to operate as if bound by rules not because they will be punished if they do not but because they believe it is the right thing for a judge to do.[98] They begin to think about cases not from their intuition about the just outcome but from the dictates of authoritative sources of law. The question that judges ask is not, as Professor Duncan Kennedy has (more or less) opined, "How do I describe the law to make it fit my preference respecting the outcome of this case?"[99] Instead, judges ask, "What is the law, and what does it mean for this case?" Those may be difficult questions in themselves, but they significantly narrow the ambit of admissible considerations.[100]

Moreover, because judges believe that this is the way they are supposed to resolve the cases before them, they feel inhibited from moving outside the bounds of authoritative sources even when their intuition strongly suggests that a particular outcome is just. A judge may feel tension between his or her initial reading of the authorities and his or her intuition and may reread the authorities looking for a means to reconcile them with a sense of justice in the particular case.[101] But this does not mean that the judge commonly reasons from outcome to rationale. Because the judge believes that the externally given law governs, his or her focus on external authorities typically will not generate a strong intuition about justice independent of his sense of the legally proper outcome. And with that belief about the primacy of externally given law, even a judge who has an instinctive sense of the just outcome may find that the case is resolved by external authorities in a contrary manner.[102]

### Differences among Courts?

This picture of judging seems to fit judges of both higher and lower courts. To be sure, there are differences among judges depending on the rank of the court and the subject matters that come before the judge.[103] But those differences suggest less variance in the approach judges take to decision of legal issues than might at first appear.

Look first at trial judges. They spend a considerable portion of their time in the role of "triage nurse"—responsible for sorting cases, determining which ones can be disposed of expeditiously (because there are clear grounds for settlement or because the claim is hopeless), which ones need considerable attention, and which of those are most pressing. Another portion of the trial judge's time is spent in the role of "game show host"—keeping the show running, keeping the participants honest, and making sure that those who make key decisions have the right instructions and understand what to do. These roles place greater stress on considerations that are not law-bound than the role played by appellate judges. Even when legal authorities provide answers to questions that trial judges must resolve in their triage-nurse and game-show-host roles, it is reasonable to expect that the issues frequently will be resolved without extensive consultation of those authorities. Perhaps judges will have developed a "feel" for the legal rules, an instinct based on prior experience, that will integrate legal authority with more practical imperatives. Such is the nature of the job, however, that judges may hope for congruence with the law but not strain much to achieve it.

Yet, when trial judges make decisions on points of law outside of those roles—for instance, when passing on significant motions—they change to a more law-bound role. In this role trial judges' behavior generally looks similar to that of the appellate judge. Trial judges typically need not explain their decisions in detail, nor are they required to gain the assent of other judges, tasks that are likely to pull judges more in the direction of adherence to external authority. In contrast, both of those requirements operate on the appellate judges, who for that reason might be expected to be more law-bound. The trial judge's decision, however, is more likely than the appellate judge's to be on an issue about which external sources of law leave little doubt (a smaller decision space). And, at least arguably, it is more likely to be subject to scrutiny if it departs significantly from the law. Those last two factors argue in favor of greater law-binding for trial judges, counterbalancing the other factors distinguishing trial judges from appellate judges.

Another difference between trial and appellate judges has less clear-cut implications. The trial judge more often will deal with a set of lawyers who are repeat players, who appear before the judge many times over the years. As in other games, repeat play is helpful in assuring fidelity to the rules, though it is not entirely clear that this aspect of trial work imposes more constraint on judges to show fidelity to law than on lawyers to show willingness to accommodate the judges.[104]

In sum, broadly similar attitudes toward resolution of serious legal questions seem likely to prevail in trial and appellate courts. The structure of judging differs between trial and appellate courts, and differences will be found in the incentives of judges on trial and appellate courts. On balance, however, American judges at both levels will be likely, in the main, to behave as if quite bound by external authorities. This inquiry has not focused, save for a glancing blow, on the Supreme Court of the United States. Toward the end of chapter 5, we return to the question of whether the Supreme Court is bound in the same way as other American courts. Putting the Supreme Court aside, American courts generally conform to a law-bound model of judging.

# CHAPTER FIVE

# The Weak Agency Model
## Judges as Translators

*Obscurity of statute or of precedent or of customs or of morals, or collision between some or all of them, may leave the law unsettled, and cast a duty upon the courts to declare it retrospectively . . . [But w]e must not let the occasional and relatively rare instances blind our eyes to the innumerable instances where there is neither obscurity nor collision nor opportunity for diverse judgment. —Benjamin N. Cardozo*

## Interpretation and Judgment

The picture of law-bound judging that emerges from chapter 4 is consistent with most versions of the Agency Model. Judges do not see their job as making law; they endeavor to determine what governing authorities dictate rather than what suits their personal sense of justice, but the governing authorities at times leave considerable scope for different judges to reach different outcomes. This *but* is an important qualification of the starkest form of the Agency Model (the Strong Agency Model), although few scholars—certainly no major scholar writing in the last seventy-five years—contend for a view of judging sufficiently mechanistic to be incompatible with this qualification. Nonetheless, to underscore acceptance of that *but,* the term *Weak Agency Model* is used to describe the reality of American judging.[1]

Although this point is often overemphasized, it must be acknowledged that the orientation of judges to applying law does not do away with the problems inherent in that task. The process of interpreting legal authority and of applying it to new cases often requires highly contextual judgments respecting the nature of the principles embodied in governing law and the circumstances relevant to the application of a given principle. Legislators and constitution framers cannot foresee all relevant circumstances, nor can they specify with clarity all applications of the principles they adopt; they cannot, in other words, always fashion meaningful rules that fully give effect to the law framers' general design. Indeed, it would be wasteful to try.[2]

The frequent inability (and undesirability) of drafting the governing legal authorities in a more fully directive mode raises the importance of core contentions of the Partnership Model's proponents—that language provides imprecise bonds and that legal principles cannot be reduced to rules so clear and simple as to eliminate controversy over their meaning and application. This fact—typically called the problem of indeterminacy—causes Partnership scholars to throw their hands in the air, exclaiming that real constraints on judging cannot exist.[3] In some measure, the base fact must be accepted as true. Judges inevitably have some interpretive room, and in some instances they may have a great deal of room.

The problem is not the same in all cases. In general, interpretive room—the range of possible interpretations compatible with external authorities—is greater as one moves from narrower legal rules to broader rules and principles as the governing authority for judges' work.[4] Unfortunately, as far as the argument for Agency goes, these less confining forms are more often sources of authority in America than in other common law countries, and much more often than in civil law regimes.[5]

That makes the role of judicial incentives here more significant. The judge is insulated from strong incentives to take particular positions and thus is free of incentives that may be at odds with principled predictability. Yet the very absence of strong incentives increases the weight of subtle influences on interpretation.[6] The position a judge takes within the relevant decision-space—which, in line with the Agency Model, is given by rule imprecision, by inter-rule conflict, or by apparent lacunae in a matrix of legal rules—must be affected by factors that the judge will not articulate and may not even be aware of, factors that will vary from one judge to another. As Judge Posner says, factors that affect all other human activity doubtless affect judging as well.[7]

Nevertheless, the most important questions in each case are the size of the decision-space left to judges and the degree to which judges find the open space, if not filled, at least shaded by legal authority.[8] In the Weak Agency Model (indeed, in any version of the Agency Model), in contrast to the Partnership Model, the judge starts by asking what the law commands rather than starting with an intuitively appealing outcome and seeking to mold legal authorities into a shape that accommodates that intuition. If other factors influence judicial answers to that question, they do so less predictably, less systematically, and less forcefully than the Partnership Model supposes.

## Interpretation as Translation

The best view of judging in America, then, is not that judges are "legislators in robes." Rather, it is that judges act primarily as "translators of law."

### The Translation Analogy

Think of the job a translator has: to reproduce in the vernacular the message from the original text's language. The translator's task on its face seems straightforward, substituting a word used in modern American English, say, for the same word in another language, word by word through the text. But the task is not so simple. It is not a mechanical process, such as applying a mathematically defined code to return an encrypted message to ordinary language, but a far more complex operation that proceeds along several vectors. Consider four examples: translation of the Holy Bible, *Beowulf, Les Misérables,* or *Les Fleurs du Mal* from Hebrew, Old English, and French, respectively. The translator must find ways to express the meaning understood at the time of the original manuscript, to capture the cadence and rhythm of the initial language, and, for the last of these works at least, to include the rhyme as well.

Often, no word in modern American English will be a perfect fit, and the translator must endeavor to find the best possible among imperfect substitutes. For different works, a single translator might choose different priorities in trying to replicate the original work. Perhaps the key judgment in translating the Bible will be fidelity to the theological message; perhaps for *Beowulf* it will be conveying a sense of the story's meaning and interest in its time; for *Les Misérables* the translator may strive to capture the flow and power of the story, to elicit the emotional response of Hugo's original audience; and for Baudelaire's work the sound of the words may be nearly as important as their message in evoking the mood of the poems. At times the translator will struggle to fit a word with the right sound and rhythm to the original meaning.[9]

At times the original meaning will be obscure, and the translator will be forced to make a choice without information sufficient to illuminate that meaning fully. The impediment to fuller understanding might trace to the translator's distance in time and place from the work's initial inscription. Or it might trace to the opacity of the work itself. Or to differences between the original author's skills (linguistic and analytical) and the translator's—differences that do not necessarily cast the translator as a journeyman painter essaying to restore DaVinci's *Last Supper*. For any of these reasons, at times connotations may be lost that were important to the initial audience or words may be chosen with connotations that distract from the initial understanding. And although individual words may pose discrete translation problems, no translation will proceed word by word, because differences in idiom, in grammar, and in structure would make that a senseless approach.

In dealing with these problems, each translator's earnest effort is to do justice to the original work.[10] But each translator makes choices that are questionable. Sometimes observers believe that a translator has altered the work in a critical way, possibly changing the meaning in some fundamental respect. Inevitably, the translator's efforts, however earnest, are affected by any number of subtle influences, and critics whose judgment differs can reasonably suggest that the translation was tainted by one or more factors personal to the translator. That sort of argument is common whenever a new translation of the Bible is released and occurs less publicly with respect to other translations.[11]

The same basic picture fits judges.[12] Judges must take the legal texts that govern and apply them to individual cases, saying what the texts mean in specific contexts. Like translators, judges are imperfectly constrained agents whose goal is to be faithful to someone else's work. Like translators, judges do indeed take the work of others as setting the framework for their tasks. Like translators, judges face numerous problems in moving from available materials to finished product. Like translators, different judges will resolve those problems in different ways. Like translators, judges are not free from influences that may skew their work products. Like the work of translators, judges' work is affected by the prospect of ex post critiques, with peers' views of the professional's skill a likely consideration. And for judges as for translators, there is little in the way of effective monitoring while the work is being done.

### Translation versus Composition

This judge-as-translator metaphor casts the judge in a different role than some other, better-known images, though it shares features with some of them. Consider, for example, Ronald Dworkin's analogy of judging to composition of a "chain novel":

> In this enterprise a group of novelists writes a novel *seriatim;* each novelist in the chain interprets the chapters he has been given in order to write a new chapter, which is then added to what the next novelist receives, and so on. Each has the job of writing his chapter so as to make the novel being constructed the best it can be. . . .
>
> Each novelist aims to make a single novel of the material he has been given, what he adds to it, and (so far as he can control this) what his successors will want or be able to add. . . . The interpretation he takes up must . . . flow throughout the text; it must have general explanatory power, and it is flawed if it leaves unexplained some major structural aspect of the text. . . .
>
> He may find, not that no single interpretation fits the bulk of the text, but that more than one does. The second dimension of interpretation then requires him to judge which of these eligible readings makes the work in progress best, all things considered. At this point his more substantive aesthetic judgments, about the importance or insight or realism or beauty of different ideas the novel might be taken to express, come into play.[13]

The chain-novel metaphor resembles translation in its attendance to the preexisting texts, in its insistence that the interpretation give coherence to those texts, and in its combination of discretion and constraint. It resembles translation also in giving the authoritative texts prominence over other sources of evidence respecting the intentions of those who wrote earlier chapters. And it recognizes the variation possible when different interpreters address the texts.

Dworkin's metaphor differs, however, in suggesting a different focus than translation does and in implying a broader discretion as the norm. The chain-novel idea is that the author is very much a creator and sees creativity—though bounded by the need to fit the material thus far in hand—as his charge. The text is a side constraint on the creative impulse that is central to Dworkin's novel image. Implicit in that image is the important—and, for Dworkin, once his *fit* criterion is satisfied, normatively attractive—role of subjective, personal choice in the interpretive process.[14]

That role is not eliminated in the judge-as-translator metaphor, in large measure because it cannot be. But in seeking fidelity to a text, the translator is self-consciously stepping back from the job of the writer. The translator seeks to carry forward faithfully the text as he finds it, though he must put it in new form and make choices in performing that task. The Dworkinian chain novelist, in contrast, essays to make a distinctive contribution to the work of the writers, to whom he or she is partner as well as heir.

### Hard Cases versus Ordinary Cases

Dworkin's construct may be an accurate description of the way some judges approach some decisions. In particular, it may be apposite to decisions for which there is no source of substantial textual guidance outside judicial opinions that are not formally binding on the decision maker—a category largely composed of controversial constitutional law cases before the Supreme Court and a small number of common law cases before state courts of last resort. These rare decisions probably are the very ones Dworkin has in mind in shaping the chain-novel metaphor. They certainly are the decisions to which he pays attention.

These cases also have been the focus of much other theorizing, indeed forming the primary focus for most academic theorizing about interpretation. The dominant focus on such cases might be explained by the difficulty of resolving them, a difficulty that requires attention to questions of interpretive mode that seldom are so obviously in play. Or the focus might be explained by the cases' utility as teaching tools (after all, there is extraordinary overlap between cases taught in law school classes and cases written about by legal scholars). The difficult cases may come out differently under different modes of interpretation even if the ordinary case would not. Hence, beyond the importance of attention to interpretation in those cases, the dispersion of results under the different interpretive theories can be instructive.

Interpretive theories for such hard cases are necessarily tricky affairs, since the absence of significant guidance in external authorities leaves the task heavily dependent on the assumptions each theorist brings to the table. Theory addressed to these cases largely prescribes ways to craft the most elegant legal fabric out of the most fragile thread—and to make the tapestry look "right" when there is no accessible picture of what the fabric should be.[15] The absence of such an accessible picture does more than make the exercise a challenge— it inevitably yields dissensus over the way the exercise should be done. Not surprisingly, Dworkin's interpretive constructs have been criticized amply by scholars whose assumptions about what *right* is diverge from Dworkin's assumptions; but most other theories of constitutional construction designed for such cases have been subjects of similar criticism.[16]

Whatever is the right approach to the rare case—we'll come back to that below—Dworkin's metaphor must be rejected as a description of what transpires in the more typical legal case. In such cases, the approach of judges is less knowingly creative and transformative than Dworkin suggests—it compares more closely to recapitulation of the directives from authoritative texts in a form useful to the specific dispute at hand. In other words, it more closely resembles translation than participation in writing a chain novel.[17]

This is obviously true for interpretation of a single, controlling authority, such as a statute. But it is true as well for the great run of legal decision making, including attempts to give a coherent account of the law when multiple authorities speak to the matter. The judge is not looking to provide an account that satisfies her or him as the most normatively attractive account that is not at odds with so much of the governing authority that it cannot be said to "fit" that authority. The judge instead is trying to determine what that authority directs, a determination that is dispositive so far as the standard case goes.

Test this description yourself. Pick up any volume of trial court or intermediate appellate court decisions at random. How many cases seem to fit the relatively determinate translation model and how many a less determinate model?

A librarian friend, asked to try this out, chose a recent volume of decisions by the Massachusetts Court of Appeals, the state's intermediate appellate court.[18] The volume reports 760 decisions. Of these, 619 were decided without published opinion, the remaining 141 with published opinion. Just over one-third of this latter group (53) were appeals from the criminal docket, and nearly two-thirds (88) were civil cases (including 27 cases appealing decisions of adminis-trative agencies). In all of the cases combined, there were only two dissents.[19] One dissent differed from the majority on whether an insurance company had properly preserved an argument for judicial decision when the argument had been made and rejected in an arbitration (the dissenting judge thought the argument was preserved).[20] The other dissent questioned the majority's dis-tinction of the case at hand, a suit over injuries sustained when the plaintiff fell into an open manhole, from a seventy-year-old decision involving similar facts.[21] The opinions cover 867 pages in total, so that opinions on average are approx-imately 6 pages, including headnotes.[22] The dissents for the entire volume cover approximately 3 pages together. Only two cases drew any comment from local media, one a garden-variety labor-law decision that was noted because it in-volved a union dispute with the troubled Boston school system.[23] The other newsworthy case reversed a family-court judge's decision that had separated twin twelve-year-old girls, awarding custody of one to each parent, an unusual custody award, to say the least.[24] Neither appellate decision prompted a dis-sent; neither involved difficult legal questions.

This is the evidence from the intermediate appellate court of a relatively populous and relatively wealthy state with a reasonably high concentration of lawyers.[25] Given the state's demographics, together with the predominance of settlement over litigation to judgment and of adjudication at only a single level of the judicial system, one would expect this volume to be on the high end for complex, contested legal issues. Yet none of these cases looks as "up for grabs" in terms of the controlling law as Dworkin's chain-novel metaphor (and more generally his interpretive model) suggests.[26] One must search hard—and with a peculiar sort of spectacles as a filter—to find such a case in the volumes reporting the mass of ordinary cases decided day in and day out in America's courts. And one must look still harder to find a case in which the judge's deci-sion seems rooted primarily in moral principles rather than in analysis of the legal authorities to see what reasonable interpretation, what reasonable trans-lation, the law can be given.

Those cases can be found, as discussion of *Brown, Belton,* and *Rincon-Pineda* illustrated.[27] But these are quite exceptional decisions. That fact, in large mea-sure, is what made Chancellor Seitz a controversial figure for many years after ordering Delaware to integrate its schools, what made Judge Arabian a con-troversial figure among California judges, and why Chief Justice Earl Warren's *Brown* decision remains a subject of discussion apart from the changes it wrought.

Of course, if *Brown, Belton,* and *Rincon-Pineda* are the truly exceptional cases, they surely are not the only cases in which hard interpretive issues are posed. There are numerous difficult issues presented in court each day, involving imprecise statutory language, apparent conflicts among statutory provisions, and real conflicts among the various materials commonly referenced to clarify textual ambiguity.[28] There are also (probably less numerous, but not by any means uncommon) difficulties born of divergent explanations in judicial decisions and of precedents that, given their most natural readings, suggest legal principles leading in different directions.[29] Of such stuff is law school made.[30]

Even so, the typical judicial approach to resolving these difficult cases is relatively straightforward: each judge endeavors to figure out what the governing authorities mean for disposition of the particular case. That much is agreed by judges across a broad spectrum of political, philosophical, and personal views.[31] The translation metaphor, thus, seems more apt than alternatives such as Dworkin's that suggest greater scope for judicial creativity, that suggest more degrees of freedom (to borrow a term from statistics) for the judge.

### *"Translation" as Composition*

The translation metaphor has been used by others, however, to suggest a process somewhat closer to Dworkin's (it is not entirely clear how much) than to the Agency Model suggested here.[32] Most notable is the work of Professor Larry Lessig, who has written several articles about constitutional interpretation as "translation."[33] With no more fairness to Professor Lessig than Professor Dworkin received above, Lessig's theory can be compressed as follows. The task of the judge is to read legal texts in light of changed circumstances so that a text's meaning today coheres with the text's meaning at a previous time, understood in the context of its time and place. That coherence is found in fidelity to a process of judicial decision making that respects the meaning of the past while allowing the reading of a text to change as the forces that supported the initial meaning erode:

> Legal discourse in part rests upon discourses outside of the law. . . . [T]hese
> backgrounded, non-legal discourses permit a discourse within the law to make

judgments about the world that appear true, and not political; fact-like, not policy-driven. But if these backgrounded discourses change—if they become contested or drawn into doubt—then just as certainly they can render a discourse within law political by removing the supports to a particular judgment that before had been supplied by the absence of contest within a given non-legal discourse.[34]

Lessig does not advocate an extreme judicial freedom. He stresses that many forces constrain judges and that judges ultimately must be sensitive to the texts they interpret although their interpretation is subject to change— even fairly dramatic change—as the subtle influences on their understanding of moral right and wrong (among other things) change.[35] And he highlights the complexity of the process by which articulated legal rules explicating constitutional text change (and perhaps Lessig's description adds further complexity to this process as well).[36]

Lessig seeks a mode of interpretation that appears faithful to instructions embedded in binding authority while changing the meaning of the instructions as social and political norms evolve. At a certain level of abstraction, that is the same project pursued by numerous legal scholars, including Edward Levi, Bruce Ackerman, Frank Michelman, and many others.[37] It is a project that in some measure has engaged scholars who are generally skeptical of giving judges authority to depart from entrenched understandings as well as writers who prefer more sail than anchor in judicial interpretation.[38]

For that reason, Sandy Levinson observes that it is no real contribution "to show that *some* 'change is consistent with interpretive constancy.'"[39] The real contribution, Levinson rightly urges, comes in providing a heuristic that helps enlighten the basis for particular changes, that helps distinguish the right from the wrong, that moves our thinking beyond the sorts of arguments about the influences over judicial motives and methods that generally fall into the Partnership or the Agency mode.[40] Professor Levinson gently suggests that Lessig's work on spelling out his version of the translation analogy does not advance argument over constitutional decisions.

Whatever it adds to discourse on interpretation, Professor Lessig's approach comfortably fits with other approaches collected here under the Partnership Model. His approach is broadly similar to that part of Professor Dworkin's referenced above, though with a markedly different lexicon. Lessig differs largely in stressing a broader array of changing circumstances, in place of Dworkin's stress on the individual interpreter's moral obligation to make the Constitution "the best it can be."[41] Each of these approaches suggests more freedom for judges than can prove consistent with a positive account of American judging outside of the rarest strata.[42] Abner Greene puts the point succinctly: "In much of Lessig's work, judges get to say what the law is without assuming responsibility for such pronouncements."[43] Those who find Partnership approaches appealing may find Lessig's translation analogy congenial (whether more or less than Dworkin's chain-novel metaphor). Clearly, Professor Lessig's translation analogy differs substantially from the translation metaphor used here. But Professor Levinson's question remains applicable: Can more be said that will make the translation metaphor useful?

## The Implications of Translation

Although translation is by no means a single, uniform exercise, the comparison of interpretation of legal texts in judging to translation as described here has several implications

First, the key element in determining the quality of our adjudication system—and what must be looked to first as cause and cure for problems in that system—is the material being translated, the legal authorities that judges interpret. The clarity of these materials—including not only the care with which legislative directives are couched but also legal authorities' internal coherence, consistency across rules, and applicability to varied circumstance—will dictate the degree to which judges must struggle to perform the translator's task. As discussed in chapter 6, problems with America's legal system can often be traced to problems with the materials judges are asked to interpret and apply.

Second, because judges at times are engaged in making choices that can vary subtly and are not obviously right or wrong, those choices cannot be effectively policed, or at least not without skewing the choices in some way. Arguments over translators' fidelity to the underlying text focus on points where the original text's meaning is questionable; no rule for translators can remove that difficulty. One would not want, for example, to require a translator to take whatever word is given in a specific dictionary as the literal equivalent for each word in the text and simply construct the translation by stringing those words together without alteration. Such a rule would threaten to distort the text in many instances; it would introduce especially significant distortions in cases such as the *Fleurs du Mal* example, in which literal text is, in some measure, of secondary importance.

So, too, with judging there will be no simple rule to direct the judges on how to decide. That is why canons of statutory construction, though useful summaries of common sense, are notoriously deficient as binding rules.[44] If the choices really are reducible to formulas, they seldom will be at issue before judges. If the choices cannot be reduced to a reasonably mechanical set of decision-rules, efforts to monitor and control the choices will introduce new errors, sometimes more costly than the errors corrected.[45] Many issues (probably most of them, and perhaps the vast majority) that currently engage American judges can be recast in relatively mechanical form only at the risk of introducing substantial errors into the process, even if "mechanization" corrects other errors.

This is a large part of the argument over the Sentencing Guidelines adopted for federal courts.[46] The Guidelines were the product of efforts to replace discretionary decision making with rule-bound decision making in order to eliminate certain disparities in criminal sentencing. Rule-bound decisions, however, tend to miss much of the welfare-enhancing interplay of relevant considerations in settings where the interactions are so complex that we can better intuit them than explain them, and we can explain them better than we can prescribe rules that properly encapsulate them. In such situations, discretionary decision making may reach outcomes that are substantively superior to those reached by rule-bound decisions often enough that welfare losses from improper decisions under the latter approach dwarf welfare gains from simpler, less costly decision processes.[47] But in line with the first implication drawn from the judges-as-translators metaphor, experience with the Guidelines— which judges generally dislike but feel bound to employ, hence the high level of judicial grousing about the rules—also shows that changing the dictates of external authority can have significant effects on judicial decisions, even in the face of judges' hostility to the change.[48]

Third, and derivative of the second implication, because the choices judges make at times involve subtle distinctions highly dependent on the particular context, efforts to influence judges can bear fruit, though probably not in large bunches. Such efforts take various guises, including attempts to embarrass judges through public criticism, to frighten judges through impeachment or recall threats, and to reduce their authority by removing issues from their jurisdiction or by limiting the weight of each judge's vote (President Franklin Roosevelt's court-packing plan is the standard example). Each of these efforts has been tried in the relatively recent past. These threats will not often persuade a judge to change an interpretation that the judge believes best fits the law, but they can be effective on less clear-cut interpretive choices without judges ever consciously thinking about them.

It is worth reiterating that if the Weak Agency Model correctly describes the basic framework for judging, the room for these effects is confined—tightly or loosely—largely as a function of the clarity of the governing authority. This means that when judges improperly translate a statutory directive, the correction for that lies not only in the higher courts but also in the lawmaking branches of government. Lawmakers are free to write clearer instructions, and proposals to revise laws are consistent both with correction of errors and with changes of lawmakers' views. Proclamations that the law will be changed if interpreted by judges in a given manner are consistent with judicial performance as faithful translators of the works already written. In contrast to models such as McNollgast's that make judges strategic players in a policy-outcome-focused game, such proclamations directed at judge-translators, though proper, should be ineffective in changing judicial decisions—just as my declaration that I will rewrite my novel if you translate it in the way you intend will not necessarily persuade you that your translation is wrong. A corollary, however, is that lawyers, legal scholars, and public officials should be on guard when we see those who have the power to rewrite the text instead engage in efforts to influence the translator.

Fourth, because the choices judges make at times require sensitivity to subtle shadings in language, which may be influenced in many invisible ways, we should expect some inconsistency in legal interpretation. As Judge Frank Easterbrook has recognized, this expectation holds even when all judges are highly skilled and are earnestly attempting to divine and apply externally generated law.[49] Although authors in the Partnership school have pointed to examples of inconsistency as proof that judges make choices in line with their own preferences, commonly derived from sources unrelated to external authority, a degree of inconsistency should be expected from judges operating as fully as possible in line with the Agency Model. Variations in skill or in earnestness, of course, will increase that inconsistency, but they are not necessary to explain it.

Fifth and finally, translation implies what was emphasized above in introducing the metaphor: that law will be predictable to lawyers. That is the essence of translation and the critical distinction between the translation metaphor adopted here and the version espoused by Professor Lessig. If judges are engaged in an activity akin to translation, not creation, their decisions should be fairly—but not perfectly—predictable to anyone familiar with the texts at issue who speaks the language of those texts.

The language of law today is the vernacular, but it is a special language nonetheless.[50] It will not be a language familiar to everyone, especially insofar as the texts to be translated (the legal authorities to be applied) are taken from judicial decisions, which tend to be constructed in an argot even less accessible to nonlawyers than statutory texts.[51]

That said, the "translation" of legal language into decisions applying the governing authority to particular situations should not be a source of substantial uncertainty to those who are conversant with the base language. Unlike models of judicial decision making that emphasize law's indeterminacy or judicial creativity, the translation metaphor suggests that there will be a large degree of predictability; most issues will be relatively confined, and there will be a very limited domain for surprising outcomes.

The specialized language of law makes it necessary, when law is likely to affect an important interest, to secure advice from someone who knows the applicable authorities and understands the language in which they are written. That is why clients hire lawyers to tell them what law applies and what it means for them. Lawyers in effect predict what judges will say if judges are called upon to interpret the relevant authorities.[52] Lawyers generally feel confident making those predictions, and clients have sufficient confidence in the law's predictability to pay good money—about $124 billion in 1997—for those predictions.[53] To be sure, there will be questions in many cases as to what is the correct interpretation of the authorities, the interpretation most faithful to the governing law's meaning. But the questions will be cabined; there will be a fairly narrow set of possible answers and an even narrower set of probable answers.[54] As the translation metaphor implies, the law will not be fully determinate in many instances, and applications of it will admit of variance, even without the overlay of varied judicial backgrounds and preferences, but the applications remain highly predictable.

## The Special Case of the Supreme Court?

If the Weak Agency Model, with its judge-as-translator metaphor, is an adequate description of judicial decision making at most levels, is a different model needed for the Supreme Court of the United States? The answer is "No, not really, but . . . "

Plainly, the Supreme Court is not the same as other American courts, and Supreme Court justices are not quite the same as other judges. The Court differs from other courts in three ways. First, the Supreme Court justices cannot be moved by one incentive that is thought to affect other judges: they will not be angling for advancement to a higher court. Second, there is no superior court to review their decisions; for all practical matters, in a great many cases there is no superintending political authority, either. Third, the caseload of the Supreme Court is unlike that of any other American court, including other courts of last resort.[55]

The absence of an advancement incentive should have relatively little impact. Few judges are likely to be motivated by prospects of advancement in the first place. Of course, the Supreme Court justices probably rank higher in ambition than the great majority of judges, so that advancement opportunity and reputation effects may be stronger incentives for them than for most judges.

Two points are relevant to this observation. The minor point is that the justices are not entirely without advancement opportunities. There is one advancement within the judicial hierarchy open to eight of the nine justices. That is not likely to have much influence, because most of the time few of the justices can expect to have even a remote prospect of becoming chief justice. Sitting associate justices have been elevated to chief justice only four times in our history, in 1795 (a recess appointment, with confirmation denied when the Senate reconvened), 1910, 1941, and 1986.[56] In addition, Charles Evans Hughes resigned his position as associate justice, ran for president as the standard-bearer for the Republican and Progressive Parties in 1916, and returned to the Supreme Court as chief in 1930. But ninety-two other associate justices have served on the Court. Statistically, an associate justice of the Supreme Court has a slightly higher prospect of becoming chief justice than a state trial judge has of becoming an appellate judge—but the odds still are twenty-five to one against elevation to chief justice.

The more important point is that reputation effects are likely to be much stronger incentives than advancement effects for justices of the Supreme Court, and reputation effects for them no longer turn primarily on the vagaries of presidential appointments. Most of the justices whose names are familiar to law students, lawyers, and legal scholars—Justices Joseph Story, Stephen Field, Joseph Bradley, John Marshall Harlan (I and II), Oliver Wendell Holmes, Louis Brandeis, Benjamin Cardozo, Robert Jackson, Felix Frankfurter, William O. Douglas, Hugo Black, William Brennan—never ascended to the chief's chair. Their reputations rest on their writings, not their position along the Court's bench. Many chief justices—such as Oliver Ellsworth, Salmon Chase, Morrison Waite, Melville Fuller, Edward White, and Fred Vinson—are minor historical footnotes in comparison. The reputation incentive of Supreme Court justices probably plays a role, though perhaps not a conscious one, in the justices' behavior, but the role it plays depends in large part on the other factors distinguishing the Supreme Court from other courts. Let us put this matter aside for the moment and take it up again after examining those other factors.

The second distinction between the Supreme Court and other courts is the absence of superintendence from a higher court or a higher political authority. Of course, the Congress can revise legislation to "reverse" a disfavored judicial interpretation, and it does so on occasion.[57] But much of the Supreme Court's caseload involves constitutional adjudication.[58] That, by and large, is the final province of the Court. This is the sense of Justice Jackson's declaration that the justices "are not final because we are infallible, but we are infallible because we are final."[59]

To be sure, that finality is not always accepted by would-be supervening authority. Congressional attempts to undo Supreme Court constitutional interpretation take many forms, including constitutional amendment, revision of the Court's jurisdiction or composition,[60] and substantive lawmaking aimed at legislative reversal of a constitutional construction.

Most such attempts, however, are unavailing, at least in the short term. The Religious Freedom Restoration Act is an example of attempted reversal by legislation,[61] and the Supreme Court dispatched it as such.[62] Constitutional amendment is the obvious legitimate route to reversing a Supreme Court interpretation of the Constitution, but constitutional amendment is an arduous process. Only three of our twenty-seven amendments result from political response to Court decisions.[63]

The natural conclusion from the absence of supervisory authority over the Court is that justices are freed from the constraint of external authority that supervision implies and therefore move away from the Agency Model toward the Partnership Model.[64] However, this conclusion is based on two erroneous assumptions. One is that the threat of reversal by higher authority substantially constrains judges' behavior. The other is that decisions of the higher authority will better conform to the external legal authorities than the decisions being reviewed.

Both points have been discussed above.[65] Suffice it to say here that whatever force those points have in general—which already has been put in doubt— they have less force in respect of the Supreme Court. The Supreme Court might well make questionable constructions of constitutional directives, and politicians might take positions that better comport with the text, history, and precedents. But politicians cannot be thought systematically more likely than the Court to construe the legal authorities thoughtfully. Politicians are moved by other considerations and often press for constructions that take manifest liberties with legal authorities.[66] That is one of the powerful reasons that thinkers concerned with the protection of constitutional directives, from James Madison and Alexander Hamilton on, have urged that constitutional interpretation be lodged in the courts and that strictures be interposed against political interference with the courts.[67] None of this refutes a greater proximity of Supreme Court decision making to the Partnership Model than other courts display. The burden of this argument simply is that the absence of meaningful supervision does not obviously move Supreme Court justices away from the sort of translation efforts—sincere efforts to apply external authorities to particular legal problems—that characterize other courts.

The most important difference between the Supreme Court and other courts is the nature of the issues presented for decision. Unlike other American courts—indeed, unlike almost any other court anywhere—the Supreme Court has virtually complete discretion over its caseload. The Court receives 7,000 to 8,500 petitions each year (as of the mid-to-late 1990s) for review of lower-court decisions, out of which it hears and decides between 80 and 100 cases.[68] The justices typically select cases for which the central issues have divided the highest level of appeal courts below the Supreme Court or cases that present issues of unusual importance.

Supreme Court cases depart substantially from ordinary cases in two respects: the issues they present are disproportionately difficult to resolve from governing legal authority, and—because they have discretion to select the cases they hear and because their winnowing task is heroic—the justices, far more than other judges, necessarily view their job as setting rules for the future rather than as resolving specific conflicts between the parties. The issues presented in cases heard by the Supreme Court, thus, are commonly situated in a larger decision space—the area within which sincere efforts at honest translation of legal directives are located—than the issues typically before other courts. The relevant legal authorities are less clear, speak less directly to the issue, or are at odds with one another to a greater degree than in the vast run of litigated cases.

The larger decision space is not entirely due to the Court's role as constitutional arbiter. Despite the spareness of the Constitution's text and the ambiguity of its historical sources, many constitutional questions can be answered from precedents with little prospect of honest disagreement over the state of current law. Those, however, are not the questions addressed by the Supreme Court.

The larger decision space means that there is greater scope for justices' decisions to be influenced by their individual views on an array of matters relevant to the interpretive task. As for other translators, the less clear the text, the more work must be done by considerations apart from the text.[69]

This loosening of bonds around their decisions is compounded by the fact that Supreme Court justices' decisions are more forward-looking than other courts' determinations, more consciously rules for the future than mere disposition of a complaint about past conduct. The Court's cases do have a retrospective focus in that no issue comes before the Court apart from a concrete problem rooted in past conduct. But the high selectivity of the Court's docket means that the justices think of their role as somewhat closer to that of the legislator than other judges would conceive their own roles. There are plenty of opportunities for parties who seek justice in their particular case to obtain it from other courts, but only the Supreme Court can definitively pronounce a rule for the future when other appellate courts have given divergent answers. Other courts are referee to the parties; the Supreme Court is referee to the courts.[70]

What of the matter put aside earlier, the reputation incentive for Supreme Court justices? Reputation incentives increase the difference between the Supreme Court and other courts, because Supreme Court justices are significantly more likely than other American judges to be remembered if they leave a body of coherent opinions forcefully pushing a point of view. This reduces incentives to compromise, and it might also reduce incentives to follow legal authority.

Those effects may be offset somewhat by the justices' expectation of repeat-play relationships among themselves. This provides both personal and strategic incentives to compromise, much as in an iterated Prisoner's Dilemma game.[71] Judge Richard Posner made much of this incentive, not only among Supreme Court justices but among all judges (at least on collegial courts).[72] Judge Posner did not view the incentive to compromise as related to decision making in accord with external authority. If, however, the dominant mode of judicial decision making is congruent with the law-bound approach of the Weak Agency Model, the instinct for compromise reinforces law-bound approaches. This will not always be the case among Supreme Court justices, but it is likely to be the common tendency, especially because the law-bound approach is more sustainable over time as a strategy for explaining judging decisions and, hence, for securing adherence from judicial colleagues. It is, in other words, a better vehicle for obtaining consensus on a collegial court than is, say, appeal to political preferences—at least so long as there is not a predictable, stable majority of like preferences.

The relative impact of the reputation incentive and repeat-play incentives depends entirely on the specific weights the justices give these factors. There is no reason to expect individual justices to give constant weighting to these factors over time or to expect consistent weighting among the justices.

For all of these reasons, the Supreme Court justices' behavior falls closer to the Partnership Model than other judges'—but even so, the operation of the Supreme Court is not closer to that model than to the Weak Agency Model. The Supreme Court justices are screened more rigorously than other justices, and evidence that justices might depart from law-bound judging is both a handy basis for opposition and a potential reason for opposition. Recall that although politicians seldom are motivated by an interest in fidelity to legal authority, such fidelity from judges generally serves politicians' interests.[73] Further, most justices come to the Supreme Court after careers as lawyers and as judges, careers in which—to some extent unlike academia[74]—success correlates positively with internalization of law-bound instincts.[75] It is not likely that a change of position will immediately lead justices to abandon those instincts.

Certainly, such a move from more to less law-bound behavior is not as likely as the opposite move—that individuals whose prior professional lives put a premium on escaping the bounds of law would, as judges, behave in quite conventional, law-bound ways.[76] Finally, the presentation, argument, conference, and written disposition of cases at the Supreme Court all militate in favor of a law-bound approach—though, as the Weak Agency Model maintains, being law-bound does not always mean being bound too tightly.[77]

The looseness of the constraint, however, leaves space for behavior that looks more like an assertion of judges' personal preferences than the sort of translation that courts, including the Supreme Court, are supposed to do. That is how many people saw the Supreme Court's decisions respecting the 2000 presidential election, especially the decision in *Bush v. Gore*[78] that effectively ended the post-election contest.[79]

Following the closest presidential vote in a generation (and projections of the closest electoral college division in more than a century), nearly four dozen lawsuits were filed contesting one or another aspect of the Florida vote for president. The national vote had divided almost evenly and so, too, had Florida's vote. Election night ended with Florida too close to call, and its twenty-five electoral votes would decide the election.

With the presidency hanging in the balance and little in the way of direct legal precedent to answer most of the questions posed, news reports on the litigation immediately turned to the most readily available information: the political background of the judges. Discussion focused on what we could expect given the party affiliations of the judges or of the executive (governor or president) who appointed them.[80] Almost none of the decisions, however, went the way those political predictors suggested. Democratic judges appointed by Democratic executives rendered decisions favorable to Republican George Bush, and Republican judges appointed by Republican executives handed down decisions favorable to Democrat Al Gore.[81]

Enter the Florida Supreme Court. In two high-profile decisions, the Florida Supreme Court reversed lower-court decisions that had hurt Al Gore's prospects.[82] In each case the Florida Supreme Court rendered a decision that could be defended as resolving ambiguities in state law. But in each case the court also reached conclusions that strained (and perhaps breached) the outer bounds of reasonable construction. The governing Florida law set a date for certifying election results and also provided a mechanism for contesting the results. The Florida Supreme Court concluded that these provisions were in conflict because, in the circumstances presented in this instance, the sort of recount provided for in the contest provision could not be accomplished in the time permitted. The court chose to harmonize these provisions by preferring the implicit direction to recount fully in a given manner to the explicit direction to complete the contest by a given date. The court therefore announced a different date for the conclusion of the contest period, without any clear support for its choice.[83] The court also looked at two provisions in Florida law respecting acceptance of late vote certifications, one stating that the Florida secretary of state *shall* reject late-filed returns, the other stating that the secretary *may* reject such returns. But the court's construction of Florida law did not choose either one of these meanings, instead interpreting the law as saying that the secretary may *not* ignore late-filed returns, an interpretation incompatible with both statutory terms.[84] Again, the Florida court's interpretation was based on inference from an implicit instruction elsewhere in the law, a form of reasoning common to judicial decisions but not easily explained when at odds with what looks like express authority to the contrary. Finally, the Florida Supreme Court concluded that the secretary of state must accept votes counted in radically different ways by different counties attempting to divine what voters intended.[85]

None of these determinations by the Florida Supreme Court was without some basis in law, but each critical decision reversed lower-court determinations, contravened the decisions of administrative authorities, and rested on extrapolation from language that could not be said directly to command the reading given it. Each of these factors can be explained; none is a dramatic departure from judicial decision-making norms; but they raise questions about the Florida court's decisions. More serious, the court's rulings allowed counting authorities to select different standards *after* knowing how the standards would be likely to affect the outcome. This is not a trivial concern. Of course, courts make decisions retrospectively, with knowledge of the way their decisions will affect the immediate parties before them. That is the basis for the many limitations on court action, for their insulation from direct influence, for the insistence on guidance by external authorities, for rules militating in favor of generality and neutrality.[86] Administrative agencies also make some decisions retrospectively.[87] These decisions are not always matters of substantial concern but typically are constrained to a significant extent nonetheless. Recall the factors that increase the importance of constraining discretion over retrospective decisions by clear externally imposed rules: high stakes, a small set of cases likely to be governed by the decision, clearly identified parties whose interests are affected by the decision.[88] All of these factors were joined in the postelection decisions. The stakes were extremely high, the decisions unlikely to affect other cases, the affected parties fully known. However well-grounded their reasoning, the Florida decisions produced a result strongly at odds with the rule of law, freeing officials to make decisions in full knowledge of who would be helped or hurt by a particular method of vote-counting without any real external constraint or guidance. And they did so in as important a contest as we can have. As these cases came to the Supreme Court of the United States, then, there was ample basis for skepticism about them, about their fit with governing law, and about the propriety of the outcome.

That did not necessarily mean that there was a well-grounded legal basis for reversal. But all nine of the justices on the Supreme Court agreed in the first case, *Bush v. Palm Beach Canvassing Board* (*Bush I*) that the Florida Supreme Court's decision at least might have rested on an incorrect construction of the law.[89] And seven of the nine justices in the second case, *Bush v. Gore* (*Bush II*), concluded that the Florida decision did violate federal law.[90] The justices disagreed sharply over the standard to use in reviewing the Florida court's construction of Florida law in *Bush II,* but that disagreement did not affect the outcome. Despite differences over other issues, seven justices agreed that the use of different standards to count votes violated the equal-protection clause of the Fourteenth Amendment to the Constitution. Although that conclusion was debatable under the precedents of equal-protection law, it had sufficient grounding in those precedents (and the outcome of the Florida decision seemed sufficiently at odds with core concepts of equal treatment) to secure a strong consensus.

What most divided the justices in *Bush II* was the remedy for this violation. The remedy agreed on by a five-justice majority was simply to stop the recount process.[91] The majority held that no constitutionally satisfactory recount was possible in time to meet the "safe harbor" provision of federal law (the provision that insulates state-certified electors from challenge if selected by December 12 in accordance with certain rules) or even by December 18, the date on which electoral college votes were to be cast. Because the Florida courts had interpreted the Florida legislation as having intended to bring Florida's electors within the safe harbor provision, the majority concluded that it would not remand for further counting but would declare the process at an end.

The four dissenters strongly condemned both the majority's reasoning and its conclusion on this matter. First, the dissenters asserted that the safe harbor provision merely provided guidance to states respecting the rules to be followed by Congress in the event a slate of electors is challenged before that body.[92] Second, they argued that it was for the Florida courts to decide whether a recount consistent with the Supreme Court's construction of equal-protection law could be conducted within the relevant time.[93]

The dissenters had the better of the argument over remedy. Had the Supreme Court reversed on the grounds emphasized by three concurring justices (that the flaws in the Florida court's interpretation of Florida law were so severe as to amount to a usurpation of power constitutionally conferred on the legislature),[94] the remedy adopted would have fit. But that route commanded the votes of only three justices. The majority no doubt did the nation a service by bringing to a close a vote-recount process that had kept the election from a conclusion for more than a month, even after it became clear that, by one route or another, George Bush would in all likelihood emerge as the victor.[95] But the legal basis for the ending is the weakest part of the majority's decision.

The Supreme Court's decision was denounced as evidence that party politics infects even the judiciary.[96] Even well-respected legal scholars leveled this complaint. Consider, for example, Sanford Levinson's assertion that the Court's action can be seen easily "as the decision by five conservative Republicans—at least two of whom are eager to retire and be replaced by Republicans nominated by a Republican President—to assure the triumph of a fellow Republican who might not become President if Florida were left to its own legal process."[97] Or take the group statement of more than three hundred law professors that "the five justices [in the majority] were acting as political proponents for candidate Bush, not as judges."[98]

Justice John Paul Stevens's dissent, though not making the claim that the majority was moved merely by politics, sounded a related theme and lamented the effect this would have on public perception of the courts:

What must underlie petitioners' entire federal assault on the Florida election procedures is an unstated lack of confidence in the impartiality and capacity of the state judges who would make the critical decisions if the vote count were to proceed. . . . The endorsement of that position by the majority of this Court can only lend credence to the most cynical appraisal of the work of judges throughout the land. It is confidence in the men and women who administer the judicial system that is the true backbone of the rule of law. . . . Although we may never know with complete certainty the identity of the winner of this year's Presidential election, the identity of the loser is perfectly clear. It is the Nation's confidence in the judge as an impartial guardian of the rule of law.[99]

Surely, these claims overstate the matter. For one thing, despite differences of party and perspective, all of the justices except Justice Stevens and Justice Ruth Bader Ginsburg found constitutional problems with the Florida court decision reversed in *Bush II.* Not only was the court largely of one mind on that critical issue, but also the divisions reflected in the decision, on both substance and remedy, were not along party lines. Stevens, a Republican appointee, and Ginsburg, a Democratic appointee, broke with the other justices over the constitutionality of Florida's decision. The other justices joining Stevens and Ginsburg in objecting to the majority's remedy were David Souter, a Republican appointee, and Stephen Breyer, a Democratic appointee. The notion that these cases were decided by politics does no better when one considers the Florida Supreme Court's decision in *Gore v. Harris.* Three of the seven justices dissented from the ruling that helped Democrat Al Gore, although all seven justices on that court were appointed by Democrats and six list their own party affiliation as Democrat (the other as an independent).

The complaint that something apart from ordinary, authority-based decision making explains the outcomes, however, is not completely off base. Any ideological map of the Supreme Court would mirror the votes in *Bush II.* Ideologies might not explain the great majority of Supreme Court votes, but they certainly influence some votes in which the governing authorities leave a larger decision space for the court's action. Looking at votes in such cases (in which the governing law is particularly unclear and vigorously contested), one would predict exactly the division that occurred on the remedy in *Bush II.* The justices voting against the immediate end to recounts were the four who

tend to align with more politically liberal interests, interests generally congruent with Democratic policies. The justices voting for the immediate end to recounts were the five who tend to align with more politically conservative interests, interests generally congruent with Republican policies. What makes
*Bush II* problematic is not just that the justices divided along predictable, ideological lines respecting the remedy. They did so in a case with strong political overtones and an analytically weak link between the substantive conclusion and the remedy ordered. These factors together give reason to question
the degree to which legal authorities controlled and the degree to which the
justices' personal preferences contributed to the result.

This focus, however, does a disservice to the legal system. Perhaps a different set of justices would have found a different remedy appropriate, but three
other aspects of the case are more important for our purposes.

First, even in such a politically charged case, there was broad consensus on
the decisive issue of law. The justices reasoned from constitutional text and
prior judicial decisions to a substantive decision that commanded seven votes
in *Bush II* (and nine votes for the result in *Bush I*). The decision is arguable,
but that is the nature of cases that make it to the Supreme Court.

Second, even by Supreme Court standards these are exceptional cases, pre-
senting unusual issues in a context that is unlikely to recur. The Supreme Court
justices, like the Florida judges, operated on a completely different schedule
than is normal, one that allowed far less time for reflection and discussion than
the court ordinarily enjoys. That undoubtedly affected the shape of the decision, the care with which it was assembled, and the opportunity to find ground
that would blunt some of the rough edges visible in the opinions. Commentators should beware of drawing heroic conclusions from decisions such as
these.

Third, the outcome was seen generally as sufficiently dictated by law to be
conclusive, to be accepted by the public and by the principals as the final word
in this drama. That is not to say that everyone applauded the decisions or credited them as neutral applications of settled law. But the overwhelming majority of the public and both of the principals conceded the authority of the
courts (federal and state) to resolve arguments over the election and acknowledged the Supreme Court's decision as conclusive. Individuals generally gave
any reservations they had about the decision less weight than their belief that
the courts properly have the final word on matters of law. That weighting is

not consistent with a view of the courts in general and of the Supreme Court in particular as just another political entity or of *Bush II* as a purely political decision. Commentators, in contrast, rushed to declare the decisions, especially *Bush II,* as illegitimate and more sweepingly as undermining the claim that our courts, and particularly our Supreme Court, function in accordance with the rule of law. That accords far more weight to the most unusual decisions than is sensible while simultaneously minimizing the contribution of legal authority to these decisions.

Dispassionate observers, viewing the broader landscape of American judging, should recognize that American judicial decision making (including Supreme Court decision making) does function in keeping with the dictates of the rule of law. The work of American judges, even of Supreme Court justices, almost always looks closer to translation than to novel writing. That is what we should expect, and it is what we find.

# CHAPTER SIX

# Problems and Progress

## The American Legal System and the Rule of Law

*It has not escaped popular attention that all is not well in the world of lawyers.* —*Mary Ann Glendon*

The Weak Agency Model, as captured by the judge-as-translator metaphor, does not make judges mere appliers of external authority free from "extraneous" influences, but it portrays the judiciary as very largely constrained by external authority. Not constrained to the same degree for all decisions and all courts, but not subject to radically discontinuous constraints. It is far from an all-or-none matter: there is a range over which constraint varies. Though no case truly reaches the total-constraint end of the range, most cases fall toward the very-constrained end of the spectrum, and that is the way judges tend to see their world. Similarly, the Weak Agency Model allows inconsistency in judicial decisions, but it also supports a general pattern of principled predictability in law.

Why then, given the consonance between this picture and attractive features of the rule of law, is there so much complaint about the American legal system? Is the rule of law an object whose attractions are visible only from afar? Are its beneficial aspects overcome by other features of our legal system? Is the disconnect between the description above and public attitude mere fiction?

This chapter sketches seven possible explanations for discontent with the American legal system, framing the primary cause of complaints as bad rules, bad principles, bad decisions, inconsistency, bad process, misperception, or misbehavior. I describe each explanation briefly and suggest the weight each of them can carry—their consonance with reality, their plausibility as explanations of public dissatisfaction, and also how changes along any of these dimensions might have decreased public regard for the legal system.

The explanations most congenial to lawyers and to lawyer-bashers—respectively, the *misperception* and *misbehavior* explanations (explanations that tell us, in the one case, that the public is wrong to believe there is a problem or, in the other, that lawyers truly are the problem)—have less power than explanations looking to flaws in various parts of the legal system's design and operation. The flaws that are highlighted in this inquiry are not so large as to undermine the rule of law, the constraint of power through rules, the overall predictability and legitimacy of our legal process. The inquiry in this chapter does, however, suggest cause for concern.

## Bad Rules

Dissatisfaction with the American legal system may arise from the nature of the rules adopted by the political branches and enforced through the legal system. If these are "bad" rules, the legal system, operating faithfully under them, will do bad things.

That is the essence of many complaints. Although there are many versions of the "bad rules" objection to American law, three types of complaint predominate. First, the rules are substantively bad; they command outcomes that reduce social welfare. Second, the rules are drafted in ways that reduce predictability and increase both the risks to ordinary behavior and the costs of legal processes. Third, even if each rule taken alone were acceptable, there are too many rules—the amount of law in the United States is greater than optimal.

### Substantive Problems

The first complaint is the most common. Scholars writing in the public-choice literature have explained why the American political system frequently—the late Professor George Stigler would say invariably—reaches results that are inimical to society's welfare.[1] Public decision processes reflect variation in the distribution of individuals' preferences respecting outcomes of potential public actions, of their preferences' intensities, of the costs of their participation in group decision making, and of individuals' budget constraints.[2] The interaction among these factors can produce government decisions that both are disfavored by a majority of citizens and reduce aggregate wealth (or aggregate utility).[3]

Many government programs, plainly mandated by law, produce results that cannot be squared with economics-based definitions of social good.[4] Bruce Ackerman and William Hassler's reconstruction of the coal-scrubbing saga, in which Congress adopted a provision in the "clean air" law that resulted in higher energy costs *and* sharp increases in dangerous pollutants, making society pay more and get dirtier air, is emblematic of the problem.[5]

Of course, economics-based (efficiency-based) norms are not the only possible metrics of social good. Moreover, efficiency-based norms (and their analytical forebears, aggregate utility-based norms) are not terribly tractable norms, and they certainly are not analytically unassailable norms.[6] But efficiency, which turns on a balancing of costs and benefits, *is* congruent with widely shared intuitions of public good in many of the settings addressed by law.[7] Although the particular assumptions that inform the weighing and balancing of interests are debatable, the basic contours of the efficiency norm broadly correspond to commonsense notions.[8] Despite efficiency's shortcomings, it is worth worrying about the divergence of law from efficient solutions of many problems.

Rejecting that view does not rescue legal rules from the assault of the efficiency-minded; critics less tied to a clear prescriptive norm for public decisions also assert that many legal rules are simply nonsensical.[9] Professor Jeffrey O'Connell, among others, argues that the rules governing liability in large portions of American tort law encourage costly litigation over assignments of fault under instructions so unhelpful that the results resemble a lottery.[10] Philip Howard's collection of legal absurdities includes the New York fire law prohibiting displays of student artwork within two feet of ceilings, within ten feet of doorways, or covering more than 20 percent of a wall—compliance with which, Howard notes, would transform the typical elementary school classroom into a place "about as inviting as a bomb shelter."[11] He adds, "No one had ever heard of a fire caused by children's art, but there was a law just to make sure."[12] Others have noted that our tax system is enormously complex and is rife with provisions that seem designed to benefit particular entities or groups that differ from the general taxpaying public primarily in their influence on those whose fingers move the levers of legislative or administrative authority.[13]

One law that has been a source of considerable public consternation is the Americans with Disabilities Act.[14] The ADA grew out of concerns about the effects of various discriminations against disabled citizens in employment, in public accommodations, and elsewhere. Supporters have hailed the statute as a long-overdue charter of civil rights for handicapped Americans.[15] Other commentators, however, have attacked the law as a triumph of rhetoric over common sense. Critics have noted, for example, that the costs of compliance with the ADA's mandate respecting public transportation services—specifically, of making public transportation accessible to those confined to wheelchairs—greatly exceeds what would be spent to buy every wheelchair-bound American a limousine and a full-time chauffeur.[16] Critics assert as well that the law has vastly increased housing costs and discouraged many worthwhile improvements and that it imposes enormous costs in money and inconvenience on the general public to solve potential problems for disabled citizens who might or might not choose to use some facilities at some time in the future.[17] To take one modest example, expanding bathroom facilities so that each one is accessible to wheelchairs reduces the number of bathroom stalls available to the public—in some instances, dramatically—without any attention in the law's requirements to the likelihood that someone in a wheelchair will use the facility.[18]

The law's detractors do not denigrate the difficulties faced by those with serious handicaps. ADA opponents recognize that even with the various mandated accommodations, handicapped individuals do not occupy a preferred position; the obvious test is that critics would not willingly trade their good health for the legal benefits that disabilities can confer. The critics do not deny a basis for sympathizing with disabled citizens, but they deny that this is an adequate basis for the law. They emphasize that in our own everyday lives, we make expenditures based on the probability that the expenditures will prove worthwhile, that the sacrifices in cost and inconvenience are offset by equally valuable benefits.[19] When parking spaces dedicated to the handicapped lie empty in otherwise overcrowded lots, when wheelchair-accessible bathrooms generate long lines but are never patronized by anyone in a wheelchair, when funds are taken from programs to educate or shelter the poor to be used to purchase new subway cars or buses that virtually no disabled person will use, the law seems to require what common sense would reject.

ADA advocates do not look at the evidence the same way. They trumpet the symbolic value of visible evidence that we are looking out for our disabled brethren. For them, empty handicapped parking spaces do not offend. But these spaces have both real and symbolic costs. So, too, for the other adjustments the law requires. For all but the most committed advocates, there is serious question whether the ADA strikes a reasonable balance.

As much irritation as these problems create, they pale in comparison with complaints about the application of the ADA to "nontraditional" handicaps, such as learning disabilities or conditions associated with drug or alcohol dependence.[20] Determination and implementation of the necessary accommodations to these disabilities has spawned a new cottage industry, especially in American higher education.[21] Critics find the law's operation in this context an even more striking departure from a proper balance of costs and benefits than its application to core physical handicaps. The problem in part is that students claim entitlements to take tests without time pressure or to grading standards that exempt them from limitations imposed by ordinary rules of grammar, syntax, and spelling that they find difficult to master.[22] The other part of the problem is the skew in educational priorities that inevitably follows the grant of at least colorable legal protection to such claims. Philip Howard laments that

> gifted students, in contrast to disabled children, receive virtually no support or attention from America's school systems: about two cents out of every hundred dollars is allocated to programs for them. According to a recent report by the US Dept. of Education, gifted students languish in classrooms bored stiff, doing their work left-handed, having mastered over half the curriculum before the school year begins. Nothing is done to nurture their skills or groom them to be future leaders of education, business, or government. The ratio of funding of special education programs to gifted programs is about eleven dollars to one cent.[23]

Rules that seem at odds with common notions of public good, thus, often lie at the heart of complaints about the legal system. Much of what judges do that draws criticism consists of adherence to the legally binding directions of the political branches. Judges direct people to constrain their behavior in ways that may seem ill-advised but are legally required; they command people to pay money in settings where the party doing the paying—along with other people who hear about the matter from that party's vantage—cannot comprehend the assignment of liability.

This is true not only with respect to cases that seem quintessentially within the judges' domain, such as cases that fall within the old common law headings of tort, contract, or property but are governed today to a significant degree by statutory command.[24] It is true as well for the vast array of activities governed by administrative decision makers. Judicial challenges to administrative actions are commonplace, but the general rule for review of such actions is one of deference.[25] Administrative appeals routinely result in affirmance of agency decisions that seem questionable to ordinary mortals, however predictable they might be to the cognoscenti.[26] Complaints about law from well-informed individuals, at least in casual conversation, often focus on administrative decisions that seem ill conceived, even though they are not likely to be declared legally invalid. "The legal system" is faulted because the complainant sees the administrative process effectively determining the shape of legal rules and shaping them in ways out of kilter with his or her expectations of how the world should work.[27]

The question remains whether bad rules—ones that command inefficient allocations of resources directly or that command deference to administrative determinations that produce such results—are a significant source of *public* dismay at the American legal system. Rules respecting the assignment of liability for various perceived ills or other government decisions at odds with the commonsense solution of a conflict do seem likely sources of at least some—perhaps significant—dissatisfaction, though it is more likely that the general public will know of a particular decision than of the underlying rule.[28] Certainly, insofar as particular publicly noted decisions are the predictable implementations of bad rules, we must blame the rules, not the implementation.

Although this may be an intuitively appealing explanation of public dissatisfaction, one important strand of academic writing might be read as casting doubt on the claim that these decisions have sufficient effect to spur much discontent with the law. Nobel laureate Ronald Coase famously observed that if the cost of engaging in market transactions (now routinely referenced as "transaction costs") were low enough, people would contract around inefficient rules on legal liability.[29] Studies of actual behavior suggest that in many settings individuals' behavior is regulated by extralegal understandings, which may be more efficient than legal rules and more efficiently enforced—through social pressure, for example—as well.[30]

Nevertheless, the same analysis that suggests limits to the efficacy of law also indicates that law will have real bite in many settings. A vast array of legal rules cannot be readily ignored in favor of arrangements the parties deem better, in large part because many rules—the great bulk of rules that writers like Philip Howard target—are backed by threat of public sanction. Typically, no individual who might benefit from a more efficient, more socially beneficial rule is authorized to waive the current rule on the public's behalf in the same manner as private parties might. Private citizens, who generally will be the ones directly affected by governmental rules, are discouraged from trying to prevent the rules' implementation: the law prevents direct exchange of payment for nonenforcement of the law (bribery) and also frustrates attempts to obtain binding agreements for nonenforcement.[31]

Howard also asserts that legislated rules increasingly prevent even those who are not directly affected by the rules (that is, the judges and administrators charged with their effectuation) from exercising discretion to reach sensible results.[32] His complaint is that legislators have substituted detailed legislative directives for administrative or judicial discretion. Clearly, in some instances legal rules leave little room for judgment and cannot internalize so full a range of relevant considerations as a less constrained decision maker might. That point was made earlier with respect to the Sentencing Guidelines.[33] Even so, the argument that overspecification is the principal vice of legal rules—or that, on balance, rules today leave less room for administrative discretion— seems unlikely. How often does the part of the legal community that gives new legislation the most intense scrutiny complain that a new enactment is too certain, too clear, too specific?

Moreover, Howard's argument treats only the legal *permissibility* of a sensible exercise of discretion—it says nothing about administrators' *incentives* to exercise discretion in a sensible way. The primary thrust of modern social science writing about government administration is that administrators' incentives systematically lead them to behave in ways that, although perfectly sensible for them, produce results wholly at odds with common notions of what would be sensible for our society.[34] Unless administrators have the incentive to exercise discretion to society's benefit, there is no point to increasing scope for administrative discretion. Discretion can be valuable in some instances, and some legislated rules that deprive officials of discretion no doubt move us away from outcomes that are socially desirable by almost any measure. Howard is right to that extent. But there is no reason to expect a systematic skew toward too little administrative discretion. Simply put, legislators would not seem to have incentives to systematically overconstrain administrators. After all, the legislative decision whether to leave matters to officials' discretion or tie their hands more securely ex ante is not random: the same factors that induce socially undesirable overspecification in some instances can also induce socially undesirable reliance on discretion in others.[35]

## Rule Ambiguity

Does that mean that the converse of Howard's hypothesis is true? That question must be answered in order to evaluate the second type of "bad rules" complaint, expressing the concern that legal rules are not sufficiently clear.

Clear rules are problematic only if they prescribe conduct that is socially undesirable. Unclear rules present a different problem. Just as some rules seem to bind decision makers in clear terms, other rules are drafted in ways that carefully camouflage any intended meaning. Consider, for example, the Occupational Safety and Health Act of 1970.[36] The act directs the secretary of labor to set occupational safety and health standards that prescribe "conditions, . . . practices, means, methods, operations, or processes, reasonably necessary or appropriate to provide safe or healthful employment."[37] The act also instructs the secretary

> in promulgating standards dealing with toxic materials or harmful physical agents . . . [to] set the standard which most adequately assures, to the extent feasible, on the basis of the best available evidence, that no employee will suffer material impairment of health or functional capacity even if such employee has regular exposure to the hazard dealt with by such standard for the period of his working life.[38]

Not surprisingly, the courts have struggled to give coherent meaning to the direction to adopt standards reasonably necessary to health and safety that, so far as feasible, prevent harm to employees. Among the possible meanings attributed to that formulation were requirements that the Secretary of Labor utilize a cost-benefit analysis, that the Secretary not use such an analysis but instead protect workers to the extent technologically feasible, and that the Secretary mandate the most worker-protective actions subject to a finding that those actions would not bankrupt the industry affected.[39] Two justices of the Supreme Court concluded that the answer was "none of the above"—that the law did not state any intelligible principle.[40]

Unclear laws do not necessarily produce rules that are substantively unattractive, but they do impose costs because they generate uncertainty.[41] These laws are also likely to be interpreted inconsistently by different courts (another source of uncertainty). There may be better and worse efforts to translate unclear laws, but the translations offered for unclear texts—even if all judges endeavor to behave as the Agency Model prescribes—will diverge more than interpretation of clear instructions. As the arguments among justices construing the Occupational Safety and Health Act have revealed, unclear laws also are likely to be interpreted in ways that seem strained. For all three of these reasons—the primary uncertainty of the law, the secondary uncertainty stemming from differing judicial interpretations, and the fact that interpretations of convoluted instructions will seem less convincing (more suspect) to those individuals who must obey the judges' commands—unclear laws will prompt complaints about both the law and the judges.

The rules that are passed today are not necessarily framed in fewer words than rules of the past; the opposite is true. Detailed statutes specifying both processes and substantive considerations for decision makers abound, certainly more so today than in previous generations. As the OSHA example indicates, however, that does not necessarily make the rules clearer.

There is reason to believe that both the substantive departure of the law from socially beneficial results and the unclarity of laws have increased over time. Joseph Schumpeter long ago explained why he believed that nations would, as they became wealthier and more secure, increasingly drift toward socialism (not a move that Schumpeter saw as social improvement).[42] Mancur Olson more recently gave a public-choice account of the reasons that groups especially interested in particular matters are increasingly prevalent in public decision making of advanced, stable societies and increasingly able to pull public decision making away from policies more in line with general public interests.[43] James Buchanan and Gordon Tullock have described the deleterious effect that a single variable, increased population within the nation or other group making a group decision, has on decision making.[44] The forces that Schumpeter, Olson, and Buchanan and Tullock identify make bad rules more likely now in America than they were a generation or two ago.

Public-choice writings assign unclear rules much the same derivation as rules favoring well-placed interest groups. Rule ambiguity can make it more costly to determine who truly benefits from a political bargain, making ambiguity especially valuable as camouflage for rules that advantage a relative few at the general public's expense.[45] That is, however, not a good of itself to those who would influence rule-making. Ambiguity has costs to them as well as benefits.[46] Plainly, it is most useful if those who implement the rule understand the deal.[47] This, then, is a theory of ambiguity better suited to ongoing regulatory relationships than to broadly applicable laws.[48] Yet, if public-choice scholars are correct, uncertainty might well be increasing for the same reasons that bad rules would be.

It is possible that these theories are incomplete or incorrect; each of them can be criticized in some particular. But they are substantial, thoughtful analyses, all pointing toward plausible bases for belief not only that judges and lawyers frequently encounter bad rules—rules misshaped by the authorities who properly have responsibility for framing the rules—but also that they do so at an increasing rate. Each theory, thus, provides support for the claim that although judges act in keeping with the rule of law, bad rules will lead to rising dissatisfaction with the system that applies the rules.

### Rule Overload

The third type of "bad rules" complaint picks up from this point, noting that even if these theories of increasingly problematic rules are wrong, a sharp escalation in the *number* of legal rules may be to blame for the increased dissatisfaction with the legal system. Whether the measure is the number of general laws adopted by Congress,[49] the number of pages of legislation, the number of pages of regulations reported in the Federal Register, or virtually any other metric, the story is the same: the amount of law in the United States has increased dramatically over the past sixty or seventy years.[50] Consider, for example, the growth in the number of pages in the Federal Register relative to the U.S. population. Between 1936 and 1980, the population increased by less than 78 percent, while Federal Register pages rose by more than 3,500 percent![51]

Two different problems might follow from growth in the law. One is that, even if the *proportion* of bad rules to good has remained unchanged, because of the increased *number* of rules the average citizen in 1980 could expect much more frequently than the citizen in 1936 to encounter a legal rule that would seem undesirable. If discontent with the legal system is driven by experience with bad rules, that could be the basis for rising dissatisfaction.

Alternatively, even if the number of bad rules remains constant, the increased number of rules alone might be detrimental. Consider this homely analogy. People who floss their teeth regularly have a lower incidence of gum disease and fewer cavities than those who do not floss. The same is true for people who brush their teeth regularly and for people who use an antibacterial mouthwash. People who use certain skin creams can not only improve their appearance but also lessen the rate at which their skin dries out, reducing the risk of some skin diseases. Washing with certain preparations, too, is helpful, as are some types of skin masks. Showering and shampooing before bed improves one's health by reducing the inhalation of bacteria and assorted pathogens. Each of these activities is beneficial and not terribly time-consuming. And the list of similar activities could be extended considerably. At some point, however, the cumulative time taken to perform these tasks is great enough that adding another procedure—even one that improves health—will not add net benefit (will not, on balance, increase the individual's overall welfare). As the time available for additional activities becomes scarcer, the value that must be conferred by another hygiene-enhancing procedure for it to be beneficially added to the established set rises.

The example is instructive not merely for its suggestion of the dangers of cumulation—the logical fallacy that if drinking one glass of wine daily is good, drinking a dozen or a hundred or a thousand glasses is that much better—but also for its divergence from the legal-rule situation. For personal hygiene, each of us can choose which steps to take, when to add new steps, and when to drop old routines, each of us assessing for ourselves the personal cost and value. But for legal rules, that is not the case, or at least not in the same way. We are not supposed to pick and choose which legal rules to obey. And the likelihood of repealing old legal commands as new ones come on-stream is substantially less than the probability that we will substitute new personal hygiene tasks for old ones (at least as long as the value of our time remains at its current level).

On this last point, take a look, for example, at the laws regulating how federal agencies make substantive rules. Professor Mark Seidenfeld found that more than a dozen separate statutory mandates for rule-making in federal agencies—requiring analyses and procedures that are overlapping and, in some respects, contradictory—have been added on top of the basic rule-making requisites of the Administrative Procedure Act.[52] Seven executive orders impose additional duties in connection with agency rule-making.[53] The various requirements—commanding attention to the needs of small businesses, examination of the proposed regulations' impact on the environment, consideration of effects on trade and technology, assessment of impact on unfunded government obligations, analysis of regulatory costs and benefits, and so on—may be independently beneficial. But they commonly have been imposed without attention to the cumulative effects of the full array of rule-making requirements.[54] There must be many such stories, and the growth in the numbers of legal rules might cause people in almost any walk of life to grumble about the degree to which the law regulates their lives.

The case for seeing increased numbers of rules alone as a major source of discontent with the legal system, however, is far from clear. Statistics such as the number of pages in the Federal Register are not unassailable proof of the growth of law; nor is it evident which of the alternative explanations linking dissatisfaction to the growth of American law, if either, is persuasive. The measure of Federal Register pages is used here (in preference to other measures) not only because of its precipitous rise but also because it actually fell over the next decade (1980-90)—a plain result of the Reagan Revolution—before resuming its upward march.[55] Despite the decline in regulation, the 1980s were not a decade of markedly good feeling toward the legal system, nor were the 1990s (which is inconsistent with a possible lagging effect of the perceived benefit from reduced regulation).

Yet the complaint about the extent to which law now affects our lives rings true as part of the assertion that bad rules are to blame for much of the public's disaffection with the legal system. Even if the statistics respecting any one measure of the increase in legal rules are misleading and the connection between the increase and dissatisfaction with the legal system is not straight-line, legal rule-making has been a growth industry over time. That fact probably has importance of itself, and it probably also implies an increase in bad rules. There is no reason to believe that good rules have increased relative to bad ones, so direct experience with bad rules, encounters with others who have had such experiences, or a general sense of being excessively "ruled" are plausible inferences from growth of government and of the legal system. For all three reasons examined under the "bad rules" explanation, the legal rules themselves are a likely source of complaint about the legal system.

## Bad Principles

A second explanation for dissatisfaction with the legal system looks more to the judiciary than to the political branches. It is not that judges have simply been ignoring the dictates of the other branches or behaving in ways at odds with the judges' assigned role (though there is a flavor of such accusations in some variants of this explanation). The heart of the argument is that judges, even when looking at the relevant external authorities and endeavoring to translate them faithfully and decide cases properly, have sent the law in directions that produce results that are at odds with society's interests. They have crafted bad principles of law, with the same effects as those that flow from legislated bad rules.

Numerous commentaries have opined that American judicial decisions increasingly rest on principles that are at odds with public interest. That, in large measure, is the thesis propounded by former professor and judge Robert Bork,[56] by Thomas Sowell,[57] and by Richard Epstein,[58] among others.[59] Bork and Sowell criticize the principles followed over the past three or four decades by American judges (especially federal judges) as unduly biased against religion, property, family, the military, and localities, shifting power to the national government and to the courts. They see those principles as disrespectful of tradition and traditionally important institutions, of ordinary citizens, and of a set of values not shared by the judges. They also see the principles as unduly focused on means rather than ends. The result is a set of decisions that produces public antipathy without reaching the ends that ostensibly justify the courts' means. Sowell puts the point bluntly:

Appellate courts have successfully imposed their will on other institutions—school boards, trial courts, universities, employers—without achieving the social end results expected. For all the countless criminals freed on evidentiary technicalities, there is no evidence that the police practices the courts attacked have been eliminated or even reduced. For all the costly and controversial procedures imposed by "affirmative action" quotas, there is little or no evidence that such policies have advanced blacks beyond what was achieved under the previous "equal opportunity" policy. For all the bitterness surrounding the busing controversy, there is no overall evidence of any social, educational, or psychological gains from these policies, and even purely statistical "integration" has been offset to a great extent by "white flight" to the suburbs. . . . That little or nothing has been achieved does not mean that there has been no cost. [In addition to the financial cost of busing, there are] such social costs as *increased* racial antagonism, and a disruption of school children's social life and reduced parental input into local schools. An "affirmative action" *report* can cost an employer hundreds of thousands of dollars, not to mention its costs in morale to officials, white male employees, and even minority and female employees feeling the backlash.[60]

Judge Bork attributes the misconceived principles to judges' ideologies, but Professor Sowell points the accusing finger at hubris: the conceit that anyone can make the sort of judgments needed to properly coordinate the myriad human actions that are at issue in running school systems or in setting employment policies. Sowell compares the judge to the central planner, in contrast to decentralized decisions informed by an enormous network of social, economic, and political relationships.[61] Socialism failed because it indulged the conceit that individual decision makers could know enough to direct in exquisite detail the fortunes of innumerable fellow citizens engaged in extraordinarily complex interactions dependent on a web of constantly changing facts and values. Sowell accuses judges of a similar conceit, with similarly dismal results.

Professor Epstein also accuses judges of following erroneous principles, but he identifies a different, though related, fundamental problem. Rather than the oversimplification that attends centralized decision making, it is the *undersim*plification of modern judicial precepts that is to blame.[62] Over time, complex rules have replaced older, simpler "rules of thumb," often because the older rule produced results in particular cases that conflicted with broadly applicable notions of fairness. Complex rules—often not *rules* at all, but merely a set of countervailing considerations to be balanced by judges—hold the promise of "perfect justice," of being able to sort more finely the cases in which one result is preferable from those in which a different outcome is better.[63]

As Professor Epstein notes, however, even if simple rules clearly work hardship in some cases—generating outcomes that are not socially ideal in those instances—abandoning them in favor of more finely tuned decision guides does not necessarily produce gains for society. The change may yield better substantive results (more appealing effects on behavior of individuals targeted by the rules the judges seek to give effect) but at the same time incur sufficiently greater administrative costs (largely what the public would call *legal costs*) to outweigh the gains in individual justice. More often, the added complexity moves the law away from social justice in substantive results as well as away from efficiency by virtue of increased costs. Results in individual, litigated cases may be more congruent with our notions of justice, but when the administrative costs and secondary effects of complex rules are taken into account, the outcomes (including nonlitigated outcomes) are less socially desirable than those obtained with the older, simpler rule.[64]

An example of the sort of change Epstein references (though not a focus for his discussion of legal complexity) is the move from broad rules of public officials' immunity from personal liability to rules that allow suit but provide defenses based on the particular official's state of mind or the particular state of the law regulating the official's conduct.[65] The shift was predicated on principles of good pedigree respecting risk-sharing, the nature of government's obligation to citizens, and the broad responsibility of those who cause harm to compensate victims. The result, however, was not congenial to interests that these principles purport to serve: the outcome has been increased litigation, increased expense, and no change in compensation to those asserting injury from official misconduct.[66] We might do well to return to the posture struck by Judge Learned Hand in defending the older, cruder immunity rule:

> It does indeed go without saying that an official, who is in fact guilty of using his powers to vent his spleen upon others, or for any other personal motive not connected with the public good, should not escape liability for the injuries he may so cause; and, if it were possible in practice to confine such com-

plaints to the guilty, it would be monstrous to deny recovery. The justification for doing so is that it is impossible to know whether the claim is well founded until the case is tried, and that to submit all officials, the innocent as well as the guilty, to the burden of a trial and to the inevitable danger of its outcome, would dampen the ardor of all but the most resolute, or the most irresponsible, in the unflinching discharge of their duties. . . . In this instance it has been thought in the end better to leave unredressed the wrongs done by dishonest officials than to subject those who do their duty to the constant dread of retaliation.[67]

Professor Epstein's argument suggests that Hand's approach was correct. And although Epstein's formulation of the problem with present-day American law is quite different from Professor Sowell's, the heart of the problem Epstein observes closely resembles that identified by Sowell: the abandonment of salutary principles of judicial modesty for principles that reach for social justice without being able to grasp it. That complaint does not require a definition of public interest at odds with the judges', although many critics see the judiciary embracing principles that, even if they could be implemented at very little administrative cost, would have untoward effects. Epstein's assertion, worked through in numerous examples, is that the modern judges' inadequate sensitivity to administrative costs is sufficient to explain why so many modern judicial ventures have produced bad results and widespread discontent.

This assertion rings true. Indeed, expanding Sowell's complaint into territory more traditionally conceded to be within judges' domain, Epstein's point applies to all of the relatively invisible costs that legal rules convey to parties whose identities, circumstances, and values cannot be known to or evaluated by the judges. The more judges earnestly endeavor to unearth and understand these costs, the more they complicate legal analysis with principles that will not be so readily comprehended by those to whom they are directed or so predictably applied through the legal system. The greater cost and reduced predictability that follow from added complexity explain why so many nonlawyers who deal with the legal system see the real punishment of modern law as being the need to spend time and money on lawyers, rather than the bad end-result of their encounter with law.[68]

The arguments advanced by critics such as Professors Sowell and Epstein can be understood without the need for any form of conspiracy theory. They can be credited without accepting the implication (veiled in Epstein, clear in Sowell, and not an implication but an explicit assertion in Bork) that judges have followed personal values that depart from values that, both historically and currently, have broad public acceptance. In contrast to the picture Professors Daniel Farber and Suzanna Sherry paint of the legal academy gone awry in just that way,[69] Epstein and Sowell offer a portrait of judging that is sympathetic to the judicial mission but that views much of the judicial effort as doomed to failure.

As the population governed by a legal rule grows, as society becomes more complex, and as judges become increasingly remote from personal acquaintance with the people and circumstances to which the rules they effectuate apply, there is less and less chance that the judges can craft legal principles that will produce attractive results. Actors performing in most professional live theater settings are made up in a fashion that appears realistic at a distance but bizarre up close. They use exaggerated movements on stage, in marked contrast to acting for film or television. Because the audience in live theater is remote, unable to see and hear the nuances that are staples of other performance media, actors and directors scale the look and sound of what they do to portray reality at a distance, even if it seems less real on stage. Judges can be conceived as actors in a form of drama that is performed in different settings. To be sure, much of the day-to-day business of the courts still takes place as a chamber presentation or as acting for the small screen. But important principles increasingly are crafted in settings where the judges perform on the functional equivalent of a Broadway stage.

Oddly, as the audience has moved away, judges have been exposed to more and more examples of wonderful movie acting and have come to believe that this is their art. Perhaps we should imagine that the judges have been given better technology to pick out a spectator here or there, to see and hear parts of their audience with greater clarity. Judges therefore have the illusion of greater proximity when in fact they are more remote; the real need for fewer, simpler, broader gestures is masked by a sense that more, subtler, and more elegant moves will be even more effective now than before.

The general problem of legal decision making in a more complex world probably is enough to explain what has gone wrong with legal principles. There is, however, more.

An argument advanced in recent years by several scholars, most notably by

Professor Clayton Gillette, adds another string to this bow. They argue that path-dependence—a common phenomenon made more remarkable by virtue of judges' precedent-based, case-by-case decision making—risks innocent divergence from socially preferred solutions.[70] In difficult cases, judges reason from principles, which are both the precursors of many rules (notably, common law rules) and the critical vehicles for resolving conflicts over and among rules.[71] Principles that guide judges are derived in large measure from other judicial decisions.[72] But a principle inherent in one decision and made explicit in other decisions that follow the first, even if wholly congenial to general public interests in its initial applications, may produce results inimical to social interests later on. Changes in social organization, in technology, or in our values may account for the subsequent divergence of principle from interest. As Professor Gillette explains, however, a precedent-based system of decision is path-dependent; that is, it is influenced by earlier steps along the way, so that altering a settled principle becomes more costly.[73] It can be done (recall *Belton* and *Brown* and *Rincon-Pineda,* for examples), but judges commonly are reluctant to depart from precedent that is still widely followed and (the Supreme Court aside) cannot readily coordinate a group response. Hence, the old principle will be sustainable for too long. Further, efforts to change to a different principle may at first produce signals that the new principle is wrong; it may generate confusion and local inefficiencies even if it makes possible a socially preferable set of results.[74]

Anyone who has looked carefully at the law, even with rose-colored glasses, finds many areas where courts have built up a body of doctrine over the past three decades—working from older authorities in traditional ways—but have created as many difficult problems as they have solved. Part of the public antipathy to courts must rest with the judicial construction of decisional principles, in constitutional and common law adjudications that lie largely outside the purview of the political branches, that have ill served their purported ends. Whether stress is placed on the path-dependence point or on more direct critiques of judicial work product, such as those offered by Professors Epstein and Sowell, it is clear that the bad results can be arrived at innocently, by judges acting from good motives within the model of how judges should behave. But however innocent the error and whatever the source, it should also be clear that principles of judges' making have indeed produced some bad results.

## Bad Decisions

A third explanation for the legal system's ill repute is that even if most judges act in accord with the Agency Model and both the rules they follow and the principles they propound are basically sound, enough bad decisions are made to give the system a black eye. Many commentaries on the legal system, from rank outsiders and sophisticated insiders alike, point to particular decisions that seem silly.[75]

It is not the intricacies of integration doctrine but the McDonald's coffee case that gets mentioned most often as an emblem of the system's ills. That case produced a $2.9 million verdict against the McDonald's fast-food chain for serving coffee too hot, resulting in injuries to 79-year-old Stella Liebeck when she spilled coffee on herself, opening the lid while holding the coffee cup between her legs in her car.[76] Few people thought McDonald's, which served something like a billion cups of coffee each year, lacked adequate market incentives to select an appropriate temperature for its coffee or that courts were better able to make that decision. And quite a few people found the aftermath of the case—new labels on coffee cups warning drinkers that coffee is hot—symbolic of a system out of control.[77]

The story is largely the same with respect to most individual court decisions that are subjects of extensive public commentary. Widespread public condemnation accompanied O. J. Simpson's acquittal on charges of murdering his wife, Nicole, and Ron Goldman, as well as the acquittal of police officers accused of wrongfully beating Rodney King on a Los Angeles highway.[78] Similar public reaction surrounded the Louise Woodward murder case—the "nanny trial," in which Ms. Woodward was charged with killing a baby left in her care by shaking the baby violently. Both the jury verdict (murder) and the judge's decision to reduce the conviction to involuntary manslaughter and the sentence to time served were controversial.[79]

Less highly publicized, but still widely noted, cases likewise appear questionable. Consider, for instance, the suit over Dr. Ira Gore's repainted BMW—he was awarded $4 million because his BMW dealer had repainted his car before delivery (without telling him) to cover minor blemishes in the finish that had occurred during shipping.[80] Or the suit by Milo Stephens, whose case against the New York City Transit Authority for injuries sustained when Mr. Stephens attempted to commit suicide by throwing himself in front of a subway train was settled for $650,000 in 1983.[81] Indeed, nearly all the commentary one sees about particular decisions—involving physician liability, criminal sentencing, product liability, or other matters—observes the failure of the legal system in a particular instance.[82]

As with other complex decisions, there are plenty of opportunities for a decision to go awry, through judicial mistake, through jury error, or even through judicial misfeasance. The last of these sources of error is relatively rare, but as Operation Greylord in Chicago revealed, judicial misconduct does occur.[83] Whatever the source of error, given the number of decisions made each year, it is no doubt true that a significant number will be at odds with the applicable legal rules and principles. It is also no doubt true that a significant number of decisions will be uncongenial to most ordinary citizens.

Moreover, those decisions that seem most at odds with common sense may be especially newsworthy, the only explanation for the extravagant attention given to the McDonald's coffee case. And news of such decisions could very well explain widespread concern about the legal system. Most people's impression of the legal system is, after all, formed by a few high-profile cases rather than by extensive knowledge of legal rules and processes.[84]

This explanation of public dissatisfaction, however, is far from complete. For one thing, surveys of public attitudes toward the legal profession reveal something at odds with this explanation: the more extensive a person's contact with the legal system, the less positive his or her impression of it is likely to be.[85] For another, there is evidence that some features of the American legal system regularly produce bad decisions: for example, the confluence of civil juries, unstructured punitive-damage liability, and minimum contacts-based jurisdiction (allowing a court to exercise authority over individuals or businesses with minimal contacts in the court's jurisdiction), arguably combine to pit homegrown plaintiffs against "foreign" defendants, producing a systemic bias toward large liability awards.[86]

The evidence of systemic bias is not compelling, but there is at least enough to sustain suspicion. Serious examinations of the evidence have produced divergent conclusions about the degree to which—or whether—our legal system tilts systematically in directions that are problematic.[87] One factor contributing to the perceived problem is that some decisions portrayed as evidence that the system has gone awry are ones that must be made when evidence is ambiguous. They do not necessarily have to be made in the exact way they have been, but they require disposition before the relevant facts can be known. These decisions can often look bad in hindsight.

Consider the breast-implant litigation.[88] Women sued manufacturers of silicon-gel breast implants, claiming that leakage from the implants produced serious health problems. When the first cases were decided, the scientific evidence was in dispute. In one suit filed in 1982 and decided in mid-1984, the jury concluded that the implants had damaged the health of the woman who was suing, awarding her $1.4 million in compensatory and punitive damages (the punitive damages were premised on evidence—to be sure, *contested* evidence—that the manufacturer knew there was a potential problem and manipulated data in one study). The case was settled while on appeal. Subsequently, plaintiffs won increasingly large verdicts, including one for $25 million. In the next decade, more than twelve thousand suits were filed, almost all coming after sensational reports about the problem and a decision by the Food and Drug Administration to ban the implants' use.[89] Years later, it became quite clear that there was no valid scientific support for the claimed link between the implants and the health problems.

The breast-implant cases plainly involve a series of wrong decisions. Not only did the court decisions based on erroneous scientific testimony reach the wrong outcome; decisions by administrators, activists, and producers of a news/entertainment program also were wrong and dramatically changed the nature and effect of the litigation.[90] The fact that many different decisions were made on the basis of bad evidence is testament to the difficulty of deciding complex scientific issues before enough scientific testing has been done. Of course, people who believe that they have been injured seriously by an action have an interest in securing compensation even if the scientific community has not yet come to consensus about long-term effects of the potential source of harm. Making decisions under conditions of uncertainty can hurt plaintiffs as well as defendants—some people who have been injured find their claims rejected on bad science.

The breast-implant cases, however, suggest a possibility that the legal system can spin out of control in a particular way when reliable information is unavailable. If there is not a firm control on the evidence admitted or a check on the cases that are allowed to go to jury decision, it is possible that the dynamics of jury deliberation will lead juries to award huge sums to appealing plaintiffs on weak evidence. Recent investigation of the operation of juries supports this fear,[91] though the courts have also taken steps to counteract the problem of decisions based on bad evidence.[92] Nonetheless, if there is a systemic jury bias toward people with apparently serious health problems and a perception that the firms defending such claims have significant wealth, the problem is not only the risk of a bad decision. The problem also is the likelihood that the risks—and costs—of bad decisions are not symmetrical. And the cost of these decisions together with the cost of contesting them can be staggering. The threat of enormous damage awards and high litigation costs prompted one producer of the implants to declare bankruptcy. Another implant producer estimated that it had spent more than $100 million in litigation costs alone.[93]

These cases may present only anecdotal evidence that the American legal system has a bigger problem than the occasional bad decision. Yet they are not the only evidence of that. Undoubtedly, the odd decision does play a role, perhaps a large one, in fueling concern about the legal system. But more is going on than that.

## Inconsistency

A fourth possible explanation for the public's dissatisfaction with the American legal system is not the nature of any rule, principle, or decision so much as the inconsistency among decisions. Two arguments support the importance of consistency to public decisions. Writings in the public-choice or rational-choice schools have emphasized the role of consistency as an attribute of minimally rational individual choice.[94] If I prefer the Mercedes Benz E430 to the BMW 5-series, and I prefer the BMW 5-series to the Lincoln Continental, then the property of *transitivity* (which is a form of consistency across preference pairs) requires that I also prefer the Mercedes to the Lincoln. To choose otherwise would be irrational.[95] Public-choice scholars have viewed such consistency as a desirable, if not readily attainable, attribute of public as well as individual decision making, at times suggesting its necessity to well-functioning public-choice mechanisms.[96] Alternatively, philosophically minded scholars have urged consistency as an aspect of fairness, a moral requirement to treat like things alike.[97] This requirement applies to small family units and to large polities. It captures a widely shared, if imprecise, concept of sound decision making for parents or princes, for juveniles or judges.

*Hard Inconsistency*

Legal scholars have often treated consistency as a similarly critical attribute of well-functioning legal systems.[98] Lon Fuller emphasized the link between consistency and the two qualities—predictability and generality (nondiscrimination)—that he believed to be of special importance to a legal system.[99] As discussed earlier, principled predictability, which describes the intersection of the concepts Professor Fuller separated into predictability and generality, is an essential attribute of the rule of law.[100] Inconsistency in the laws themselves or in their application can erode the rule of law; inconsistency can call a legal system's legitimacy into question.[101]

To see that, consider instances in which two matters addressed within the legal system seem in all respects identical (except, perhaps, for the identity of the parties or of the legal decision maker) but are treated dissimilarly. Consider, for example, the Florida court decisions about the 2000 presidential election. Several judicial decisions were challenged as embracing standards—and reaching results—flatly inconsistent with prior decisions.[102] What authority did the Florida Secretary of State have to decide when to certify election results and whether to accept certain modifications of those results? Should partially punched ballots count in determining the results? The assertions most corrosive of trust in our legal system are that judges decide these questions in one manner when that decision helps Democrats and in a contrary manner when applying those standards would advantage Republicans. The open expression of suspicion that courts reach different outcomes depending on the identity of the parties involved and on the political preferences of the judges is rare and unlikely to explain broader public attitudes toward our legal system. However, some segment of the public does believe that in critical cases politics can produce inconsistent decisions—not out of judges' fear of retribution or hope of reward from those in positions of power, but out of personal inclination insufficiently constrained.

More typical examples of inconsistency might involve different criminal sentences for a rich and well-known defendant than for a poor one or different rules for access to government benefits.[103] These differences could be—and most often will be—the result of legitimate evaluation of factors that affect different defendants differently. A person with a good job, stable family life, and valuable property holdings in the community sensibly is treated as less of a flight risk for bail purposes than a vagrant. In the same manner, the mere fact of criminal conviction may impose a greater penalty on some defendants than on others, and incarceration for a given period of time may be a greater deterrent to some classes of potential transgressor. But boldly divergent treatment that appears inexplicable except as favoritism to a particular person presents a different case. Such instances are very likely to be matters of public controversy if they come to light. Witness, for example, the outcry when it was revealed that Speaker of the House Jim Wright's chief aide had attempted murder in a particularly brutal fashion and, after only a short time in a local jail (not the state penitentiary), had been released into Wright's custody.[104] Public dismay at the verdict in the O. J. Simpson case was not simply a reaction to what was seen as a wrong outcome; it was even more an expression of disapproval of a system that appeared to provide different justice for the rich (who could afford to hire the "Dream Team" of defense lawyers) and the poor.[105]

The concern over inconsistency in such settings may manifest the more general human concern with status: focusing on relative wealth or relative treatment by a powerful individual or entity rather than solely on absolute wealth or absolute measures of treatment.[106] The perception that different legal outcomes reflect differences in status predictably triggers dissatisfaction with the legal system and may partially explain the system's poor public image.

The number of these inconsistencies associated with the American legal system may be on the rise. That possibility follows from the increase in numbers of cases and of judicial decision makers. I may be perfectly consistent and so may you, but we still can reach strongly inconsistent decisions in some cases. The more of us there are and the more decisions we make, the greater the risk of such inconsistency. The possibility that inconsistency has increased also is enhanced by the increasing number of decisions that turn on judgments of decision makers other than judges. The most obvious examples are jury decisions; the American legal system is unique in its heavy reliance on juries.[107] The case that systemic biases promote bad jury decisions, noted in the preceding section, is plausible, but the case that the use of juries increases inconsistency is conclusive. Unlike judges, jurors are not repeat players and also lack the professional (peer pressure) incentives to consistency across cases that influence judges. The impact of reduced incentives to consistency is most evident for decisions for which there is relatively little guidance available for the one-time player. So, for example, we should expect to observe gross inconsistency more frequently in damage awards on nearly identical facts than on liability determinations on nearly identical facts.[108]

The mere existence of inconsistent decisions should not be enough to create concern. Our legal system, like other decision-making systems, has mechanisms that exist to correct inconsistencies. Appellate courts correct lower courts when their decisions are inconsistent. The Supreme Court typically exercises its discretionary power over case selection to hear cases when the intermediate appellate courts reach inconsistent results. And jury decisions often are amended by judges to conform to a consistent pattern. Even so, these mechanisms do not completely eliminate inconsistency. In particular, it is unlikely that judges will fully correct inconsistency in jury decisions.

The problem may be even worse for some decisions by administrative agencies, where decision-making incentives may strongly *encourage* inconsistencies dependent on the identity of the parties involved.[109] As noted above, the share of decisions affecting our lives in which administrators play a key role doubtless has increased over the past few decades. But blatant inconsistencies are not commonly observed in judges' decisions and certainly are the exception, not the rule, even for most other decision makers in our legal system—at least inconsistencies that cannot be predicted in advance by knowledgeable observers, reduced to some pattern or probability distribution, and accounted for appropriately in fashioning our activities. Here, too, judicial review can substantially reduce the effect of inconsistency. But again, some measure of inconsistency will remain.

### Soft Inconsistency

As Fuller observed, there is another form of inconsistency in law that is less significant (as far as systemic legitimacy is concerned) but more pervasive. It might be termed a *soft* inconsistency in contrast to a *hard* inconsistency. It involves legal decisions that may seem inconsistent but whether that is so turns on more complex debate over the relevance of factors that make two situations (two cases, two rulings) alike or dissimilar. The frequency with which these soft inconsistencies occur owes to the complexity of the law and of the human interactions it regulates. With a sufficiently large number of variables coming into play in each legal decision, it is hard to be sure that in fact there *is* an inconsistency when one observes outcomes that vary—after all, typically the observer will only be able to assess similarities across a relatively small sub-set of those variables.[110] Further, as Professor Fuller and Dean Edward Levi instructed, most of these inconsistencies cannot be cured without creating other inconsistencies.[111]

The point Fuller makes about the sources of inconsistency also explains why inconsistency is an ineluctable traveling companion of increases in the size and number of legal regulations and decisions. As these increase, it becomes ever more costly to account for all the variations in the settings that produce legal decisions and to maintain the same outcomes for the same sets of variables. As just noted, we seldom observe all of the relevant variables, nor are we able to assess them accurately. Hence, the prospect of keeping all decisions consistent decreases as their number and complexity rises.

This is true even if there is a single decision maker and a single set of express decisional criteria, as anyone who has graded a large number of law school exams soon realizes, but it is even more true if we allow the possibility of nonidentical decision makers. Consider, for instance, the following situations. Start with a single judge deciding a single issue, the appropriate sentence for bank robbery. The law gives the judge a range of possible sentences and discretion to set the sentence within that range. Our lone judge believes that a showing of genuine remorse is important, because it suggests that the defendant is less likely to return to a life of crime. Defense lawyers soon learn that their convicted clients would do well to confess their crime, acknowledge responsibility, and express regret.

Now introduce a second judge, who believes that the age of the defendant is far more important than expressions of remorse, because age correlates closely with certain criminal proclivities. The pattern of sentences will be less consistent with two judges than with one. Then posit a third judge, who believes that criminal sentences should vary less with characteristics of the individual defendant than of the specific crime (for example, how much was stolen, whether force was used, whether the defendant carried a weapon, how many people were present at the time). Again, consistency will decline. Add a fourth judge, who is also concerned with the nature of the specific crime but who puts more stress on *relative* than *absolute* considerations (how great a percentage of the bank's assets was stolen, for instance) and add a second sentencing issue (sentences for grand theft, not from banks). Consistency declines further with the fourth judge, and new inconsistencies—among the sentences for the second crime and across the two types of crime—will emerge with the addition of the second legal issue.

Over the past three decades, both the number of judges in America and the number of cases decided have grown considerably. Judge Richard Posner, commenting on the changes in litigation over the course of the twentieth century, traces a major shift in litigation. He notes that the rate of growth in litigation was both relatively low and quite stable over the period 1900-1960, averaging roughly a compound annual rate of 1.8 percent.[112] Since 1960, however, there has been explosive growth in litigation, especially in federal litigation, even though rates of both population growth and (measured) economic growth have slowed substantially.[113] For example, between 1960 and 1983 the "number of cases filed in the district courts more than tripled, compared with a less than 30 percent increase in the preceding quarter-century."[114] During that period, federal civil cases increased 330 percent, federal appellate cases increased by nearly 700 percent, and federal civil appeals rose by nearly 800 percent.[115] Appellate filings have continued to rise, by another 73 percent from 1983 to 1999, a much more modest increase in relative terms; but because it comes on top of the earlier growth, this represents annual increases that are larger in absolute terms than those in the earlier period.[116]

The increases in decisions and decision makers doubtless have increased the number of instances in which decisions are likely to be softly inconsistent. Take the Dr. Gore case, mentioned above. The lawyers who brought Dr. Gore's suit had filed two dozen other suits on the same theory that repainting a new car prior to delivery without informing the buyer amounted to fraud. One had been tried before Gore's in the same circuit court. No punitive damages, however, were awarded in the prior case.[117] When Dr. Gore's suit was tried, the jury awarded him $4,000 in compensatory damages and tacked on $4 million in punitive damages, multiplying the compensatory award by the approximate number of refinished BMWs sold in the United States.[118] It is possible that Dr. Gore's case differed in some meaningful way from the other case of alleged "repainting fraud." It is more likely that the decisions are inconsistent—perhaps not flatly inconsistent, decided on completely opposed standards, but inconsistent in which facts and factors gain decisive weight. The different results in these cases appear to be illustrations of the "lawsuit lottery" that Professor O'Connell says characterizes American tort litigation.[119]

The lottery analogy, though useful, overstates the case against the legal system. Professor O'Connell does not believe, nor do other critics, that every claimant stands an equal chance of recovery, regardless of the merits of the individual case (the overlap between the circumstances—or at least one party's honest estimation of the circumstances—and the black-letter law's definition of bases for liability).

The case O'Connell mounts against the legal system, however, does not collapse merely because his analogy exaggerates his point. If inconsistency within the legal system generates a lottery-like aspect for some class of cases, that will affect the behavior of potential litigants, perhaps even beyond the cases actually at issue. That is the easy part, understanding that there is likely to be an effect from inconsistency.

The more difficult part is calculating the effect, mapping its influence across cases. The effects of inconsistency do not fit a single, homogeneous pattern. Inconsistency can encourage some people with questionable claims to litigate, because it becomes less certain that such claims necessarily will fail.[120] Inconsistency also can discourage some people with reasonably strong claims from pursuing those claims, because it becomes less certain that such claims necessarily will succeed. The same contrary effects hold for those who face legal claims.

How the different effects play out depends on the relationship between the costs of bringing and pursuing claims, the costs of defending against claims, the rewards to successful claimants, and the penalties for unsuccessful defendants.[121] In the scenario that is most likely to raise concerns, defendants face asymmetrically high costs (because it is harder to defend against a particular claim than to assert it) and penalties (for instance, because losing a suit imposes negative reputational effects that are not the mirror image of gains to the plaintiff from winning). In such (not unrealistic) circumstances, inconsistency will increase both litigation and payments from targets of litigation.[122] The payments will be made directly to plaintiffs in the form of settlements, and they will also be made indirectly in the form of altered behavior, such as "defensive medicine" or the refusal to answer questions when asked about former employees.[123]

Defendants who pay in either form to avoid litigation often feel as if they have been blackmailed.[124] They sense that the direct payment is not to a "meritorious" claimant, even though the payment typically is based on a recognition that the claimant might win. Similarly, potential defendants may resent the steps—altering behavior or paying for liability insurance—made necessary (which is to say, rational) by the prospect that a low-probability complaint might impose high defense and penalty costs. The fact that it *is* a low-probability complaint may be what engenders the belief that in a righteous world it would not pay off.

The low probability, of course, reduces the real costs of such litigation— actual payments in court cases are less because of that, as are payments to insure against liability (whether in standard, commercial insurance, in funds set aside against the possibility of an adverse judgment, or in altered behavior). But a low-probability claim can still impose substantial costs on a potential defendant who faces prospects of follow-on litigation with greater burdens because of the way a court might dispose of certain issues or who faces substantial reputational harm or greater opportunity costs for litigating. To see the last point, imagine the different cost of time spent on litigation by an ordinary person, such as you or me, or even by someone with fewer and less remunerative options for her or his time, versus an executive—say, Bill Gates of Microsoft— whose time has enormous value and whose talents are not easily replicated (his second-in-command's instincts on key issues may be substantially less reliable than his own).

Soft inconsistency, thus, is problematic primarily because of its interaction with other aspects of the legal system, such as the prospect for a complaint with a low probability of success to generate high costs. The most obvious costs are the damages that can be assessed when a low-probability claim succeeds: witness Dr. Gore's case or Stella Liebeck's suit against McDonald's. Inconsistency with low payouts is uninteresting as well as untroubling (putting aside cases in which the low amount of money nominally at risk masks a much higher-stakes contest over reputation or other valuable, though not immediately monetized, item). If there is not much at stake, there is not much worry about whether decisions are right or wrong, consistent or not. If these obvious costs are small, the less apparent costs of socially undesirable changes in behavior are likely to be small as well.[125]

*Reducing the Costs of Inconsistency*

The interplay of inconsistency with high stakes in much highly publicized litigation explains why many proposals for reforming the legal system address features that appear to contribute either to the prospect for inconsistency (for allowing the occasional low-probability claim to prevail) or to the prospect that such a claim could lead to a high payout. Calls for reexamination of the civil jury, which is seen as a primary source of unpredictability in our legal system, fall in the first category.[126] So, too, do recommendations to abandon the "American rule" for apportionment of litigation expenses (each party bears its own legal costs, regardless of outcome) in favor of the "English rule" (the loser pays).[127] The proposals for cost-shifting are designed to address the problem of low-probability claims at the front end by discouraging claimants from filing; abolishing or cutting back on jury trials is intended to tackle the problem at the back end. The risk that low-probability claims will result in high payouts is the target of attempts to eliminate or cap punitive damages.[128]

*Punitive damages* play an especially large role in debates over reform of the American legal system today. Many of the decisions that seem to be off target gained notoriety more for the size of the punitive-damage award than for the mere fact of liability. If Dr. Gore appeared an undeserving winner, because his claim of harm from undisclosed repainting sounded so weak, the difference between interest in the story and outrage over it lies in the fact that the initial verdict put more than $4 million in his pocket. The same holds true for Stella Liebeck's suit against McDonald's. Had she received compensation for medical expenses and nothing more, it seems improbable that this case would be so widely known. An award of punitive damages approaching $3 million, however, focuses public attention quite nicely.

The public also took notice of the award of $145 billion—yes, *billion* dollars—to Florida smokers who sued tobacco companies for selling nicotine-rich cigarettes that induced Floridians to keep smoking long enough to ruin their health.[129] For many years, tobacco companies prevailed in one suit after another. Almost invariably, juries rejected claims on the ground that the smokers themselves had notice that cigarettes were harmful and chose to continue smoking nonetheless; in fact, smokers' claims were rejected in more than three hundred suits before the tobacco companies lost.[130] The Florida suit was the first class-action suit in which a jury verdict went against the tobacco companies.[131] However plausible it is that facts could come to light that change the liability calculus from negative to positive, something seems amiss when the change produces a verdict that exceeds the gross national product of 172 nations—about 85 percent of the world's sovereign states.[132]

Cases such as Dr. Gore's and Ms. Liebeck's are intuitively troubling. It seems wrong on its face that every now and then a plaintiff will succeed in a case based on a firm's repainting cars at no cost to the new owner or selling coffee that is hot enough to burn.[133] Even if tobacco companies are to be held liable for the sale of legal products that long have been known to be harmful to one's health, the assessment of staggering punitive-damage awards as a form of public condemnation seems wrong. Those intuitions give weight to the proposals for legal reform.

The step from intuition to systemic reform, however, though probably salutary, is a tricky one. All of the proposed reforms have effects more complicated than appear at first blush, and all of them must be viewed in tandem with other aspects of the American legal system that affect and are affected by their operation.[134]

Consider, for instance, the change that has been examined most carefully—a shift to the "loser pays" rule. The change may on balance be beneficial, but it will also have adverse effects: it is likely to prompt higher expenditures for cases that go to trial, even though it will discourage some case filings and some trials.[135] Further, the impact of this change on the pattern of settlements and trials is not so obviously what its proponents would like. If litigants have significantly different information about the facts underlying their conflict, and thus about the actual strength of their legal positions, a shift to the loser-pays rule could *increase* litigation of relatively weak cases that might settle under the standard American rule on litigation costs.[136]

Or look at what may be the most seemingly compelling cure: a cap on punitive damages. The case for such a cap rests largely on the observation that punitive-damage awards are growing in frequency and in amount yet cannot be readily reduced to an insurable risk. If punitive damages were restricted to occasions of egregious wrongdoing, insurance would be unlikely because there would be a serious "moral hazard" problem—the insured would be best able to avoid the damages by acting properly but, once insured, would lose the incentive (or face a substantially reduced incentive) to do so.[137] The bigger problem is that punitive damages are not confined to these instances. They are used at times and for reasons that defy ready classification. And there is no clear basis for calculating what the magnitude of these damages should be, even if we could identify the proper occasions for imposing them.[138] As one review observed, "In its current state, the doctrine of punitive damages has a questionable logical basis, is difficult to apply, and is unpredictable."[139] We know that jury verdicts have been increasing and have included some staggeringly high awards, but we do not know what to expect in any given case or even across a range of cases.[140] The absence of a basis for predicting what the universe of punitive-damage awards will look like is a strong impediment to efficient insurance against the possible imposition of such awards.

Yet there are instances in which punitive damages may make sense. Cases in which a defendant's wrongdoing is plainly established, but its effects are difficult to detect or sufficiently difficult to trace, can leave a substantial gap in deterrence.[141] Imagine, for example, a bank that routinely cheats its customers but is seldom caught or, when it is, faces a penalty that does not cover the full extent of the harm its action causes. Conduct that imposes real costs on society, then, will be engaged in too often with too little precaution. One antidote is the use of punitive damages to make up for the "deterrence shortfall."[142] Although other antidotes exist—criminal or administrative sanctions, for example—their costs, including error costs, well might exceed those associated with punitive damages. Caps on punitive damages may be justified, given the costs of current practices, but for some classes of activity they doubtless will increase the divergence between the ideal and the actual incentives provided by the legal system. The point is not that caps are a bad idea, only that even the most intuitively compelling idea will turn out on closer scrutiny to have effects that are more varied, and often less desirable, than a quick consideration suggests.

Apart from the particular steps to be taken, the intuition that low-probability, high-stakes decisions are a problem for the American legal system is open to question. At least, the intuition is not readily turned into a principle that comfortably identifies who can litigate or who is entitled to large recoveries or when high costs should attach to a legal decision. Recall, for example, that the plaintiffs in *Belton v. Gebhart* and *Brown v. Board of Education* had low probabilities of success with their claims.[143] Does that mean that we should have made it more difficult for those claims to be brought or should have limited the remedies available to successful plaintiffs in those instances?[144]

Although inconsistency does have consequences, most complaints that focus on cases such as Dr. Gore's or Ms. Liebeck's properly belong to the preceding category, complaints about bad decisions. The real culprit is not that those decisions were sufficiently inconsistent with other decisions to have a low probability of success—indeed, that is the good news. The complaint about those cases is that the decisions were just wrong. Hard inconsistencies trouble us wholly apart from the result in any one case. Soft inconsistencies are an inevitable product of a large system with many decisions and many decision makers; they are unlikely to account for much of the discontent with our legal system. They are, however, harbingers of problems that may not only account for discontent: they may also point to trouble that, unchecked, threatens the predictability of legal decisions and ultimately the rule of law.

## Bad Process

Another possible source of complaint about the American legal system is that there is something wrong with the process for making decisions. Process defects primarily are objected to on the ground that they produce a bad result—generating either more bad decisions or greater inconsistency than a better-designed procedure. But they also can produce higher administrative costs (costs unrelated to the result) and undue delay. Two problems with civil juries—decision biases and inconsistency—are discussed earlier in this chapter. Proponents of civil juries will contest the validity of the first criticism and the magnitude of the second. But even the most ardent fans of civil juries must concede that juries contribute to both cost and delay in the American legal system.[145]

Juries aside, how does the American legal process stack up? Law professors and lawyers talk a great deal about the virtues and vices of specific procedures, almost always providing grist for virtually any view of the desirability or undesirability of a given procedural feature. Consider, for example, two much-criticized features of the American legal system: expanded discovery opportunities and increased use of class-action suits. Proponents defend expanded discovery as permitting better development of cases so that less time is wasted during the trial and parties are better informed when deciding how to structure their case or a possible settlement.[146] Critics assail expanded discovery for allowing plaintiffs with no evidence of wrongdoing to launch "fishing expeditions" that impose costs on innocent defendants, costs that then can be used strategically to encourage settlement of frivolous claims.[147] Similar division characterizes discussion of the class-action mechanism. Depending on your perspective, class actions either are mechanisms for efficient adjudication of claims and for improving the alignment of deterrent incentives with social value, or they are tools that allow lawyers to sue essentially on their own behalf with the assistance of procedures so costly that, for many defendants, settlement becomes a more economical alternative.[148]

The truth, not surprisingly, is that the procedural devices most debated by insiders do not have a single cost-benefit balance across cases or across time. Even relatively general conclusions about them often are problematical. There are good defenses for the adoption of more lenient discovery rules and for relaxing impediments to class actions, but both devices can be used strategically to advance the interests of parties whose claims (or defenses) are unlikely to be found meritorious. Both can increase the cost of legal actions; both can exacerbate delay. We should understand the costs *and* the benefits of process features before evaluating whether and how to change them.

Take discovery first. Broad discovery can require a party to search through thousands of documents, through warehouses of paper (or the electronic equivalent), or to answer questions that do not admit of simple responses in ways that risk opening the respondent to further difficulty if answers seem inaccurate or incomplete or in tension with later statements.[149] But the risk of abuse must be balanced against the risk that one party will hide—or that one simply will not discover—crucial information. In some cases, that information allows litigation to align the law's incentive effects appropriately; without it, too few or too many cases will be brought, and too little or too much money will be assessed for a given activity.[150] Search costs can be too high to make it worthwhile to pursue certain information in many settings (not only in legal processes). But people also can underinvest in searching; they can fail to make efforts to uncover information that is more valuable than the expected costs of additional search activity.[151]

Which risk is greater? In the individual case, that depends on the particular parties and issues presented, on the specific rules governing discovery, on the advantages accruing to lawyers who gain reputations for a given attitude toward litigation, and on the way individual judges control proceedings within their purview. It depends on the substantive laws themselves and on the error costs associated with them. If the laws generate higher error costs from overenforcement than from underenforcement, the discovery rules should lean toward reducing errors associated with overenforcement. Analysis of these issues often takes on a partisan tinge: after all, broad discovery commonly (and probably rightly) is thought to advantage plaintiffs and thus is staunchly defended by plaintiffs' lawyers and attacked by defense counsel. But fuller consideration of the costs and benefits of discovery would also take into account that it can be used by defendants as well—and, as with plaintiffs, it can be used either strategically or sincerely.[152]

Although a full evaluation of the factors pertinent to designing the ideal discovery rule plainly would require extended analysis, well beyond what can be done here, it is almost certainly not worth answering the question for individual cases or for specific classes of cases. Altering procedure in particular cases may prove beneficial for those cases; but insofar as our focus is directed to particular litigation, it is likely to be both easier and more rewarding to alter the substantive law than to fine-tune procedures.[153] This route is likely to be preferable in part because there is a substantial cost saving associated with a relatively clear, stable set of procedures that would apply across a range of cases.[154] Of course, this is only one side of the equation. The costs and benefits of particularity cannot be given in so small a nutshell. It is worth adding, however, that where the legal system opts for more general procedural rules, the benefits of fine-tuning can, to some extent, be captured through individual agreement, with the general rules serving as the default.

A global analysis of the costs and benefits of broad discovery could yield more valuable lessons for reform, but this is an even more daunting task. Without taking on that burden, it is possible in short compass to offer two thoughts about the contours of proper discovery rules. First, recognize that, no matter how it is structured, discovery is rife with opportunities for game-playing. Limiting discovery does cut off opportunities to uncover useful information, but it also reduces the costs of the game. One process reform that is likely to pay dividends is a reduction in the time allowed for discovery. Early experiments with such reforms have been well received.[155] Second, so long as the primary cost of discovery is borne by the responder, there is ample incentive to overuse this device. Whatever the optimal amount of discovery, eliminating this distortion should move the process in a positive direction. Placing all of the cost on the requester would risk a different strategic problem, that is, giving responders reason to wastefully raise the cost of response, but a division of discovery expenses should help reduce its abuse.

Class actions, likewise, though neither all blessing nor all curse, probably merit reform. Let us begin with the recognition that here again there is a balance to be struck.

Class-action cases are prominent among the lawsuits—and decisions—that have outraged observers of the American legal scene. The breast-implant litigation described earlier in this chapter, much of the tobacco litigation, and many other "mass tort" cases have been brought as class actions. In each of these instances, commentators have declaimed that the class-action device distorted the legal process.[156]

Despite the fervor of the assertions, many complaints about the use of class actions in cases such as these can be put aside quickly. The costs of class-action litigation, though substantial, probably are considerably less—not more—than the costs of individual actions. Defendants, plaintiffs, and the public (which bears some cost of ordinary private litigation) all are likely beneficiaries of cost savings in any class-action case that has been properly certified—any case, that is, where issues common to the class in fact predominate.[157] That, of course, is the justification for creating this process in the first place. There is a fair question in many instances whether a class has been certified properly, but that is a question about the propriety of a specific decision. Bad decisions do happen. But, as discussed above, that is probably not sufficient to explain the degree of public discontent expressed with the American legal system.

The serious complaint about the use of class actions in these cases is not that the process becomes too costly but that the aggregation of claims makes the stakes too high. The class action can become, in common parlance, a "bet the company" case; look again at the breast-implant cases, which saw the bankruptcy of one defendant long before the scientific community concluded that there was no basis for these suits.[158] It is very largely the magnitude of the stakes that explains the great investments made in litigation. Some litigation costs are fixed, regardless of the stakes, a point we return to momentarily. But most can vary with the parties' assessments of the value of an additional test or witness or investigative tool. That value depends in part on the nature of the evidence, both the specific evidence under consideration and the other evidence in the case; and, critically, it is also a derivative of the stakes. A small increase in the prospect of winning is worth a lot more litigation investment when a billion dollars is at stake than when parties are fighting over a hundred thousand dollars. If class actions raise the stakes in litigation, they will increase litigation costs as well.

The high-stakes objection, though serious, looks questionable on its face. If class actions merely aggregate individual claims that could be brought anyway, why would a class action present higher stakes for the opposing party (typically, the defendant) than the sum of the individual actions? The answer, in the main, is that class actions aggregate claims that *in theory*—but only in theory—could be brought individually.

Two factors make the prospect of similarly high-value claims in individual litigation less likely in practice than it is in theory. Both trace to the fact that a class action can vindicate rights that are very valuable in the aggregate but of small individual weight.

First, for some claims, the individual interest is simply too small to justify the fixed costs of litigation. Would a single claimant be able to afford the research necessary to prove the link between lung disease and exposure to asbestos? Would a bank customer whose account has been routinely (and unlawfully) rounded off in the bank's favor have enough at issue to pursue a claim against the bank? Frequently, the individual claim will not merit any action.

Second, for other claims, the problem is not the fixed cost of litigation but the asymmetry between stakes for the two sides. If one individual claimant wins an asbestos claim or a suit charging a bank with illegal accounting practices, the plaintiff wins a small amount. The defendant, however, has much more at issue. In many settings, asymmetrical stakes arise because the defendant is a commercial venture with a substantial reputational stake in the litigation.[159] A special case of asymmetrical stakes traces to the rules allowing "one-way preclusion" (what procedure buffs refer to as nonmutual offensive preclusion). A defendant, say, having lost once, can be precluded from relitigating the issue of asbestos's contribution to lung disease in future cases. Because he has had the opportunity to contest the issue, it is not thought unfair—and it is thought to advance efficiency interests—to allow that finding in evidence in subsequent court contests.[160]

The asymmetrical-stakes case potentially folds back into the analysis above, because it may discourage individual litigation. The asymmetry in stakes gives the defendant (the party with more at stake in this example) incentive to invest more in the litigation. That translates into a greater prospect of prevailing in individual, case-by-case litigation. Potential claimants who understand this dynamic may choose not to bother filing claims in the first place if they only stand to vindicate their own individual interests—if their investment is limited to that justified by their own individual stakes.

Yet the matter is not so simple. Under plausible assumptions, the opportunity to leverage a potential victory into a settlement that accounts for the asymmetrical costs to the defendant is more likely to *induce* than to inhibit litigation. That will occur if the asymmetrical costs and risks to the defendant dominate the greater chance of a defendant victory. With asymmetrical investment, the defendant is more likely to win. But settlement talks will take into account that the defendant must spend more to win and will spend more because losing is asymmetrically costly to the defendant—both factors that should drive up settlement values.

In a world of class actions, however, the real expected payoff from one-way preclusion lies in follow-on litigation through class actions. Because class actions allow aggregation of individual interests that cumulatively can approach the defendant's stakes, they will support more comparable investment in litigation. Even if individual litigation is a realistic possibility, the strongest incentive to the initial litigation in these cases is its utility in later class-action litigation, transforming the individual asymmetrical-stakes lawsuit into a part of the class-action strategy. Although the asymmetry in stakes will support some net increase in the settlement value of individual litigation, the settlement value of that litigation will be less than the settlement value of litigation in which plaintiffs are more likely to succeed. That, in turn, requires more comparable stakes, which is exactly what the class-action device provides. Thus, contrary to the initial assumption that this was a questionable proposition, for both sets of cases—those that would not be brought individually without the class-action device and those more likely to be brought because of the availability of subsequent class-action suits—class actions do indeed create a higher-stakes game than the sum of individual lawsuits.

In addition to the increase in nominal stakes that is likely with class actions, there may also be an increase in the stakes for punitive damages. We have already seen that punitive damages play a substantial role in raising the payouts for high-profile cases. Class actions, such as the Florida tobacco litigation, make particularly attractive vehicles for punitive-damage claims.

This, too, might seem odd on its face, especially to those who recall the deterrence-based explanation for punitive-damage awards. If punitive-damage awards are justified in part on what cases are *not* brought, individual litigation—proceeding piecemeal and without knowledge of what other cases will be filed—could well lead to exaggerated punitive-damage awards, awards based on an erroneously low estimation of the claims that will be filed in the future.[161]

And most American jurisdictions have no formal mechanism for offsetting earlier punitive-damage awards against later ones, so that the aggregate punitive-damage awards in individual litigation could be exceedingly high.

Yet, despite the theoretical possibility of higher awards in individual cases, it seems more likely that punitive-damage awards will rise disproportionately with the magnitude and the number of the claims against a defendant.[162] Cases with large numbers of claims and very large compensatory-damage claims often are the cases in which it is easiest to urge juries to "send a message" to the defendant in large, round numbers.[163] Jury verdicts are not final decisions: judges very often order some portion (and, increasingly, a very large portion) of punitive damages awarded by juries to be set aside (remitted).[164] Nevertheless, the class action is likely to present a peculiarly frequent vehicle for high-stakes litigation, with the "wager" set above what would be expected aggregating the stakes in a comparable class of individual suits.

All of this brings us to the question, Why is that bad? Of course, parties that face a greater prospect of litigation with larger potential losses will object. But that objection should be a mirror image of the potential gain to other parties.

The social problem with class actions comes from the interplay between high stakes, soft inconsistency, and risk aversion. If parties to litigation are "risk-neutral," they have no preference between a certain loss of fifty thousand dollars and a one-in-one-hundred chance of losing $5 million. If they are risk-averse, they see the chance of a large loss as more threatening than a statistically equivalent certain cost. That preference could allow strategically minded claimants to extract settlements exceeding the amount they could expect to win in court. The higher the degree of inconsistency—the larger the spread of values across possible outcomes for trial—the more likely this scenario. Even if the stakes stay the same for one decision with one hundred class members as for one hundred individual decisions, with expected losses exactly equal in the two settings, aggregating suits into a single class action increases the variance of expected returns (in fact, raising it by a factor of 100 in this example).

With risk-averse defendants, that increased possibility that a single decision—one often hears it described as a single roll of the dice, though that metaphor overstates the part chance plays in the outcome—will produce a disaster raises the likely settlement value of the suit. A corporate counsel or CEO may feel much more sanguine about explaining a $250 million settlement of litigation he or she expects to win three times out of four than about the possibility of having to explain a billion-dollar adverse judgment if she or he spins the cylinder and clicks on the one loaded chamber. The greater the sums paid in this manner to avoid that risk, the greater the likely dislocation of behavior from the social ideal, because people adjust their activities to avoid the prospect of payments that could be very large but are, nonetheless, bad bets.

This complaint about class actions should be taken seriously; it probably explains some of the angst about the American legal system. Some reform of class-action rules probably is in order. It should, for instance, be easier for judges to refuse to certify class actions when cases appear substantively weak, removing one lever to settlement of low-probability suits. Perhaps judges should give greater scrutiny as well to the alignment of attorney fees with class recoveries.[165]

Though reform of class actions is merited to address the problems associated with them, we should be careful not to overstate the impact of class actions, either in fact or in perception of the U.S. legal system. They contribute to difficulties with the legal system, but their effects are not even so clear as the (highly qualified) first-order analysis offered here suggests. Consider this: the most likely targets for high-stakes class-action suits are profitable corporations. They will be the targets for the same reason Willie Sutton gave for robbing banks—that's where the money is. But profitable firms can take actions that minimize the dislocative effects of excessive litigation and settlement costs. If the basis for suit is a practice that is common to firms in a given line of business—the use of asbestos insulation, for example—the firms in that line of business can respond to litigation costs by altering both their behavior and their prices. As consumers, we see price increases as bad. Other things being equal, lower prices are better. But what matters more is the accuracy of prices in reflecting the real costs of economic activity. Price increases by firms with risk-averse managers should dampen what otherwise would be an overreaction to litigation risks.

A final caution is in order to make certain that the qualifications sprinkled across this section, including the one immediately above, are kept in perspective. Saying that the merits or defects of specific procedures are less than clearcut does not mean that the American legal system should receive a pass on process issues. Procedures are integral to the rule of law; bad procedures can make the law in practice less certain, less predictable, or less consistent with coherent principles. Any procedure that allows underlying asymmetries to be exploited, so that more "bad" claims are rewarded with settlement payments or more "bad" defenses are rewarded with dropped suits (or significantly reduced settlement awards), is problematical even if it is not a dramatically bad procedure on all counts. The defenses offered here for procedures such as broadened discovery rules and the use of class actions are merely that the cases against them are not clear-cut and, as yet, not proved. Further, though the focus of this section is on individual procedures, that may not be where the greater fault lies. Even if no given procedure generates untoward results in a substantial number of cases, the combination of several procedures can do so.

Even if it is not demonstrated analytically that there is a process problem in American courts, telling evidence that a problem exists can be found outside the law journals and editorials and books about the legal system. The most persuasive evidence may be the frequency with which litigants are turning to private alternatives to the judicial system. "Alternative dispute resolution" (ADR), a congeries of procedures that allows disputants to tailor their litigation processes, to use procedures more to their liking than standard court-centered litigation, has been quite popular over the past decade.[166] Some ADR approaches look very much like trials, though with smaller juries, less discovery, or relaxed rules of evidence. Some substitute a private judge—often a judge recently retired from the more traditional side of the legal system—for a public judge. Some involve considerable limitations on the time allowed prior to trial, on the time taken for trial, or on other factors contributing to the costs associated with the litigation. Some look a lot more like cooperative problem-solving sessions than like adversarial dispute resolution. All of the ADR methods allow parties more control over the identity of the decision maker, with some forms allowing the parties almost unlimited control over the selection of the arbitrator/decision maker *after* a dispute has arisen. And almost all ADR mechanisms reduce the litigation stakes by eliminating the prospect of one-way preclusion and by rejecting punitive damages.[167]

The increased demand for ADR suggests that potential litigants are dissatisfied with the procedures used in American courts, with their slowness, costliness, intrusiveness, and complexity and with the commitment of decisional authority to individuals who seem less well suited to render reasonable decisions than the litigants would like.[168] Litigants seldom adopt rules for dispute resolution that put aside the substantive, governing law (though private contracts do so to some degree). But if the parties are experienced, have a substantial stake in the issue potentially to be resolved, and have the opportunity to agree in advance, they very often will prescribe a process that is not simply the handiest, publicly provided legal process.

Again, however, a note or two of caution is in order. First, at the same time as ADR's popularity has risen, court processes have been modified as well. Measures have been introduced in many jurisdictions to provide courts some of the flexibility, speed, and cost savings that ADR approaches promise.[169] These changes may be less important than the procedural improvements not yet made, but the gap between public and private processes may be narrower today than it was a decade ago. Second, the continued growth of litigation in American courts raises questions about the degree to which potential litigants are dissatisfied with the system. Given the plaintiff's first-mover advantage in selecting a venue, the 90 million or so legal actions filed each year in America may indicate that there is substantial satisfaction with our legal system, even if parties who are especially disadvantaged by particular aspects of the litigation process (or especially advantaged by an ADR process), for obvious reasons, would prefer a process more to their—not their adversary's—taste. Interpreting litigation rates is a tricky business, and it surely is open to question what to make of our very full judicial plates. But whatever the right interpretation of that statistic, there is room for improvement in our procedures.

## Misperception

The sixth possible explanation for the legal system's perceived difficulties is that they are only *perceived* difficulties, not real ones. This is the explanation that will be most congenial to judges and lawyers. It also has some force.

The point here is not simply that, as explained in chapters 2 through 5, America truly does live under the rule of law. The point, rather, is that there are reasons why the public's impression of the legal system is inaccurate, why the public is aware of problems with the system but not of ways in which the system corrects itself.

Look at some of the highly publicized cases that inform public opinion. Start with the two cases discussed immediately above, those of Dr. Gore and Ms. Liebeck. The initial awards in those cases were $4 million and almost $3 million.[170] Dr. Gore's award was cut in half by the Alabama Supreme Court and set aside by the Supreme Court of the United States. Ultimately, Dr. Gore settled for an award of $4,000 compensatory damages and $50,000 punitive damages, a figure $3.95 million lower than the initial award.[171] Ms. Liebeck's punitive-damage award was reduced to $480,000 (less than 20% of the $2.7 million punitive-damage verdict) by the trial judge and ultimately settled for what is reported to have been considerably less than even that.[172] The initial verdicts were much more widely reported and commented on than the subsequent reductions for the same reason that "man bites dog" makes a bigger, better story than "dog bites man"; one is a surprise, whereas the other is very much in line with our expectations.

To some extent, the same holds true for cases such as O. J. Simpson's and Rodney King's. Both of these cases resulted initially in acquittals in the state criminal trial (of O. J. Simpson for murder and of the police officers filmed beating King for assault). Both acquittals were greeted with dismay in many quarters, O. J.'s acquittal prompting a flood of criticism and the acquittals in the King case sparking a destructive riot in Los Angeles.[173] And both were followed by second trials—a civil suit against O. J. for wrongful death and a second criminal trial of the police officers accused of beating King, this time on federal charges of violating King's civil rights. Of course, these cases got enormous publicity the second time around as well as the first. But the second verdict did not stick in the public mind the way the first did. There was not the same drama surrounding the verdict in O. J. II. There were no riots following King II. Neither became instant fare for comedians and other commentators in quite the way that round one in these cases had. Most of the post-trial comment on the second round of O. J. and of King focused on the contrast with the earlier round. The reason in each case for greater attention to the first round is the same as for attention to the initial verdicts for Dr. Gore and Ms. Liebeck.

Public perception of these cases is skewed by more than the different prominence given to the surprising and unsurprising actions. It is also biased by selective reporting of the underlying facts. Every casual observer of current events as this is written knows that Ms. Liebeck spilled coffee on herself and then recovered money from McDonald's. But almost no one knows how much hotter McDonald's served its coffee than is the norm in restaurants—apparently, twenty to thirty degrees hotter, enough to account for the difference between causing a mild burn and a severe (third-degree) burn.[174] Almost no one knows how extensive Ms. Liebeck's burns were, or the length of her hospitalization, or that she required skin grafts. Almost no one knows the number—many hundreds—of complaints McDonald's had received about burns from coffee spills. These facts do not mean that McDonald's should have been liable at all, much less that the magnitude of the initial verdict was justified. But they make the story less obviously one of legal error than is generally supposed, as opposed to one involving a difficult judgment about which of two possible "insurance" mechanisms is more efficient—letting people like Ms. Liebeck recover from their health insurance, with costs spread across others in the same insurance system, or allowing recovery from McDonald's, with costs spread across the purchasers of McDonald's products. When coupled with the substantial reduction in payment, the Liebeck case may not stand so readily for what we all know to be wrong with our legal system after all.

As with these individual cases, some of the well-known facts about the legal system either are not true or were moderated by subsequent, less publicized developments. So, for example, the growth of tort liability had slowed and even reversed (at least for a time) by the time it was widely reported.[175] Studies find the growth of defensive medicine to be largely fictitious and, so far as it is demonstrable, tied to insurance rules rather than directly to liability concerns.[176] Despite the understood difference between the American rule and the English rule with regard to litigation costs, legal costs are shifted to losing parties in a significant number of American cases and in the United Kingdom are shifted to losing plaintiffs less than half the time.[177] Statistics on overall litigation rates are seriously flawed.[178] And contentions about the degree to which the United States is "overlawyered" often rest on comparisons of noncomparable data. For example, although Japan has a tiny coterie of *bengoshi* (lawyers who are licensed to appear in court), those who are law-educated make up between four and five times as great a proportion of Japan's population as those with law-school education in America make of the U.S. population.[179] The number and size of punitive-damage awards has risen, as claimed, but the frequency and size of remittiturs—judge-mandated reductions in these awards—has risen concomitantly.[180]

When all is said and done, however, some aspects of our legal system that have created controversy are undeniably true, and our system plainly is not just like others. The U.S. legal system is more costly than any other in the world, generates more litigation, has greater impact on the society, and is more adversarial than any other legal system. There may well be legitimate bases for each of these facts—they may be bound up with parts of our character that affect numerous other aspects of American life so that it is fruitless or even counterproductive to think of changing parts of that system as if they stood alone.[181] But our system has changed over time in ways that make these facts more true, suggesting that the present shape and cost of our legal system is not a simple, inevitable derivation of national character.[182] Plainly, these facts, as well as common misperceptions, inform public opinion respecting our legal system.

## Misbehavior

The final explanation focuses on the behavior of lawyers, attributing our legal system's reputational ills to lowered standards of behavior within the profession. That, in large measure, is the accusation leveled by such critics as Mary Ann Glendon,[183] Tony Kronman,[184] Sol Linowitz,[185] Susan Koniak,[186] and John Silber.[187]

The dominant criticism is that lawyers have gone from a group of civic-minded, public-spirited men who served justice (as they saw it) to self-centered, mean-spirited men and women who seek money above all. Professor Glendon reaches back to the legendary figures in the law whose words shaped our concept of the law as a noble profession and whose actions pointed the way to combine public service and private practice. She contrasts those lawyer-statesmen with the lawyers of today. Ambassador Linowitz laments the change in attitude, contrasting the world of law practice today with the different profession recalled from his early years at the bar. "In my generation, we thought of the law as a *helping* profession, not a continuation of war by other means," and "The law we spoke of was not an 'adversary system' but a framework for cooperative activity."[188]

> Fair contracts were not a game, where the lawyer for one side or another won advantages for his client by cleverness, but the fundament of civilized economic activity. . . .
>
> Today there are too few lawyers who see it as part of their function to tell clients . . . that they are damned fools and should stop. . . . The public pays, because the rule of law is diminished. Coal companies falsify the data from the gauges that measure air quality in the mines, tobacco companies sponsor research that confuses people about the dangers of smoking, automobile com-

panies conceal data about product defects, makers of breast implants misstate the results of their tests of the toxicity of silicone. . . . Too many times, lawyers have been willing to look the other way, or even plan out the defenses in advance, while their clients violated the law.[189]

Dean Kronman, like Glendon and Linowitz, sees the good lawyer as one who serves not narrowly defined client interests but broader social interests. Like Glendon and Linowitz, too, Kronman sees the good lawyer as one who serves the truer interests even of the immediate client. And, like Glendon and Linowitz, Kronman also sees that vision as one of old-fashioned virtue, a vision not shared by many modern lawyers.[190]

To a large degree, these authors argue that the present market for legal services has gotten things wrong, that clients and lawyers are behaving in ways that do not serve the real interests of either. They recognize the forces that shape the market for lawyers and legal services. But implicitly they assert that these markets are inefficient. That certainly is possible. Markets tend to be less efficient for customized services that are provided on a one-shot basis than for standardized or repeat-play services, and some of the market for legal services fits the one-shot description.

That is not answer enough: much of the market for legal services, including the market segment on which these authors primarily focus, is major corporate clients. These clients tend to be repeat players with enough at stake to invest in obtaining the sort of services they desire and to attract price competition from would-be suppliers. Yet even here, agency costs, which distort the incentives of individual actors from what would be in the best interests of the corporation's owners if it were possible to achieve those interests in a "frictionless" manner, make inefficiencies of some sorts plausible.[191] Thus, a corporate general counsel might hire a law firm that is known to the bosses as a blue chip firm with a strong reputation, even if better service could be obtained at a lower price from another firm with less name recognition in the critical circles. At this level, the argument is not a strong statement of market inefficiency but the fairly banal observation that this market—like so many others—operates at less than perfect, textbook efficiency.

The more important argument for Glendon, Linowitz, and Kronman is that even if the market for such legal services is efficient in that sense, so that we can trust the market to see that lawyers' and clients' interests are protected, it is inefficient from a societal perspective because it does not account for the impact those services have on others. So, for example, the "Rambo litigator" may gain an immediate advantage for his or her client, but the costs of the "scorched earth" tactics are paid more generally, spread across the society that faces a legal system that is more expensive, more time-consuming, and more contentious than necessary to resolve the issues it confronts. Yet clients often seek out litigators precisely because they are reputed to be partial to the sort of no-holds-barred excess and plain nastiness that thoughtful commentators deplore. Some clients, indeed, litigate because they are so angry at their adversary that inflicting pain (economic or psychological) becomes a more important goal than success in court. That explains why entreaties to lawyers to play nice have been ineffective and why Glendon, Linowitz, and Kronman recognize the jeremiad quality in their commentaries: asking people to act against their immediate self-interest seldom is the quickest route to success.

John Silber and Susan Koniak, among others, add another note to this criticism. They suggest that lawyers today are *not* acting to advance the narrow interest of clients. Instead, they assert, lawyers are acting in their own interests and against those of clients.[192] Some of the ways in which this is alleged to occur (or the *motivations* alleged for conduct that is, at least from the vantage of efficiency, socially harmful) are questionable: it is doubtful, for instance, that lawyers intentionally write vague legislation to make more work for themselves and their professional brethren or that lawyers' billing practices are systematically at odds with client interests.[193] But other criticisms seem on target, identifying practices that advantage lawyers at the expense of their less sophisticated, less well informed, one-shot (not repeat-play) clients.[194] Critics of professional self-regulation, including regulation of the legal profession, have long seen it as a vehicle for advancing the profession's self-interest at the expense of everyone else, clients not least.[195] There is plenty of reason to believe that the legal profession, though increasingly competitive, retains sufficient slack to allow misbehavior to occur.

Ultimately, the serious problem for these authors is not the individual lawyer's misbehavior but the design of a system that allows, and gives incentives for, socially harmful behavior. That problem takes us back to concerns with rules, principles, and processes—each of which requires our attention if we are to maintain a system that conforms to the rule of law.

# Conclusion

*If we are to speak of the law as our mistress, we who are here know that she is a mistress only to be wooed with sustained and lonely passion,—only to be won by straining all the faculties by which man is likest to a god. —Oliver Wendell Holmes, Jr.*

*I have never seen any reason why law should make any more sense than the rest of life. —William L. Prosser*

The ideal of the rule of law, so captivating to people around the world and so commonly assigned an American face, often seems at odds with Americans' perception of their own legal system. The two halves of that sentence are signals, best heeded by American lawyers, lawmakers, judges, and law teachers, that something is—and something else is not—amiss.

There is enough wrong with the American legal system and the behavior of lawyers to sustain many complaints. Those who care about the legal system and about its effects should look carefully at ways in which it is off track and needs fixing. In particular, we should look carefully at laws that—as written or as effectuated by administrators exercising lawful discretion or by judges essaying faithfully to implement the legal authority at hand—depart from what seems normatively attractive and democratically appealing. We should examine the increasing tendency, fostered by the impulse to do perfect justice in an imperfect world and abetted by academicians of many stripes, to give complex answers where simple ones fit better with the public good. And we should look as well to procedural attributes of the American legal system that exacerbate ill effects of too much or too vague or misdirected law.

Merely to state the first failing, the failing of *bad laws,* is to reveal the difficulty of fixing it. Laws are not randomly generated. They are products of rational responses to interests of various members of society, channeled through particular mechanisms of social choice. The responses may vary over time even though very similar interests exist in society; small changes in factors not immediately related to a given policy question may alter the politically salient response. Along with normative differences among individuals, that is why politicians and pundits and scholars and other citizens spend time arguing over government policies.

Saying that we have laws for understandable reasons—that laws are rationally generated given the nature of the interests involved, the mechanisms of social choice, and the host of exogenous factors that influence the alignment of political agendas and winning coalitions—however, is not the same as saying that the laws serve our best interests. That individuals disagree about what our best interests are and how they can best be protected does not mean that there are not better answers about what laws we should have. The answers here, building on the review in chapter 6 of the possible bases for criticism of the American legal system, will not be congenial to everyone, but everyone should at least see in them some truth.

What ties the answers together is a sense that in some areas the imbalance between widely dispersed interests and concentrated interests has tipped the laws in directions that encourage too much litigation at too much expense in order to prevent harms that, however real and serious, are not so frequent and so injurious as to justify the legal armaments now deployed. Concern about our health and safety, for example, at times has extended beyond the realm of reason. Our laws and legal regulations have protected us against trivially small risks while delaying the availability of needed medical treatments or advances in health or safety protection, substituting far greater risks from older technologies and treatments, and discouraging innovation and investment.[1] These defects represent the victory of the visible over the invisible, of the hypersensitive over the average citizen's interests, of official self-interest over the greater public good.[2]

So, too, the proliferation of antidiscrimination laws has gone beyond categories correlated with pervasive discrimination based on group animus to categories for which legitimate judgments of individual competence and ille-gitimate biases are interwoven in far subtler fashion. The difficulty of disen-tangling them and the costs—reputational, financial, psychological—of doing battle over them far too often make employment decisions in America ques-tions not of what would make business sense in a world where efficiency and fairness rule but rather what makes business sense in a world where businesses must prove their fairness and their efficiency to skeptics.[3] An exaggerated con-cern over the division of our national economic pie has become a significant constraint on its growth—not, to be sure, as compared to the rest of the world, but as compared to the ideal or to the not-too-distant past. Or so it seems to me.

At the same time, we have largely ignored the effects that division of the economic pie, in combination with other changes in our laws and our gov-ernment, has had on rights to liberty and to life. The problem notably surfaces in our criminal process. We have allowed the criminal law's reach to grow far beyond our limited investment in enforcement resources.[4] In 1964, for exam-ple, the U.S. Code's criminal provisions ran to 179 pages.[5] By 1994 that num-ber had increased to 485, and by 1997 to 684.[6] Not only has the number of crimes grown, but the law's commitment to longer and more certain punish-ment has also grown, a factor that necessarily raises the stakes in prosecution, with strong implications for the cost of taking a case to trial. These circum-stances produce a system in which mass processing through deal-making is the norm and financial wherewithal is critical to the deal you get.[7]

Money does not buy the favor of the judge or the prosecutor, but it does affect the balance between prosecutor and defendant, altering the result the prosecutor thinks acceptable under all the circumstances. Although counsel pro-vided for indigent defendants at public expense has raised the floor for defen-dants' rights (a bit), wealthy defendants still stand in a privileged position rel-ative to others. They can afford to do more investigation on and more analysis of potential jurors, to demand more complete discovery, to make more inde-pendent tests of evidence, to contest more points of the prosecution's case, to submit more thoroughly researched memoranda in support of more motions on more points of law—in short, to provide a more formidable opponent to the prosecution, increasing the cost of that prosecution relative to other pros-ecutions and decreasing the chances that the prosecutor will gain the desired result through trial. At times, the prosecutor will find it advantageous to invest in a case against a wealthy defendant; among other reasons, it can bring fame of a sort that is difficult to come by and helpful to careers, especially to those who see a future in politics. But more often, the prosecutor may be inclined for wholly rational reasons respecting his or her enforcement budget and mission to strike deals that may be more lenient to wealthier defendants than to impecunious ones.[8] If the consequent division between rich and poor defendants is troubling, that is but one aspect of an investment of substantial discretion in the hands of prosecutors. Instances of serious abuse may not be common, but that is no defense of the system we have.

These are vices of government grown too big in its reach into everyday life; and those who should be our most vigorous guardians against the abuses attending such growth, our judges, sometimes are more than merely complicitous in those defects. Sometimes judges bear direct responsibility for creating the problem. Tort law in America very largely is judge-made law. The principal doctrines were judicially generated, and major expansions of tort law, especially product liability law, have been judges' creations. Some of these creations have improved the law, making those best positioned to take care that products are safe responsible to those who use them.[9] But too often the judicial creations have substituted cumbersome, expensive judicial processes aimed at perfect justice for the rough justice of a competitive marketplace—and have dramatically overshot their mark.[10] Many judges have scant understanding of the second- and third-order effects of their decisions, the spider's web of interrelated adjustments that makes the real world so difficult to control through directives, however well-intentioned.

Judges do seem attentive to the effects that surface visibly in cases that come before them, and they adjust judge-made doctrines over time to correct the apparent flaws, to bring their doctrines more in line with a vision of public good.[11] But well-meaning efforts, though they may correct one problem, often miss the mark by just as much: reform efforts in official liability law, for instance, at times have wandered far from a suitable line, though clearly designed to serve public interests.[12] And not all judicial decisions garner even that modest laurel as well-intended; in some instances, the judicial creation looks remarkably like self-interested legislation.[13]

These systemic flaws are exacerbated by our reliance on juries. The jury has a resonance with our democratic impulses. It provides a check against some abuses of prosecutorial authority and from time to time brings officialdom back in line with broadly shared public sentiments. And it generally produces decisions similar to those our judges would reach. But reliance on juries also increases the variance within our legal system, especially with respect to the magnitude of civil damages.[14] The variance of juries' decisions threatens the predictability necessary to the rule of law and adds to the cost of a system that seems already too costly.

Juries are not the only process problem. Discovery processes that are not cabined in time and scope, where litigants can externalize the cost of the process to their opponents, also undermine the operation of the legal system. So does too-ready certification of class actions in settings where the potential for settlement may dominate decisions of parties and, what often is more significant, of counsel. The rise of alternative dispute resolution as a preferred locus for deciding many important legal matters is one datum that speaks of the problems with our legal system.

These are serious problems, and they deserve to be taken seriously. They are not readily established as fact, and the normative authority of the assertions that these *are* problems will be contested vigorously. If that were not enough, the problems are not easily fixed, and every potential solution will raise new difficulties. Chapter 6 offers some modest steps toward fixing the legal system's process problems and toward reorienting judicial thinking about the principles they craft. These proposals are not worked through in sufficient detail or buttressed by sufficient attention to their effects to persuade doubters. That is not the goal of this book.

Although not all readers will agree with the descriptions of the legal system, of its problems, or of potential solutions, the complaints about the system identified here should not be dismissed as the phantasms of the misinformed. They should not be put aside as the inventions of misanthropes who would avoid responsibility for their conduct. They should not be rejected as the contrivances of the solipsistic wealthy who distrust a system that risks transferring some of their abundance to the poor. Nor should they be cast aside as complaints by advocates for an unattainable equality, complaining of preferences for the wealthy that are the inevitable by-products of a free society. Whatever truth there is to skepticism of any given complaint from any given source, the fact remains that the system we have is flawed.

Preoccupation with our problems, however, should not obscure more fundamental truths: despite our problems, the rule of law is alive and well in America, and America is well served by the rule of law. Although the reach of government today is vast, the power of individual government officials is limited. Individual rights generally are protected, and even our most powerful and prominent officials respond to judicial command.

The complaint that is most common among academicians—that decision making by judges is largely shaped by politics, and bad politics at that—should be seen in perspective both as directed to an exceedingly narrow slice of judicial decisions and as overstated even there. The complaint is not, to be sure, without foundation. Our judges, we know, make judgments that inevitably require discretion beyond what simple models of a mechanistic legal system admit. And in some instances those judgments look uncomfortably close to judgments common in the political arena.

Yet emphasizing this aspect of judicial decision making does a disservice to our judges and our legal system. It mistakes the marginal influence for the motive force in judging. It transforms judges from translators to creative writers whose fictions bear the titles of other works but with no necessary similarities of character or plot.

Academic theorists have devoted extraordinary attention to proving that law cannot control judicial decisions (so that politics, at least if seen expansively, must infect judging) and to explaining how judges should decide the cases that cannot be decided without a complex guide to interpretation, but the world of law these theorists speak to is a very small one. The far larger world that is the vast bulk—indeed, all but a tiny fragment—of the American legal system is quite controlled by law. That is not to say it is controlled by a set of words abstracted from the larger world we inhabit, from our conventions of language and thought, from our ordinary understandings, from our training as lawyers. Although this extreme position often is assigned to anyone who would say that formal law controls judges' decisions, that assignment reflects a desire to oppose a position so extreme as to be untenable.

The tenable position—the *correct* assessment of what actually is transpiring—is, instead, that American judging is controlled by law, giving that word its more common meaning as a set of understandings fused with authoritative instructions that judges see as binding; as directives that come through formal channels for authoritative instruction, substantially but imperfectly directing official action; as instructions clarified as needed by judges who rightly appreciate that theirs is an interpretive, not a starkly creative, role. Given the judges' common understandings of the language, of formal instructions, and of their role, American judging operates overwhelmingly as an exercise directed by formal law, conforming to external guidance, and predictably independent of the identity of the individual judge. Contrary to the frequent assertion that it is independent of the law, judging in America very strongly conforms to the rule of law.

The standard academic complaint about American judging, hence, clearly fails as positive description, but it fails on normative ground as well. If it were taken seriously by judges as a statement of the professional norm, this emphasis on the impossibility of judicial constraint by formal authority almost certainly over time would undermine a salutary aspect of our present judicial practice—judicial commitment to be bound by external authority, which is crucial to the rule of law. The argument that judges cannot be constrained by law, along with theories of interpretation emphasizing aspects other than formal constraint of judges by authoritative texts, encourages judges to try a hand at creating the legal solutions they deem best suited to solve whatever problems they see. Taken seriously, this would be a likely source of ill-considered ventures at finding first-best outcomes in a costly second-best world.

We should listen to those who say that our legal system needs change, for the willingness to change and adapt is an essential aspect of our system and of its common law roots. We should listen to complaints about our system because, left untended, its flaws can threaten the rule of law. And we should listen as well to those around the world who aspire to the legal system we in America have, because that system has contributed to a level of freedom, of stability, and of material well-being that rightly are the envy of the world. The rule of law may be only an indistinct notion even to those within the legal system, and adherence to the rule of law surely is not a full guarantee of justice. It is, nonetheless, a pillar of our society. We should spend less energy making it seem pâpier-maché and more making it secure.

# Notes

## Introduction

1. ALEXIS DE TOCQUEVILLE, DEMOCRACY IN AMERICA 272 (Alfred A. Knopf 1945; vol. I, orig. pub. 1835).

2. *See, e.g.,* 145 CONG. REC. S63, S74 (daily ed. Jan. 14, 1999) (Trial Memorandum of the U.S. House of Representatives); 145 CONG. REC. S221 (daily ed. Jan. 14, 1999) (statement of Mr. Manager Hyde).

3. *See, e.g.,* 145 CONG. REC. S191, S192 (daily ed. Jan. 14, 1999) (Trial Memorandum of Pres. William Jefferson Clinton); 145 CONG. REC. S832 (daily ed. Jan. 21, 1999) (statement of Mr. Counsel Kendall).

4. For similar, divergent invocations of the "rule of law" concept with respect to the impeachment and trial of President Clinton, see Akhil Reed Amar, *It's a Democracy Thing,* LEGAL TIMES, Feb. 1, 1999, at 26; David Cole, *An Ounce of Discretion,* LEGAL TIMES, Feb. 1, 1999, at 23; Mike France, *Impeachment: Does the Rule of Law Really Rule?* BUS. WEEK, Feb. 8, 1999, at 60; Thomas Sowell, *What Is at Stake Here?* WASH. TIMES, Jan. 31, 1999, at B1.

5. *See, e.g.,* Richard L. Berke, *Spin the Battle: Fierce Contest to Woo Public,* N.Y. TIMES, Nov. 19, 2000, at 1, 26; Kenneth R. Berman, *Headed for Court, as It Should Be,* BOSTON GLOBE, Nov. 19, 2000, at C2; Lynda Gorov & Anne E. Kornblut, *Gore to Challenge Results,* BOSTON GLOBE, Nov. 24, 2000, at A1, A46.

6. *See, e.g.,* Robert Kagan, *American Power—A Guide for the Perplexed,* COMMENTARY, Apr. 1, 1996, at 21; Joseph S. Nye, Jr., *Future Wars: Conflicts after the Cold War,* WASH. Q., Winter 1996, at 5–24; Walt Williams, *The "New American Century" Must Be Put in Perspective,* SEATTLE TIMES, May 8, 1998, at B5. *See also* HAROLD EVANS, THE AMERICAN CENTURY 656–58 (Alfred A. Knopf 1998). For a prediction that this would be the view by the late 1990s, see HENRY R. NAU, THE MYTH OF AMERICA'S DECLINE: LEADING THE WORLD ECONOMY INTO THE 1990S (Oxford Univ. Press 1991).

7. *See, e.g.,* Gary A. Hengstler, *Vox Populi,* ABA J., Sept. 1993, at 60; Chris Klein, *Poll: Lawyers Not Liked,* NAT'L L.J., Aug. 25, 1997, at A6.

8. *See, e.g.,* MARY ANN GLENDON, A NATION UNDER LAWYERS: HOW THE CRISIS IN THE LEGAL PROFESSION IS TRANSFORMING AMERICAN SOCIETY (Farrar, Straus & Giroux 1994); PHILIP K. HOWARD, THE DEATH OF COMMON SENSE: HOW LAW IS SUFFOCATING AMERICA (Random House 1994); PETER W. HUBER, LIABILITY: THE LEGAL REVOLUTION AND ITS CONSEQUENCES (Basic Books 1988); ANTHONY T. KRONMAN, THE LOST LAWYER: FALLING IDEALS

OF THE LEGAL PROFESSION (Belknap Press 1993); SOL M. LINOWITZ & MARTIN MAYER, THE
BETRAYED PROFESSION: LAWYERING AT THE END OF THE TWENTIETH CENTURY (Chas. Scrib-
ner's Sons 1994); RICHARD NEELY, THE PRODUCT LIABILITY MESS (Free Press 1988); JEFFREY
O'CONNELL, THE LAWSUIT LOTTERY (Free Press 1979); WALTER K. OLSON, THE LITIGATION
EXPLOSION: WHAT HAPPENED WHEN AMERICA UNLEASHED THE LAWSUIT (Dutton 1991) [here-
inafter EXPLOSION]; WALTER K. OLSON, THE EXCUSE FACTORY: HOW EMPLOYMENT LAW IS
PARALYZING THE AMERICAN WORKPLACE (Free Press 1997).

9. *See, e.g.,* Duncan Kennedy, *Legal Formality,* 2 J. LEGAL STUD. 351 (1973); Duncan
Kennedy, *The Structure of Blackstone's Commentaries,* 28 BUFF. L. REV. 205 (1979); Gary Peller,
*The Metaphysics of American Law,* 73 CAL. L. REV. 1151 (1985); Joseph Singer, *The Player and
the Cards: Nihilism and Legal Theory,* 94 YALE L.J. 1 (1984); Mark Tushnet, *Following the Rules
Laid Down: A Critique of Interpretivism and Neutral Principles,* 96 HARV. L. REV. 781 (1983).

10. *See, e.g.,* ROBERT H. BORK, THE TEMPTING OF AMERICA: THE POLITICAL SEDUCTION
OF THE LAW 51, 65–67, 71–73, 91, 110, 153, 346–49 (Free Press 1990); HUBER, *supra* note 8,
at 3–18; NEELY, *supra* note 8, at 30–56; OLSON, EXPLOSION, *supra* note 8, at 285–89, 346–47;
John Hasnas, *The Myth of the Rule of Law,* 1995 WIS. L. REV. 199; Margaret Jane Radin, *Reconsidering the Rule of Law,* 69 B.U. L. REV. 781 (1989). *See also* O'CONNELL, *supra* note 8.

11. This point has been made by others. *See, e.g.,* GEORGE P. FLETCHER, BASIC CONCEPTS
OF LEGAL THOUGHT 11 (Oxford Univ. Press 1996); Steven G. Calabresi & Gary Lawson, *Intro-
duction: Prospects for the Rule of Law,* 21 CUMB. L. REV. 427, 428 (1991); Richard H. Fallon,
Jr., *"The Rule of Law" as a Concept in Constitutional Discourse,* 97 COLUM. L. REV. 1, 1–3 (1997).

12. *Compare* Joel B. Grossman, *Social Backgrounds and Judicial Decisions: Notes for a Theory,* 29 J. POLITICS 334 (1967); *and* Tushnet, *supra* note 9; *with* HENRY M. HART, JR., & ALBERT
M. SACKS, THE LEGAL PROCESS: BASIC PROBLEMS IN THE MAKING AND APPLICATION OF LAW
(William N. Eskridge, Jr., & Philip P. Frickey eds., Foundation Press 1994); Daniel A. Farber, *Statutory Interpretation and Legislative Supremacy,* 78 GEO. L.J. 281 (1989); *and* Sanford Levinson, *Escaping Liberalism: Easier Said than Done,* 96 HARV. L. REV. 1466 (1983). For an examination of both the attitudinal or preference-based conception of judging (represented by
the first group of authorities immediately above) and the law-based conception (represented
by the second group), see Edward P. Schwartz, Judging Our Judgment of Judges: Can Positive Political Theory Be the Answer? (Aug. 1995) (on file with author); Edward P. Schwartz,
The Concurrence Dilemma (Sept. 1997) (on file with author).

# 1. The Rule of Law

1. ARISTOTLE, THE POLITICS 141–48 (Ernest Barker trans., Oxford Univ. Press 1958);
PLATO, THE LAWS (Trevor J. Saunders ed., Penguin Books 1970).

2. *See, e.g.,* H. L. A. HART, THE CONCEPT OF LAW 195–207 (Oxford Univ. Press 1961);
THOMAS HOBBES, LEVIATHAN 183–200 (Richard Tuck ed., Cambridge Univ. Press 1996)
(1651); Michael Oakeshott, *The Rule of Law, in* ON HISTORY AND OTHER ESSAYS 119, 157–64
(Barnes & Noble Books 1983) [hereinafter *Rule*]. *See also* Oliver Wendell Holmes, Jr., *The
Path of the Law,* 10 HARV. L. REV. 457 (1897) [hereinafter *Path*]. The meaning of the term *pos-*

*itivist* in this context is different from its meaning in most other contexts. *See* RICHARD A. POSNER, THE PROBLEMS OF JURISPRUDENCE 20 n.31 (Harvard Univ. Press 1990) [hereinafter JURISPRUDENCE].

3. *See, e.g.*, A.V. DICEY, AN INTRODUCTION TO THE STUDY OF THE LAW OF THE CONSTITUTION 198 (8th ed., Macmillan 1915); JOSEPH RAZ, THE AUTHORITY OF LAW: ESSAYS ON LAW AND MORALITY 211–13, 228–29 (Clarendon Press 1979) [hereinafter AUTHORITY] (advocating a positivist conception that includes constraints on the source and character, but not the goal or morality, of law).

4. *See, e.g.*, GEORGE P. FLETCHER, BASIC CONCEPTS OF LEGAL THOUGHT 11–12 (Oxford Univ. Press 1996); Richard Flathman, *Liberalism and the Suspect Enterprise of Political Institutionalization: The Case of the Rule of Law, in* NOMOS XXXVI; THE RULE OF LAW 297, 299–303 (Ian Shapiro ed., New York. Univ. Press 1994) [hereinafter NOMOS XXXVI]. *But see* GERALD I. NEUMAN, THE U.S. CONSTITUTIONAL CONCEPTION OF THE RULE OF LAW AND THE RECHTSSTAATSPRINZIP OF THE GRUNDGESETZ (Colum. L. School, Public L. & Legal Theory Working Paper No. 5, June 1999) (the Rechtsstaatsprinzip under the current German constitution incorporates substantive principles, including the principle of proportionality, in distinction to the more formal Anglo-American conception of the rule of law).

5. *See, e.g.*, FLETCHER, *supra* note 4, at 38.

6. *See, e.g.*, FRIEDRICH A. HAYEK, THE ROAD TO SERFDOM 80–96 (Univ. of Chicago Press 1944) [hereinafter SERFDOM]; Oakeshott, *Rule, supra* note 2.

7. *See, e.g.*, ROBERT COVER, JUSTICE ACCUSED: ANTISLAVERY AND THE JUDICIAL PROCESS (Yale Univ. Press 1975); FLETCHER, *supra* note 4, at 12, 34–35; Lawrence B. Solum, *Equity and the Rule of Law, in* NOMOS XXXVI, *supra* note 4, at 120–47.

8. *See, e.g.*, RAZ, AUTHORITY, *supra* note 3, at 211–13, 218–19, 223–29; Steven Macedo, *The Rule of Law, Justice, and the Politics of Moderation, in* NOMOS XXXVI, *supra* note 4, at 148, 157. *See also* ROBERT NOZICK, PHILOSOPHICAL EXPLANATIONS 503 (Belknap Press 1981) ("In no way does . . . the realm of the state exhaust the realm of the morally desirable or moral oughts. . . . Rights are not the whole of what we want a society to be like, or of how we morally ought to behave toward one another").

9. *See, e.g.*, COVER, *supra* note 7; FLETCHER, *supra* note 4; Judith N. Shklar, *Political Theory and the Rule of Law, in* THE RULE OF LAW: IDEAL OR IDEOLOGY (Allan Hutchinson & Patrick Monahan eds., Carswell 1987).

10. *See, e.g.*, Randy Barnett, *Foreword: Can Justice and the Rule of Law Be Reconciled?* 2 HARV. J.L. & PUB. POL'Y 597 (1988); Solum, *supra* note 7. *See also* POSNER, JURISPRUDENCE, *supra* note 2, at 228–38. Judge Posner stakes claim to an approach that diverges from typical moralist account critically in its rejection of ethical priors from natural law or moral philosophy. This approach, which Judge Posner labels *pragmatic* (rejecting both moralist and positivist labels), lies closer to the views of moralists such as Fuller than to positivists such as Hart.

11. *See, e.g.*, ALEXIS DE TOCQUEVILLE, DEMOCRACY IN AMERICA 273–80 (Alfred A. Knopf 1945; vol. 1, orig. pub. 1835) (discussing benefits of American deference to law, judges, and lawyers); ROSCOE POUND, AN INTRODUCTION TO THE PHILOSOPHY OF LAW 5–7, 9, 18–19, 26

(rev. ed., Yale Univ. Press 1954) (describing ancient law's association with security and stability and the recurrence of those themes over time).

12. *See, e.g.,* FRIEDRICH A. HAYEK, THE CONSTITUTION OF LIBERTY 153–54, 227–28 (Univ. of Chicago Press 1960) [hereinafter CONSTITUTION]; HAYEK, SERFDOM, *supra* note 6, at 80–84; MICHAEL OAKESHOTT, RATIONALISM IN POLITICS AND OTHER ESSAYS 387–89 (Liberty Press 1991) [hereinafter RATIONALISM].

13. *See* RAZ, AUTHORITY, *supra* note 3, at 225–26. Raz defines the rule of law as a concept rooted in efficiency (in a sense closer to *efficacy* than to *efficiency* as that term is used in normative economic analysis), but he would have the concept serve normative goals of restraint of the illegitimate exercise of arbitrary power, promotion of individual freedom, and protection of human dignity. *Id.* at 219–22. For a view of the rule of law's relation to efficiency that gives efficiency its more typical meaning, see POSNER, JURISPRUDENCE, *supra* note 2.

14. *See* JEREMY BENTHAM, A FRAGMENT ON GOVERNMENT 236 (Oxford Univ. Press 1931) (1776).

15. *See* RANDY BARNETT, THE STRUCTURE OF LIBERTY: JUSTICE AND THE RULE OF LAW 89–90 (Clarendon Press 1998); LON FULLER, THE MORALITY OF LAW 38–40 (Yale Univ. Press, rev. ed. 1969) (embracing a set of requirements for a legal order that provide a structure conducive to equality, predictability, and other values; Fuller eschewed the positivists' content-neutral stance toward law but did not adopt a formal moral structure for substantive law).

16. *See, e.g.,* COVER, *supra* note 7; FLETCHER, *supra* note 4; Shklar, *supra* note 9.

17. CONST. OF MASS.: DECLARATION OF RIGHTS, Art. 30 (1780) [hereinafter MASS. DECLARATION]; DAVID HUME, ESSAYS, MORAL, POLITICAL, AND LITERARY 94 (Eugene F. Miller ed., LibertyClassics 1985) (1742) (stating that this now can be said of enlightened monarchies as well as of republics). *See also* JAMES HARRINGTON, COMMONWEALTH OF OCEANA (Cambridge Univ. Press 1992; orig. pub. 1656) (aspiration to "an empire of laws not of men").

18. *See, e.g.,* RAZ, AUTHORITY, *supra* note 3, at 212 ("The ideal of the rule of law is . . . often expressed by the phrase 'government of laws and not of men'"); Owen M. Fiss, *The Bureaucratization of the Judiciary,* 92 YALE L.J. 1442, 1451 (1983) ("Adherence to rules is required . . . by the maxim that insists upon a 'government of laws and not of men'"); Orrin Hatch, *Senate Trial Ought to Be Adjourned,* PORTLAND OREGONIAN, Feb. 3, 1999, at B13 ("The integrity of our government of laws—not men—depends on our fidelity to the basic principle that society will hold each of its members accountable to the rule of law"); Ronald Sanborn, *Controversy over Flag,* L.A. TIMES, Jun. 24, 1990, at M6 (relating ideal of government of laws, not men, to flag-protection amendment).

19. The phrase has been invoked in essentially its present form for more than three centuries, and similar locutions can be found scattered across even wider expanses. *See, e.g.,* J. M. KELLEY, A SHORT HISTORY OF WESTERN LEGAL THEORY (Oxford Univ. Press 1992) (describing Greek, Roman, medieval, and modern conceptions of the rule of law). The modern phrase, for example, is similar to a phrase used by Aristotle. ARISTOTLE, *supra* note 1, at 141, 146, 148. It is, however, worth heeding Professor Harvey's caution that, though the core of the rule of law as a concept consistent with the Hume-Adams phrase has broad appeal,

the conception of the rule of law that is dominant at different times and places varies. *See* W. Burnett Harvey, *The Rule of Law in Historical Perspective,* 59 MICH. L. REV. 487 (1961).

20. *See, e.g.,* HAYEK, SERFDOM, *supra* note 6, at 80–81; OAKESHOTT, RATIONALISM, *supra* note 12, at 390–91. *See also* KENNETH J. ARROW, SOCIAL CHOICE AND INDIVIDUAL VALUES 30 (Yale Univ. Press, 2d ed. 1963) (including "non-dictatorship" as an essential element in rational decision making); RAZ, AUTHORITY, *supra* note 3, at 220; JOSEPH RAZ, THE CONCEPT OF A LEGAL SYSTEM 170–71 (Oxford Univ. Press, 2d ed. 1980) [hereinafter CONCEPT].

21. *See, e.g.,* HOBBES, *supra* note 2; JOHN LOCKE, TWO TREATISES OF GOVERNMENT 272–73, 361–63 (Peter Laslett ed., Cambridge Univ. Press 1988) (1689); Michael P. Zuckert, *Hobbes, Locke, and the Problem of the Rule of Law, in* NOMOS XXXVI, *supra* note 4, at 63, 67–75; JAMES A. BUCHANAN & GORDON TULLOCK, THE CALCULUS OF CONSENT: LOGICAL FOUNDATIONS OF CONSTITUTIONAL DEMOCRACY (Univ. of Michigan Press 1962).

22. This was common ground for both Hobbes and Locke. Hobbes answered this objection by making law derive from a divinely inspired sovereign; Locke answered the objection by entrusting law's creation and application to political institutions designed to guard against the evils expected from granting power to individual men. *See* Zuckert, *supra* note 21. *See also* JOHN FINNIS, NATURAL LAW AND NATURAL RIGHTS 275, 281–90 (Clarendon Press 1980); Frank I. Michelman, *Law's Republic,* 97 YALE L.J. 1493, 1513–14 (1988) [hereinafter *Republic*].

23. *See* Zuckert, *supra* note 21, at 68.

24. *See, e.g.,* FULLER, *supra* note 15, at 33–94, 209–19; HAYEK, SERFDOM, *supra* note 6, at 80–92; RAZ, AUTHORITY, *supra* note 3, at 213–14. *See also* Richard H. Fallon, Jr., *"The Rule of Law" as a Concept in Constitutional Discourse,* 97 COLUM. L. REV. 1 (1997).

One of the best-known descriptions of elements of the rule of law is Professor Lon Fuller's list of eight ways a society could fail in its legal system. His first route to failure—by failing to adopt rules—is encompassed by elements 1 and 4 here. His last route to failure—"a failure of congruence between the rules as announced and their actual administration"—includes aspects of elements 1 and 4 as well. As discussed in the text, five of Fuller's routes to failure mark aspects of principled predictability, element 2. Fuller's sixth route to failure—"rules that require conduct beyond the powers of the affected party"—is more complicated. Fuller might mean that the rule of law will not abide laws requiring conduct that *no one* can perform. In that case, the command of the impossible necessarily would lead to other rule-of-law failures, most commonly the absence of principled predictability in the rules governing official behavior and the absence of constraining (as opposed to merely authorizing) external authority. Such rules either become dead letters—they are never enforced—or they provide authority for officials to choose the occasions for enforcement on the basis of considerations not reflected in predictable, valid, external authority. In either case, the result contravenes element 2 and element 3 or 4 or both. *See* text accompanying notes 62–87. If, however, Fuller means that rules should not command action that is "beyond the powers of" a *particular* individual (as seems to be Fuller's intention [see FULLER, *supra* note 15, at 71–73), the requirement looks to be a mandate for substantive justice of a sort that falls outside the Hume-Adams conception of the rule of law, the conception that is embraced here.

25. The greater flexibility inherent in the term *fidelity* may explain why scholars, such as Ronald Dworkin, whose theories of interpretation contain substantial play in the joints (even while stressing the imperative of being governed by legal authority) employ that term. *See* RONALD DWORKIN, LAW'S EMPIRE 7–8 (Belknap Press 1986) [hereinafter EMPIRE].

26. *See, e.g.,* RONALD DWORKIN, TAKING RIGHTS SERIOUSLY 35–36 (Harvard Univ. Press 1977) [hereinafter RIGHTS]; FULLER, *supra* note 15, at 63–65; FREDERICK SCHAUER, PLAYING BY THE RULES: A PHILOSOPHICAL EXAMINATION OF RULE-BASED DECISION-MAKING IN LAW AND LIFE 137–45 (Oxford Univ. Press 1991). *See also* discussion, text accompanying notes 39–61 *infra*.

27. *Compare* DWORKIN, EMPIRE, *supra* note 25, at 37–43; FULLER, *supra* note 15, at 225–34, *with* HART, *supra* note 2, at 119–20.

28. It is, for example, the nub of the argument between Lon Fuller and H. L. A. Hart or between Ronald Dworkin and his critics. *See, e.g.,* ROBERT H. BORK, THE TEMPTING OF AMERICA: THE POLITICAL SEDUCTION OF THE LAW 176–77 (Free Press 1990); DWORKIN, EMPIRE, *supra* note 25, at 117–24, 142–43, 217–28; RONALD DWORKIN, FREEDOM'S LAW: THE MORAL INTERPRETATION OF THE AMERICAN CONSTITUTION 74–76 (Harvard Univ. Press 1996); FULLER, *supra* note 15, at 133–45; HART, *supra* note 2, at 136–44; ANTONIN SCALIA, A MATTER OF INTERPRETATION: FEDERAL COURTS AND THE LAW 67–68 (Princeton Univ. Press 1997); Ronald Dworkin, *The Arduous Virtue of Fidelity: Originalism, Scalia, Tribe, and Nerve,* 65 FORDHAM L. REV. 1249 (1997); Lon Fuller, *Positivism and Fidelity to Law—A Reply to Professor Hart,* 71 HARV. L. REV. 630 (1958); H. L. A. Hart, *Legal Positivism and the Separation of Law and Morals,* 71 HARV. L. REV. 593 (1958); Antonin Scalia, *Originalism: The Lesser Evil,* 57 U. CIN. L. REV. 849 (1989).

29. *See, e.g.,* discussion *infra* text accompanying notes 89–92.

30. *See, e.g.,* DWORKIN, RIGHTS, *supra* note 26, at 22–28, 72–80; RICHARD A. POSNER, ECONOMIC ANALYSIS OF LAW 590–93 (5th ed., Aspen Law & Bus. 1998) [hereinafter ECONOMIC ANALYSIS]; SCHAUER, *supra* note 26, at 12–14, 93–100; Colin S. Diver, *The Optimal Precision of Administrative Rules,* 93 YALE L.J. 65 (1983); Louis Kaplow, *Rules versus Standards: An Economic Analysis,* 42 DUKE L.J. 557 (1992); Duncan Kennedy, *Form and Substance in Private Law Adjudication,* 89 HARV. L. REV. 1685, 1687–1713 (1976).

31. The distinctions are stated in short compass in Larry Alexander & Ken Kress, *Against Legal Principles, in* LAW AND INTERPRETATION: ESSAYS IN LEGAL PHILOSOPHY 279 (Andrei Marmor ed., Oxford Univ. Press 1995), *reprinted in* 82 IOWA L. REV. 739, 740–41 (1998) [citations will be to pagination in the law review version].

32. *See, e.g.,* CONN. GEN. STAT. ANN. §§ 30–91 (West Pub. Co. 1990 & Supp. 1998); MASS. GEN. LAWS, ch. 138, § 33 (1996). Although guidance that does not fit this description at times is referred to as a "rule," Professor Schauer makes the case that the category of rules relevant to legal analysis is that of "regulative rules"—rules that have effects different from those of other forms of argument or of analysis. These rules necessarily share the qualities referenced in text. *See* SCHAUER, *supra* note 26, at 1–6.

33. *See, e.g.,* POSNER, ECONOMIC ANALYSIS, *supra* note 30, at 590–93; POSNER, JURISPRU-DENCE, *supra* note 2, at 44–48; Diver, *supra* note 30. These authors generally recognize standards as one form of rule.

34. *See, e.g.,* Lillian R. BeVier, *The First Amendment and Political Speech: An Inquiry into the Substance and Limits of Principle,* 30 STAN. L. REV. 299 (1978); Robert H. Bork, *Neutral Principles and Some First Amendment Problems,* 47 IND. L.J. 1 (1971); Alexander Meikeljohn, *The First Amendment Is an Absolute,* 1961 SUP. CT. REV. 245.

35. *See* SCHAUER, *supra* note 26, at 12–14, 102–4, 104 n.35.

36. *See, e.g.,* DWORKIN, RIGHTS, *supra* note 26, at 22–28; POSNER, JURISPRUDENCE, *supra* note 2, at 44–48, 318–21; SCHAUER, *supra* note 26, at 12–18, 93–100, 135–37; Alexander & Kress, *supra* note 31; Michael Moore, *Authority, Law, and Razian Reasons,* 62 S. CAL. L. REV. 827 (1989); Joseph Raz, *Legal Principles and the Limits of Law,* 81 YALE L.J. 823 (1972); Jeremy Waldron, *The Need for Legal Principles,* 82 IOWA L. REV. 857 (1997).

37. *See, e.g.,* POSNER, JURISPRUDENCE, *supra* note 2, at 320; SCHAUER, *supra* note 26, at 135–45, 167–81, 224–28.

38. *See* FULLER, *supra* note 15, at 39, 63–65.

39. *See, e.g.,* Holmes, *Path, supra* note 2, at 461.

40. HAYEK, SERFDOM, *supra* note 6, at 80.

41. Hayek's opposition to rules controlling specific individual activities, in addition to their direct conflict with his conception of freedom, was based on the assertion that such rules generally are not sufficiently clear to provide predictability of themselves, depending for real content on decisions by officials charged with their implementation. *See id.* at 81–96.

42. *See, e.g.,* Holmes, *Path, supra* note 2. *See also* FULLER, *supra* note 15, at 209–10; Herbert Wechsler, *Toward Neutral Principles in Constitutional Law,* 73 HARV. L. REV. 1, 15–17 (1959).

43. *See, e.g.,* BENTHAM, *supra* note 14, at 232; FULLER, *supra* note 15, at 39. Accessibility is a minimal predicate; in some instances, negligent failure to gain familiarity with the law is, and should be, required before one incurs penalties under the law. *See, e.g.,* Lambert v. California, 355 U.S. 225 (1957); HERBERT L. PACKER, THE LIMITS OF THE CRIMINAL SANCTION 129–30 (Oxford Univ. Press 1968); Ronald A. Cass, *Ignorance of the Law: A Maxim Reexamined,* 17 WM. & MARY L. REV. 671 (1976).

44. Ronald H. Coase, *The Problem of Social Cost,* 3 J.L. & ECON. 1 (1960). *See also* FULLER, *supra* note 15, at 46–70, 209–19.

45. *See, e.g.,* FULLER, *supra* note 15, at 46–49; HART, *supra* note 2, at 121–32; RAZ, AUTHORITY, *supra* note 3, at 215–16.

46. Concerns over specific legislation inform a number of constitutional constraints that in the United States can be observed at both the state and the national level. These include state prohibitions on "specific legislation," the Bill of Attainder clause in the U.S. Constitution, and restriction of the national government's taxing authority to taxes that were difficult to manipulate in ways that would specially disadvantage particular individuals or even particular states. *See, e.g.,* US CONST., art. 1, § 9, cl. 3–6; CAL. CONST., art. 1, § 9; ME. CONST., art. 1, § 11; N.J. CONST., art. 4, § 7, ¶ 3; Clayton P. Gillette, *Fiscal Federalism and the Use of Municipal Bond Proceeds,* 58 N.Y.U. L. REV. 1030 (1983).

47. *See, e.g.,* CASS R. SUNSTEIN, LEGAL REASONING AND POLITICAL CONFLICT 116–18 (Oxford Univ. Press 1996) (noting questions respecting the requisite degree of generality in legal rules).

48. *See* GERALD W. BROCK, THE TELECOMMUNICATIONS INDUSTRY: THE DYNAMICS OF MARKET STRUCTURE 198–233, 294–300 (Harvard Univ. Press 1981); GERALD R. FAULHABER, TELECOMMUNICATIONS IN TURMOIL: TECHNOLOGY AND PUBLIC POLICY 23–35 (Ballinger 1987); David S. Evans, *Introduction, in* BREAKING UP BELL: ESSAYS ON INDUSTRIAL ORGANI-ZATION AND REGULATION 1 (David S. Evans ed., North-Holland 1983) [hereinafter BREAK-ING UP BELL]; Robert Bornholz & David S. Evans, *The Early History of Competition in the Telephone Industry, in* BREAKING UP BELL, *supra,* at 7–8; Leonard Waverman, *U.S. Inter-exchange Competition, in* CHANGING THE RULES: TECHNOLOGICAL CHANGE, INTERNATIONAL COMPETITION, AND REGULATION IN COMMUNICATIONS 62, 64 (Robert W. Crandall & Ken-neth Flamm eds., Brookings Inst. 1989).

49. *See* BROCK, *supra* note 48, at 198–233.

50. So, for example, although the high barriers to constitutional amendment in the United States generally are thought to work well, efforts to assure consistency over time in administrative agencies' rules have been far less effective and more questionable even in their basic design. *See* RONALD A. CASS, COLIN S. DIVER & JACK M. BEERMANN, ADMINIS-TRATIVE LAW: CASES AND MATERIALS 982–83 (Aspen Law & Business, 3d ed. 1998); Ronald A. Cass, *RKO: Another Kind of Lottery,* 9 MEDIA L. NOTES 2 (May 1982).

51. Wechsler, *supra* note 42.

52. *See* Kent Greenawalt, *The Enduring Significance of Neutral Principles,* 78 COLUM. L. REV. 982 (1978).

53. *See, e.g.,* Mark Tushnet, *Following the Rules Laid Down: A Critique of Interpretivism and Neutral Principles,* 96 HARV. L. REV. 781, 804–24 (1983).

54. *See, e.g.,* POSNER, JURISPRUDENCE, *supra* note 2, at 71–98; Steven J. Burton, *Law as Practical Reason,* 62 S. CAL. L. REV. 747 (1989); Steven J. Burton, *Particularism, Discretion, and the Rule of Law, in* NOMOS XXXVI, *supra* note 4, at 178–201; Daniel A. Farber & Philip P. Frickey, *Legal Pragmatism and the Constitution,* 72 MINN. L. REV. 1331, 1336 (1988); Daniel A. Farber & Philip P. Frickey, *Practical Reason and the First Amendment,* 34 UCLA L. REV. 1615, 1640–43 (1987); Anthony T. Kronman, *Alexander Bickel's Philosophy of Prudence,* 94 YALE L. REV. 1567 (1985).

55. FULLER, *supra* note 15, at 39.

56. *Id.* at 5–9, 20–24, 39–41, 209–10. *See also* RAZ, AUTHORITY, *supra* note 3, at 225–26 ("Conformity to the rule of law does not always facilitate realization of the indirect pur-poses of the law, but it is essential to the realization of its direct purposes. . . . [I]f the direct purposes of the law are not to be frustrated, it must be capable of guiding human behav-iour, and the more it conforms to the principles of the rule of law, the better it can do so").

57. FULLER, *supra* note 15, at 39–44.

58. As will be seen, even this modest requirement may overstate the rule-of-law man-date, at least if viewed as a requirement that does not permit any delegations of sweeping discretion. The issue of an instruction's canonicity is addressed in element 4.

59. *See infra* chap. 4, text accompanying notes 15–52.

60. The *manner* in which predictability must be given, within the general contours of principled predictability, also is a matter of debate. *See* FULLER, *supra* note 15, at 38–81, 153–67, 197–219; HART, *supra* note 2, at 197–202.

61. *See* Michael Dorf, *Prediction and the Rule of Law*, 42 UCLA L. REV. 651 (1995) (arguing that predictability based on identity of decision maker is incompatible with rule of law). This does not mean that *formal* compliance with features associated with principled predictability is what is critical to the rule of law. A legal system may encompass external rules that, if applied transparently, would produce principled predictability yet fail utterly in practice to conform to that model. *See, e.g.,* HERNANDO DE SOTO, THE OTHER PATH: THE INVISIBLE REVOLUTION IN THE THIRD WORLD 131–87 (Harper & Row 1989). The reverse may also be true. For explication of how a legal system can embody decisional criteria of principled predictability, without formal rules or precedent, see LLOYD A. FALLERS, LAW WITHOUT PRECEDENT: LEGAL IDEAS IN ACTION IN THE COURTS OF COLONIAL BUSOGA (Univ. of Chicago Press 1969).

62. HART, *supra* note 2, at 92–93, 98–104.

63. *See* FULLER, *supra* note 15, at 134–42.

64. *See infra* text accompanying notes 72–77.

65. *See* HANS KELSEN, THE PURE THEORY OF LAW 99–100 (Max Knight trans., 2d ed., Univ. of California Press 1967); SCHAUER, *supra* note 26, at 199.

66. *See, e.g.,* SCHAUER, *supra* note 26, at 198–201.

67. For treatment of the relation between rules directed at primary (public) conduct and rules directed at official (enforcement) conduct, see Meir Dan-Cohen, *Decision Rules and Conduct Rules: On Acoustic Separation in Criminal Law*, 97 HARV. L. REV. 625 (1984). *See also* HART, *supra* note 2, at 26–48.

68. FULLER, *supra* note 15, at 138.

69. *See, e.g.,* FLETCHER, *supra* note 4, at 12–26.

70. *See* RAZ, AUTHORITY, *supra* note 3, at 211, 213–14, 224–26.

71. *See, e.g.,* HAROLD J. BERMAN, LAW AND REVOLUTION: THE FORMATION OF THE WESTERN LEGAL TRADITION 39 (Harvard Univ. Press 1983) ("Legal philosophers have always debated . . . whether law is founded in reason and morality or whether it is only the will of the political ruler"); FLETCHER, *supra* note 4, at 34–35 (describing positivist and antipositivist conceptions of law); HART, *supra* note 2, at 195–207; NOZICK, *supra* note 8, at 503; POSNER, JURISPRUDENCE, *supra* note 2, at 9–11. RAZ, AUTHORITY, *supra* note 3, at 211–13, 223–26; DAVID A. J. RICHARDS, THE MORAL CRITICISM OF THE LAW 7–38 (Wadsworth Pub. Co. 1977); George P. Fletcher, *Law and Morality: A Kantian Perspective*, 87 COLUM. L. REV. 533 (1987).

72. *See, e.g.,* Fletcher, *supra* note 71.

73. *See, e.g.,* WILLIAM L. SHIRER, THE RISE AND FALL OF THE THIRD REICH: A HISTORY OF NAZI GERMANY 117–23, 135–49, 182–87 (Simon & Schuster 1960).

74. *See id.* at 119–21, 309–21, 354–55, 357.

75. *See, e.g.,* JOHN HOPE FRANKLIN, FROM SLAVERY TO FREEDOM: A HISTORY OF NEGRO AMERICANS 126–30, 138–49, 171–90 (Vintage Books, 3d ed. 1969); Staughton Lynd, *Slavery*

*and the Founding Fathers, in* BLACK HISTORY 117–31 (Melvin Drimmer ed., Anchor Books 1969).

76. *See, e.g.,* David Lyons, ETHICS AND THE RULE OF LAW 68–74, 107–9 (Cambridge Univ. Press 1984); Henry David Thoreau, CIVIL DISOBEDIENCE (D. R. Godine 1969; orig. pub. 1849).

77. *See* Ronald H. Coase, *The Market for Goods and the Market for Ideas,* 64 AM. ECON. REV. 384 (Papers & Proceedings, May 1974); Aaron Director, *The Parity of the Economic Marketplace,* 7 J.L. & ECON. 1 (1964).

78. *See, e.g.,* JOHN HART ELY, DEMOCRACY AND DISTRUST: A THEORY OF JUDICIAL REVIEW 43–72 (Harvard Univ. Press 1980); Paul Brest, *The Misconceived Quest for the Original Understanding,* 60 B.U. L. REV. 204 (1980); Paul Brest, *Who Decides?* 58 S. CAL. L. REV. 661 (1985); Thomas C. Grey, *Origins of the Unwritten Constitution: Fundamental Law in American Thought,* 30 STAN. L. REV. 843 (1978); Frank Michelman, *The Supreme Court 1985 Term—Foreword: Traces of Self-Government,* 100 HARV. L. REV. 4 (1986) [hereinafter *Traces*]; Henry P. Monaghan, *Our Perfect Constitution,* 56 N.Y.U. L. REV. 353 (1981).

79. *See* Dorf, *supra* note 61. This general tendency does not mean that the content of rules or the fit between the content of rules and the preferences of rule enforcers is irrelevant to the predictability of outcomes. And external authority will not *always* increase predictability. But, other things being equal, in conditions of uncertainty with respect to the identity of rule enforcers, indicia of enforcers' (as a class) acceptance of external guidance should increase predictability.

80. *See, e.g.,* FULLER, *supra* note 15, at 115, 148; Dorf, *supra* note 61. That does not, however, mean that the external authority must be fully binding on all aspects of decision. *See, e.g.,* FULLER, *supra* note 15, at 86–91, 149; RAZ, AUTHORITY, *supra* note 3, at 206–9.

81. For Professor Fuller, that understanding is embodied in the concept of "law." *See* FULLER, *supra* note 15, at 137–40.

82. Scholars have debated whether decisions in equity, a branch of Anglo-American judicial authority long distinguished from decisions controlled by "law," conform to the rule of law. *See, e.g.,* Burton, *supra* note 54, at 178–201; Macedo, *supra* note 8, at 148–177; Solum, *supra* note 7. This debate is serious in its reach to define the limits of discretion in judicial decision making acceptable under the rule of law. That should not, however, be mistaken for a serious debate that the actual practices of equity adjudications in Anglo-American jurisdictions conflict with reasonable definitions of the rule of law. *See* Burton, *supra* note 54, at 191–98.

83. *See, e.g.,* Felix Cohen, *Transcendental Nonsense and the Functional Approach,* 35 COLUM. L. REV. 809 (1935); Kennedy, *supra* note 30, 90; Joseph Singer, *The Player and the Cards: Nihilism and Legal Theory,* 94 YALE L.J. 1 (1984); Tushnet, *supra* note 53, at 781; Note, *'Round and 'Round the Bramble Bush: From Legal Realism to Critical Legal Studies,* 95 HARV. L. REV. 1669 (1982).

84. This is the problem that induced Professor Hart's distinction between the "core" and the "penumbra" of legal meaning. HART, *supra* note 2, at 119–20.

85. *E.g.,* DICEY, *supra* note 3, at 198.

86. *See* discussion *infra,* chap. 5, text accompanying notes 8–31, 47.

87. *See, e.g.,* DWORKIN, RIGHTS, *supra* note 26, at 31–38; HENRY M. HART, JR., & ALBERT M. SACKS, THE LEGAL PROCESS: BASIC PROBLEMS IN THE MAKING AND APPLICATION OF LAW 145–58 (William N. Eskridge, Jr., & Philip P. Frickey eds., Foundation Press 1994). Indeed, even arbitrariness may at times be compatible with the rule of law. *See* RAZ, AUTHORITY, *supra* note 3, at 219. *But see* HAYEK, SERFDOM, *supra* note 6, at 91–92.

88. *See* discussion *infra,* chap. 5, text accompanying notes 8–47.

89. For Raz, stability is a subordinate value, contributing to freedom and dignity. *See* RAZ, AUTHORITY, *supra* note 3, at 214–15.

90. A similar point is made in McNollgast, *Politics and the Courts: A Positive Theory of Judicial Doctrine and the Rule of Law,* 68 S. CAL. L. REV. 1631 (1995).

91. *See, e.g.,* THE FEDERALIST No. 51 (Hamilton or Madison) (explaining the need for government to be organized so as to check human ambition with contrary ambition: "If men were angels, no government would be necessary. If angels were to govern men, neither internal nor external controls on government would be needed. In framing a government which is to be administered by men over men, the great difficulty lies in this: you must first enable the government to control the governed; and in the next place oblige it to control itself"); RAZ, AUTHORITY, *supra* note 3, at 224–29.

92. *See, e.g.,* RAZ, AUTHORITY, *supra* note 3, at 214–15; DANIEL E. TROY, RETROACTIVE LEGISLATION (AEI Press 1998) (discussing effects of lawmaking when protections against retroactive legislation are weakened).

93. For cogent criticism of perhaps the best-known effort to establish an overarching norm for a legal system, that of Hans Kelsen, see RAZ, CONCEPT, *supra* note 20, at 100–109. A more general criticism of the reliance on moral philosophy in legal analysis is Richard A. Posner, *The Problematics of Moral and Legal Theory,* 111 HARV. L. REV. 1637 (1998).

94. The term *democratic republic* here encompasses nations ruled by constitutional monarchies, such as Great Britain and Spain, that function in very similar fashion to the governments of nations organized as democratic republics, such as France, Germany, and the United States.

95. To be sure, there has been a vigorous challenge to this perception, mounted by Marxist writers in Europe and American academicians in the Critical Legal Studies movement. *See, e.g.,* Duncan Kennedy, *The Structure of Blackstone's Commentaries,* 28 BUFF. L. REV. 205 (1979); Gary Peller, *The Metaphysics of American Law,* 73 CAL. L. REV. 1151 (1985).

96. *See, e.g.,* J. W. GOUGH, THE SOCIAL CONTRACT: A CRITICAL STUDY OF ITS DEVELOPMENT (Clarendon Press, 2d ed. 1957); BARNETT, *supra* note 15; JOHN RAWLS, A THEORY OF JUSTICE 17–22 (Belknap Press 1971); JOHN RAWLS, POLITICAL LIBERALISM 22–28 (Columbia Univ. Press 1993).

97. *See, e.g.,* JOSEPH A. SCHUMPETER, CAPITALISM, SOCIALISM, AND DEMOCRACY (Harper & Row 1975) (1942).

98. This goal is often discussed in connection with the American constitutional system. *See, e.g.,* THE FEDERALIST No. 10 (Madison); THE FEDERALIST No. 51 (Hamilton or Madison); Bruce Ackerman, *Discovering the Constitution,* 93 YALE L.J. 1013 (1984); Jonathan

Macey, *Competing Economic Views of the Constitution*, 56 GEO. WASH. L. REV. 50 (1989). For discussion of the privilege aggregate welfare gives to binding limits over time, *see, e.g.,* THE FEDERALIST No. 49 (Hamilton or Madison); David Richards, *Constitutional Legitimacy and Constitutional Privacy*, 61 N.Y.U. L. REV. 800, 818–20 (1986).

99. THE FEDERALIST No. 10 (Madison); THE FEDERALIST No. 51 (Hamilton or Madison); THE FEDERALIST No. 78 (Hamilton); James Madison, *Vices of the Political System of the United States, in* 2 THE WRITINGS OF JAMES MADISON 361, 368 (Gaillard Hunt ed., G. P. Putnam's Sons 1901) ("The great desideratum of Government is such a modification of the sovereignty as will render it sufficiently neutral between the different interests and factions, to controul one part of the society from invading the rights of another and at the same time be sufficiently controuled itself from setting up an interest adverse to that of the whole society").

100. Indeed, *general welfare* very likely had a different meaning to our founders than the term *aggregate welfare* has today—which explains the inclusion of a series of other goals alongside "promot[ing] the general welfare" in the Constitution's preamble. *See, e.g.,* Ronald A. Cass, *Money, Power, and Politics: Governance Models and Campaign Finance Regulation*, 6 SUP. CT. ECON. REV. 1, 25–26 (1998) [hereinafter, *Governance Models*].

101. *See, e.g.,* Randy Barnett, *Introduction: Implementing the Ninth Amendment, in* 2 THE RIGHTS RETAINED BY THE PEOPLE: THE HISTORY AND MEANING OF THE NINTH AMENDMENT 1 (Randy Barnett ed., Geo. Mason Univ. Press 1993); Terry Brennan, *Natural Rights and the Constitution: The Original "Original Intent,"* 15 HARV. J.L. & PUB. POL'Y 965 (1992); Calvin R. Massey, *The Natural Law Component of the Ninth Amendment*, 61 U. CIN. L. REV. 49 (1992); Suzanna Sherry, *The Founders' Unwritten Constitution*, 54 U. CHI. L. REV. 1127 (1987).

102. *See, e.g.,* John Hart Ely, *Foreword: On Discovering Fundamental Values*, 92 HARV. L. REV. 5 (1978); Philip A. Hamburger, *Natural Rights, Natural Law, and American Constitutions*, 102 YALE L.J. 907 (1993); Thomas B. McAffee, *The Original Meaning of the Ninth Amendment*, 90 COLUM. L. REV. 1215 (1990); Frederick Schauer, *Constitutional Positivism*, 25 CONN. L. REV. 797 (1993).

103. *See, e.g.,* MAX FARRAND, THE FRAMING OF THE CONSTITUTION OF THE UNITED STATES 68–123, 147–52 (Yale Univ. Press 1913); JOSEPH STORY, A FAMILIAR EXPOSITION OF THE CONSTITUTION OF THE UNITED STATES 57–66, 324–36 (Regnery Gateway 1986) (1840); THE FEDERALIST No. 57 (Hamilton or Madison); Edward S. Corwin, *The Basic Doctrine of American Constitutional Law*, 12 MICH. L. REV. 247 (1914); John Hart Ely, *Wages of Crying Wolf: A Comment on* Roe v. Wade, 82 YALE L.J. 920 (1973). *But see* Laurence Tribe, *The Puzzling Persistence of Process-Based Constitutional Theories*, 89 YALE L.J. 1063 (1980).

104. *See, e.g.,* Schlesinger v. Wisconsin, 270 U.S. 230, 241 (1926) (Holmes, J., dissenting) (legislature given authority to define public interest within broad sphere); Cass, *Governance Models, supra* note 100, at 22; Daniel A. Farber, *Democracy and Disgust: Reflections on Public Choice*, 65 CHI.-KENT L. REV. 161, 174 (1989); Oliver Wendell Holmes, *The Gas-Stokers' Strike*, 7 AM. L. REV. 582, 583 (1873), *reprinted in* 1 THE COLLECTED WORKS OF JUSTICE HOLMES 323, 324 (Sheldon M. Novick ed., Univ. of Chicago Press 1995); Norman R. Williams II, *Note: Rising above Factionalism: A Madisonian Theory of Judicial Review*, 69 N.Y.U. L. REV. 963, 990 (1994).

Many legal scholars would urge a different construction of our constitutional tradition and of its relation to public interest. A common argument for American scholars over the past twenty years has been that something other than the evident framework for government decision making (together with expressly stated side-constraints) is embedded in the Constitution and in our constitutional tradition. That extra something is a trust that, in a properly functioning polity, citizens will behave in ways consonant *not* with assertion of preferences but rather with attention to our best ideals—defining a *best* aggregate welfare—and by doing so will create a legal order worthy of respect. *See, e.g.,* Anne C. Dailey, *Constitutional Privacy and the Just Family,* 67 TULANE L. REV. 955 (1993); Michelman, *Republic, supra* note 22, at 1495–96, 1500–1503; Michelman, *Traces, supra* note 78; Cass R. Sunstein, *Interest Groups in American Public Law,* 38 STAN. L. REV. 29 (1985) [hereinafter *Interest Groups*]. *See also* Gregory Alexander, *Time and Property in the American Republican Legal Culture,* 66 N.Y.U. L. REV. 273 (1991). The proper role of courts and scholars, for these writers, is to deny force to governmental actions that do not reflect the proper respect for our best selves, that seem animated by mere preferences, that do not conduce to a healthy dialogue over civic virtue. *See, e.g.,* Michelman, *Republic, supra* note 22, at 1532–37; Michelman, *Traces, supra* note 78, at 65–77; Sunstein, *Interest Groups, supra,* at 52.

Like much academic writing, this approach might be dismissed as merely clever pleading of personal values, a better-disguised version of exactly what the civic republicanism scholars deplore when other people's values win. This seems a fair criticism, but it is no more applicable to this approach to constitutional adjudication than to most academically advocated approaches.

There is, however, a more serious problem that is peculiar to civic republicanism: this approach turns the constitutional understanding on its head. The Constitution was the product of battles informed by just the kinds of personal, partisan preferences that advocates of "civic republicanism" would read out of the constitutional tradition. And the Constitution was expressly intended to combat the ill effects of disfavored preferences *not* by heavy reliance on the virtue of "dialogue" or on judicial policing but through structural limitations. *See, e.g.,* THE FEDERALIST No. 10 (Madison), No. 47 (Madison), No. 48 (Madison), No. 49 (Hamilton or Madison), No. 51 (Hamilton or Madison), No. 66 (Hamilton), No. 69 (Hamilton), No. 79 (Hamilton). In other words, knowing that we are moved by personal interests and disagreeing among themselves for that very reason, the framers put in place a structure that would check the worst effects of our human nature. *See* THE FEDERALIST No. 10 (Madison), No. 51 (Hamilton or Madison). Today's civic republican legal scholars would have the framers intending to revise human nature and trusting courts to do the job when ordinary government processes do not. For thoughtful critiques of the "civic republicanism" debates, see LAURA KALMAN, THE STRANGE CAREER OF LEGAL LIBERALISM (Yale Univ. Press 1996); Larry Simon, *The New Republicanism: Generosity of Spirit in Search of Something to Say,* 29 WM. & MARY L. REV. 83 (1987); Naomi M. Stolzenberg, *A Book of Laughter and Forgetting: Kalman's "Strange Career" and the Marketing of Civic Republicanism,* 111 HARV. L. REV. 1025 (1998) (book review).

105. *See, e.g., Americans Rate Their Society: The NORC Series on Confidence in National*

*Institutions,* PUB. PERSPECTIVE, Feb./Mar. 1997, at 2, 6. To be sure, Americans send mixed messages about our government and our legal system. In one recent survey of Americans, the U.S. Supreme Court garnered a higher confidence rating than any other institution, and 80% of the survey audience opined that our legal system is "the best in the world"—but more than half also said that the system "needs a complete overhaul." *See* James Rodgers, *Message Bearers Wanted,* ABA J., Apr. 1999, at 89.

106. *See, e.g.,* C. EDWIN BAKER, HUMAN LIBERTY AND FREEDOM OF SPEECH (Oxford Univ. Press 1989) (favoring a form of personal liberty as the norm); GARY L. BAUER, OUR HOPES, OUR DREAMS: A VISION FOR AMERICA (Focus on Family Pub. 1996) (a version of traditional values and Christian morality); WILLIAM J. BENNETT, THE DEATH OF OUTRAGE: BILL CLINTON AND THE ASSAULT ON AMERICAN IDEALS (Free Press 1998) (personal responsibility and traditional Judeo-Christian values); ROBERT H. BORK, SLOUCHING TOWARD GOMORRAH: MODERN LIBERALISM AND AMERICAN DECLINE (HarperCollins 1996) (personal responsibility); BORK, *supra* note 28, at 28–34 (same); RICHARD A. EPSTEIN, TAKINGS: PRIVATE PROPERTY AND THE POWER OF EMINENT DOMAIN 19–31 (Harvard Univ. Press 1985) (individual liberty); Thurgood Marshall, *The Constitution's Bicentennial: Commemorating the Wrong Document?* 40 VAND. L. REV. 1337 (1987) (equality); Thurgood Marshall, *Reflections on the Bicentennial of the United States Constitution,* 101 HARV. L. REV. 1, 4 (1987) (same); Richard A. Posner, *The Ethical and Political Basis of the Efficiency Norm in Common Law Adjudication,* 8 HOFSTRA L. REV. 487 (1980) (wealth maximization).

107. Ronald A. Cass, *Perils of Positive Thinking: Constitutional Interpretation and Negative First Amendment Theory,* 34 UCLA L. REV. 1405, 1438–44 (1987) [hereinafter *Constitutional Interpretation*]; Frederick Schauer, *The Role of the People in the First Amendment,* 74 CALIF. L. REV. 761, 782 (1986) [hereinafter *The People*].

108. *See, e.g.,* LEONARD W. LEVY, THE EMERGENCE OF A FREE PRESS (Oxford Univ. Press 1985); Cass, *Constitutional Interpretation, supra* note 107; Schauer, *The People, supra* note 107. This approach is redolent of philosophical argument on the importance of negative liberties, freedoms *from* things as opposed to freedoms *for* things. *See, e.g.,* ISAIAH BERLIN, FOUR ESSAYS ON LIBERTY 122–31 (Oxford Univ. Press 1969); Friedrich A. Hayek, *The Legal and Political Philosophy of David Hume (1711–1776), in* 3 THE COLLECTED WORKS OF F.A. HAYEK: THE TREND OF ECONOMIC THINKING: ESSAYS ON POLITICAL ECONOMISTS AND ECONOMIC HISTORY, at 101, 117 (W. W. Bartley III & Stephen Kresge eds., Univ. of Chicago Press 1989; lecture orig. pub. 1963) ("[Hume] knew that the greatest political goods, peace, liberty, and justice, were in their essence negative, a protection against injury rather than positive gifts").

## 2. Limited Government

1. *See, e.g.,* THE FEDERALIST Nos. 10, 32, 47, 48 (all by James Madison).

2. THE FEDERALIST No. 47 (Madison).

3. THE FEDERALIST No. 10 (Madison).

4. *Id. See also* THE FEDERALIST No. 51, at 351 (Madison) (Jacob E. Cooke ed., Wesleyan Univ. Press 1961) ("It is of great importance in a republic not only to guard against the

oppression of its rulers, but to guard one part of the society against the injustice of the other part"); letter from James Madison to Thomas Jefferson (Oct. 17, 1788), *in* 1 THE CONSTITUTION AND THE SUPREME COURT: A DOCUMENTARY HISTORY 121, 122 (Louis H. Pollack ed., World Pub. Co. 1966) ("Wherever the real power in a Government lies, there is the danger of oppression. In our Government, the real power lies in the majority of the Community, and the invasion of private rights is chiefly to be apprehended, not from acts of Government contrary to the sense of its constituents, but from acts in which the Government is the mere instrument of the major number of constituents").

5. ROBERT A. DAHL, A PREFACE TO DEMOCRATIC THEORY 6–32, 131–34 (Univ. of Chicago Press 1959).

6. Since Dahl's monograph, a considerable body of work has elaborated on these propositions. *See generally* DENNIS E. MUELLER, II PUBLIC CHOICE (Cambridge Univ. Press 1989); MANCUR OLSON, THE LOGIC OF COLLECTIVE ACTION (Harvard Univ. Press 1965) [hereinafter LOGIC].

7. JOHN HART ELY, DEMOCRACY AND DISTRUST: A THEORY OF JUDICIAL REVIEW (Harvard Univ. Press 1980). In his opinion for the Court in United States v. Carolene Products Co., 304 U.S. 144 (1938), upholding a federal ban on the interstate shipment of "filled milk," Justice Stone articulated a standard for judicial review of legislation that was generally deferential where the basis for constitutional challenge was an asserted infringement of economic (*property*) interests. The particular application of that standard to the statute at issue in *Carolene Products* has been criticized as turning a blind eye to the use of legislative process to advantage a set of powerful business interests at the expense of the public. *See* Geoffrey Miller, *The True Story of* Carolene Products, 1988 SUP. CT. REV. 397. Far better known is Justice Stone's footnote reserving the possibility of a less deferential review for legislation that "appears on its face to be within a specific prohibition of the Constitution," "legislation which restricts those political processes which can ordinarily be expected to bring about repeal of undesirable legislation," or "statutes directed at particular religious, or national, or racial minorities [or laws motivated by] prejudice against discrete and insular minorities." *Id.* at 152 n.4 (citations omitted).

8. *See, e.g.,* JOHN HOPE FRANKLIN, FROM SLAVERY TO FREEDOM: A HISTORY OF NEGRO AMERICANS 324–43 (Vintage Books, 3d ed. 1969); CIVIL RIGHTS AND AFRICAN AMERICANS: A DOCUMENTARY HISTORY 283–84 (Albert P. Baustein & Robert L. Zangrando eds., Northwestern Univ. Press 1991); C. Vann Woodward, *Capitulation to Racism, in* BLACK HISTORY 326, 328–32 (Melvin Drimmer ed., Anchor Books 1969).

9. *See, e.g.,* MAX FARRAND, THE FRAMING OF THE CONSTITUTION OF THE UNITED STATES 68–123, 147–52 (Yale Univ. Press 1913).

10. *E.g.,* JOHN SILBER, STRAIGHT SHOOTING: WHAT'S WRONG WITH AMERICA AND HOW TO FIX IT 216–17 (Harper & Row 1989).

11. ALEXIS DE TOCQUEVILLE, DEMOCRACY IN AMERICA 278–80 (Alfred A. Knopf 1945; vol. 1, orig. pub. 1835).

12. *See, e.g.,* ROBERT ELLICKSON, ORDER WITHOUT LAW: HOW NEIGHBORS SETTLE DISPUTES (Harvard Univ. Press 1991).

13. Contrast with this the utility of religious law in certain small groups and the stability this imparts to arrangements within a single group. *See, e.g.,* Lisa Bernstein, *Opting Out of the Legal System: Extralegal Contractual Relations in the Diamond Industry,* 22 J. LEGAL STUD. 115 (1992).

14. *See, e.g.,* New York Times v. Sullivan, 376 U.S. 254, 270–79 (1964); Pennekamp v. Florida, 328 U.S. 331 (1946). *See also* Time, Inc. v. Hill, 385 U.S. 374, 389 (1967); Speiser v. Randall, 357 U.S. 513, 526 (1958).

15. *See, e.g.,* Harry Kalven, Jr., *The New York Times Case and the "Central Meaning" of the First Amendment,* 1964 SUP. CT. REV. 191.

16. Most of the attention devoted to America's legal system by academicians focuses on the system as a means of dispute resolution, whereas other discourse about the rule of law concentrates more on direct application of state authority.

17. For discussion of why this is so and what distinguishes such examples from other settings where legal outcomes are less predictable, see, e.g., Vincent Blasi, *The Checking Value in First Amendment Theory,* 1977 AM. B. FOUND. RES. J. 521; Ronald A. Cass, *Perils of Positive Thinking: Constitutional Interpretation and Negative First Amendment Theory,* 34 UCLA L. REV. 1405, 1451–84 (1987) [hereinafter *Constitutional Interpretation*]; Frederick Schauer, *Easy Cases,* 58 S. CAL. L. REV. 399 (1986). *See also* Larry Alexander & Paul Horton, *The Impossibility of a Free Speech Principle,* 78 NW. U. L. REV. 1319 (1983) (explaining why there is not a single, overarching principled explanator for free-speech cases); Steven Shiffrin, *The First Amendment and Economic Regulation: Away from a General Theory of the First Amendment,* 78 NW. U. L. REV 1212 (1983) (making a similar argument from a different perspective).

18. *See, e.g.,* Planned Parenthood v. Casey, 505 U.S. 833, 868 (1992) (United States has "principled character . . . of a Nation of people who aspire to live according to the rule of law"); William F. Buckley, Jr., *Strange Uses of Tolerance,* SAN DIEGO UNION-TRIB., Jan. 27, 1985, at C2 ("The overwhelming majority of Americans believe in the rule of law").

19. *See, e.g.,* Ronald A. Cass, *Judging: Norms and Incentives of Retrospective Decision-Making,* 75 B.U. L. REV. 942 (1995).

20. This is true both of criminal prosecutions and administrative actions analogous to prosecution. *See, e.g.,* Heckler v. Chaney, 470 U.S. 821 (1985); United States v. Nixon, 418 U.S. 683 (1974); Vaca v. Sipes, 386 U.S. 171 (1967).

21. *See* discussion, *infra,* text accompanying notes 38–43, chap. 5, text accompanying notes 37–47, chap. 6, text accompanying notes 22–30.

22. *See* discussion *infra,* chaps. 4 & 5.

23. *See, e.g.,* Papachristou v. City of Jacksonville, 405 U.S. 156, 162 (1972); Lambert v. California, 355 U.S. 225 (1957); Winters v. New York, 333 U.S. 507, 515 (1948); United States v. Sharp, 27 F. Cas. 1041, 1043 (No. 16,264) (C.C. Pa. 1815).

24. *See, e.g.,* Smith v. Goguen, 415 U.S. 566, 572–77 (1974); Papachristou v. City of Jacksonville, 405 U.S. 156, 168–71 (1972); Shuttlesworth v. City of Birmingham, 394 U.S. 147 (1969); Kunz v. New York, 340 U.S. 290 (1951). For a more accurate statement of the tests actually used in these and related cases, see Cass, *Constitutional Interpretation, supra* note 17, at 1451–84; Daniel A. Farber, *Free Speech without Romance: Public Choice and the First Amend-*

*ment,* 105 HARV. L. REV 554 (1991); Frederick Schauer, *Language, Truth, and the First Amendment: An Essay in Memory of Harry Canter,* 64 VA. L. REV. 264 (1978); Frederick Schauer, *The Second-Best First Amendment,* 31 WM. & MARY L. REV. 1 (1989); Geoffrey Stone, *For a Americana: Speech in Public Places,* 1974 S. CT. REV. 233; Geoffrey Stone, *Content Regulation and the First Amendment,* 25 WM. & MARY L. REV. 189 (1983).

25. *See, e.g.,* National Cable Television Assn. v. United States, 415 U.S. 336 (1974); Kent v. Dulles, 357 U.S. 116 (1958); Schechter Poultry Co. v. United States, 295 U.S. 495 (1935); Panama Refining Co. v. Ryan, 293 U.S. 388 (1935). *But see* Skinner v. Mid-America Pipeline Co., 490 U.S. 212 (1989); Haig v. Agee, 453 U.S. 280 (1983); Yakus v. United States, 321 U.S. 414 (1944). Judicial success with the antidelegation doctrine as a first line of defense against broad grants of discretion has been extremely modest. Judicial review on substantive grounds, though frequently deferential in some measure, generally is credited with imposing greater constraint on administrative actions. *See* discussion *infra,* text accompanying notes 38–43; chap. 5, text accompanying notes 2–5; chap. 6, text accompanying notes 22–30.

26. Heard at White House Correspondents' Association Annual Dinner, April 21, 1988.

27. *See* Seth Faison, *E-Mail to U.S. Lands Chinese Internet Entrepreneur in Jail,* N.Y. TIMES, Jan. 21, 1999, at A10; Julie Schmit, *China Punishes Internet "Dissident" with 2–Year Sentence,* USA TODAY, Jan. 21, 1999, at 7A.

28. *See* Seth Faison, *Beijing Journal: Politics, Sex, and Murder! A Banned Best Seller!* N.Y. TIMES, Sept. 15, 1997, at A4.

29. *See* Rone Tempest, *China Editor Gets Life in Prison,* L.A. TIMES, Aug. 31, 1993, at A4.

30. New York Times Co. v. United States, 403 U.S. 713 (1971) ("The Pentagon Papers Case").

31. *See, e.g.,* Ana de Juan, Miguel Lasheras & Rafaela Mayo, *Voluntary Tax Compliance Behavior of Spanish Income Tax Payers,* 49 PUB. FIN. 90 (1994). *See also* Larry Rohter, *Latin America's Contagion: Where Taxes Aren't So Certain,* N.Y. TIMES, Mar. 21, 1999, § 4 at 3 (less than 40% of taxpayers in Ecuador pay income tax).

32. *See, e.g.,* INTERNAL REVENUE SERVICE, FEDERAL TAX COMPLIANCE RESEARCH: INDIVIDUAL INCOME TAX GAP ESTIMATES FOR 1985, 1988, AND 1992 (U.S. Dept. of Treasury 1996). The assertion that individuals comply with the law does not mean that individuals "correctly" interpret the law. Where the law is as complex as the tax code, those who earnestly endeavor to understand and conform to the law will be unable to ascertain a pinpoint right answer to the law's meaning, as illustrated annually near "tax day" by reports of the widely divergent answers given by tax experts to what is owed by a hypothetical taxpayer on a single set of stylized facts. *See Replacing the Federal Income Tax: Hearings before the House Comm. on Ways & Means,* 104th Cong., 2d Sess., vol. 2, 17–18 (statement of Frank Lalli); Joan Caplin, *Tax Test,* MONEY, Mar. 1998, at 104. For discussion of the difficulty caused by this aspect of law, see *infra,* chap. 6, text accompanying notes 22–27, 44–50. For discussion of the concept of tax compliance and its complications, see James Andreoni, Brian Erard & Jonathan Feinstein, *Tax Compliance,* 36 J. ECON. LIT. 818 (1998).

33. *See, e.g.,* JAMES A. BUCHANAN & GORDON TULLOCK, THE CALCULUS OF CONSENT: LOG-

ICAL FOUNDATIONS OF CONSTITUTIONAL DEMOCRACY (Univ. of Michigan Press 1962); OLSON, LOGIC, *supra* note 6; KENNETH A. SHEPSLE & MARK S. BONCHEK, ANALYZING POLITICS: RATIONALITY, BEHAVIOR, AND INSTITUTIONS (W. W. Norton 1997). *See also* RICHARD A. EPSTEIN, TAKINGS: PRIVATE PROPERTY AND THE POWER OF EMINENT DOMAIN (Harvard Univ. Press 1985).

34. *See generally* OLSON, LOGIC, *supra* note 6.

35. *See, e.g.,* Roland McKean, *Property Rights within Government and Devices to Increase Government Efficiency,* 39 S. ECON. J. 177 (1972).

36. *See, e.g.,* MORRIS FIORINA, CONGRESS: KEYSTONE OF THE WASHINGTON ESTABLISHMENT (Yale Univ. Press 1977); McNollgast, *Structure and Process, Politics and Policy: Administrative Arrangements and the Political Control of Agencies,* 75 VA. L. REV. 431 (1989).

37. *See, e.g.,* Ronald A. Cass, *Damage Suits against Public Officers,* 129 U. PA. L. REV. 1110 (1981); Ronald A. Cass & Clayton P. Gillette, *The Government Contractor Defense: Contractual Allocation of Public Risk,* 77 VA. L. REV. 257 (1991); Jerry Mashaw, *Civil Liability of Government Officers: Property Rights and Official Accountability,* 42 L. & CONTEMP. PROBS. 8 (Winter 1978); Susan Rose-Ackerman, *Reforming Public Bureaucracy through Economic Incentives?* 2 J.L. ECON. & ORG. 131 (1986). The relative invisibility of government action cannot be separated from the incentives of government managers to monitor subordinates' behavior. *See, e.g.,* Ronald A. Cass, *Privatization: Politics, Law, and Theory,* 71 MARQ. L. REV. 449, 481–88 (1988).

38. In the popular BBC series *Yes, Minister,* the civil servants routinely frustrate the wishes of their nominal boss, the Minister, for reasons that could be categorized as benign or self-interested, depending on one's vantage.

39. *See* Glen O. Robinson, *The Federal Communications Commission: An Essay on Regulatory Watchdogs,* 64 VA. L. REV. 169, 217 (1978).

40. PETER H. SCHUCK, SUING GOVERNMENT: CITIZEN REMEDIES FOR OFFICIAL WRONGS xii (Yale Univ. Press 1983).

41. *See, e.g.,* John M. Broder, *Demonizing the I.R.S.,* N.Y. TIMES, Sept. 20, 1997, § D at 1–2.

42. *See, e.g.,* David Johnston, *F.B.I. Leader at 1992 Standoff in Idaho Says Review Shielded Top Officials,* N.Y. TIMES, May 10, 1995, § D at 21; *Jewell Theft,* N.J.L.J., Nov. 11, 1996, at 26.

43. *See* discussion *infra,* chap. 5, text accompanying notes 2–5, chap. 6, text accompanying notes 33–41.

44. RONALD DWORKIN, TAKING RIGHTS SERIOUSLY 31 (Harvard Univ. Press 1977).

45. *See* PHILIP K. HOWARD, THE DEATH OF COMMON SENSE: HOW LAW IS SUFFOCATING AMERICA 22–31, 50–53 (Random House 1994); discussion *infra,* chap. 6, text accompanying notes 33–41.

# 3. Judges' Rule

1. ALEXANDER M. BICKEL, THE LEAST DANGEROUS BRANCH: THE SUPREME COURT AT THE BAR OF POLITICS (Bobbs-Merrill 1962), drawing on THE FEDERALIST No. 78 (Hamilton).

2. 418 U.S. 683 (1974).

3. A fourth Nixon appointee, Justice William Rehnquist, did not participate in the decision.

4. 418 U.S. at 694–95 (footnote omitted).

5. *Id.* at 704–5.

6. 418 U.S. at 703–5. *But see* Gerald Gunther, *Judicial Hegemony and Legislative Autonomy: The Nixon Case and the Impeachment Process,* 22 UCLA L. REV. 30 (1974).

7. 418 U.S. at 705–6 n.16.

8. *Id.* at 705–7.

9. *Id.* at 711.

10. *Id.* at 708–11.

11. *Id.* at 707.

12. 520 U.S. 681 (1997).

13. The Court did not discuss a suit against President Thomas Jefferson, filed while he was president, complaining of actions taken in his capacity as president. The suit was tried after he left office, and no defense of immunity was claimed in the litigation. Livingston v. Jefferson, 15 F. Cas. 660 (C.C.D. Va. 1811). *See* JEAN EDWARD SMITH, JOHN MARSHALL: DEFINER OF A NATION 398–406 (Henry Holt & Co. 1996).

14. Harlow v. Fitzgerald, 457 U.S. 800, 818 (1982). *See also* Davis v. Scherer, 468 U.S. 183, 190–91 (1984).

15. 520 U.S. at 695.

16. Clinton also argued that presidential subjection to judicial process threatened the separation of powers provided in the Constitution. This argument essentially reduces to the functional argument described in the text.

17. 520 U.S. at 710–24 (Breyer, J., concurring).

18. *Id.* at 702.

19. There is ample reason to suppose that had President Clinton's behavior more clearly and directly attacked the judicial process—had his dishonesty under oath been more blatant or his efforts to keep evidence out of court less deft—the outcome of his impeachment trial would have been different.

20. *See, e.g.,* THE FEDERALIST No. 78 (Hamilton) ("it is indispensable that [courts] should be bound down by strict rules and precedents, which serve to define and point out their duty in every particular case that comes before them"); JOSEPH RAZ, THE AUTHORITY OF LAW: ESSAYS ON LAW AND MORALITY 217, 219 (Clarendon Press 1979) [hereinafter AUTHORITY]; Paul G. Kauper, *The Supreme Court and the Rule of Law,* 59 MICH. L. REV. 531, 541 (1961); Michael Oakeshott, *The Rule of Law, in* ON HISTORY AND OTHER ESSAYS 119, 157–64 (Barnes & Noble Books 1983). Some scholars, especially in Europe, identify the rule of law simply with judicial control of other government officials, not with limitations on judges. *See, e.g.,* André Tunc, *Government under Law: A Civilian View, in* GOVERNMENT UNDER LAW 35, 43–45 (Arthur E. Sutherland ed., Harvard Univ. Press 1956) (discussing French view of the rule of law, focusing specifically on judicial control of executive and administrative officers, not of judges or legislators). This conception of the rule of law is too narrow to be useful. Of what value is such a rule, substituting judicial despotism for executive or legisla-

tive despotism? The ultranarrow conception of the rule of law appeals only when coupled with an assumption that the judges are constrained by law. Extensive debate over the appropriate degree of judicial discretion does not extend to the proposition that judges should be freed of constraint by law (although that accusation could be made against some authors who would have judges march to the tune of particular norms of justice extrinsic to positive law). *See* discussion *supra* text and notes, chap. 1, at notes 25–38.

21. Gunther, *supra* note 6.

22. *See, e.g.,* Chevron U.S.A., Inc. v. Natural Resources Def. Coun., 467 U.S. 837 (1984). *But see* Clark Byse, *Judicial Review of Administrative Interpretation of Statutes: An Analysis of* Chevron's *Step Two,* 2 ADMIN. L.J. 255 (1988).

23. 418 U.S. at 705–7.

24. 520 U.S. at 719. *See id.* at 710–19.

25. Nixon v. Fitzgerald, 457 U.S. 731 (1982).

26. 457 U.S. at 751–53.

27. U.S. CONST., Art. 1, §§ 2, 3, Art. 2, § 4.

28. To be sure, the Constitution's text is not clear on this point, but the placement of the statement respecting subjection to criminal process is more compatible with a suggestion that criminal process preceding impeachment and conviction is barred. The statement comes after a statement respecting the extent of punishment accompanying impeachment and conviction, and it is preceded immediately by a colon. It is contained in Article I, dictating the manner and effect of congressional exercise of the impeachment power, not in Article II (where it would logically serve as a statement of Executive officials' exposure to criminal process *while* in office) or in Article III (where it would logically serve as a statement of the extent of federal judicial process at any time). The practice with respect to other federal officers, however, has been contrary to this inference.

29. U.S. CONST., Art. 2, § 4.

30. *See, e.g.,* Ex Parte Young, 209 U.S. 123 (1908); Bates v. Clark, 95 U.S. 204 (1877); Buck v. Colbath, 70 U.S. (3 Wall.) 334 (1865); Wise v. Withers, 7 U.S. (3 Cranch) 330 (1806); Marbury v. Madison, 5 U.S. (1 Cranch) 137 (1803). As noted earlier, officers of the United States have been subject to both civil and criminal process during their terms of office.

## 4. Ruling Judges

1. *See, e.g.,* JEROME FRANK, LAW AND THE MODERN MIND (Brentano's 1930); MORTON J. HORWITZ, THE TRANSFORMATION OF AMERICAN LAW 1780–1860 (Harvard Univ. Press 1977); GLENDON SCHUBERT, THE JUDICIAL MIND: THE ATTITUDES AND IDEOLOGIES OF SUPREME COURT JUSTICES 1946–1963 (Northwestern Univ. Press 1965); JEFFREY A. SEGAL & HAROLD J. SPAETH, THE SUPREME COURT AND THE ATTITUDINAL MODEL (Cambridge Univ. Press 1993); Rafael Gely & Pablo Spiller, *The Political Economy of Supreme Court Decisions: The Case of Roosevelt's Court-Packing Plan,* 12 INT'L REV. L. & ECON. 45 (1992); Karl Llewellyn, *A Realistic Jurisprudence—The Next Step,* 30 COLUM. L. REV. 431 (1930) [hereinafter *Realistic Jurisprudence*]; Gary Peller, *The Metaphysics of American Law,* 73 CAL. L. REV. 1151 (1985); Theodore

Schroeder, *The Psychologic Study of Judicial Opinion*, 6 CAL. L. REV. 89 (1918); Mark Tushnet, *Following the Rules Laid Down: A Critique of Interpretivism and Neutral Principles*, 96 HARV. L. REV. 781 (1983). Other writings take a similar approach but are substantially less sweeping in their claims of judicial independence from external constraint. *See, e.g.*, CASS R. SUNSTEIN, LEGAL REASONING AND POLITICAL CONFLICT (Oxford Univ. Press 1996); Sanford Levinson, *Law as Literature*, 60 TEX. L. REV. 373 (1982); Edward Rubin & Malcolm Feeley, *Creating Legal Doctrine*, 69 S. CAL. L. REV. 1989 (1996).

2. RICHARD A. POSNER, THE FEDERAL COURTS: CRISIS AND REFORM 17 (Harvard Univ. Press 1985) [hereinafter, FEDERAL COURTS].

3. KENNETH A. SHEPSLE & MARK S. BONCHEK, ANALYZING POLITICS: RATIONALITY, BEHAVIOR, AND INSTITUTIONS 418–31 (W. W. Norton 1997).

4. *See, e.g.*, HORWITZ, *supra* note 1; Derrick Bell, *Who's Afraid of Critical Race Theory*, 1995 U. ILL. L. REV. 893; John Hasnas, *The Myth of the Rule of Law*, 1995 WIS. L. REV. 199, 201–21; David Kairys, *Law and Politics*, 52 GEO. WASH. L. REV. 243 (1984). *See generally* THE POLITICS OF LAW: A PROGRESSIVE CRITIQUE (David Kairys ed., Pantheon 1990). *See also* Joseph Singer, *The Player and the Cards: Nihilism and Legal Theory*, 94 YALE L.J. 1 (1984) (offering a similar view, though qualified at various points). Social scientists frequently have been sympathetic to at least a modified version of this point but have had difficulty documenting their intuition. *See, e.g.*, Jeffrey A. Segal & Harold J. Spaeth, *The Influence of Stare Decisis on the Votes of the United States Supreme Court Judges*, 40 AM. J. POL. SCI. 971 (1996).

5. *See, e.g.*, Jerome M. Culp, *Judex Economicus*, 50 L. & CONTEMP. PROBS. 95 (Autumn 1987); Stephen Gillers, *The Compelling Case against Robert H. Bork*, 9 CARDOZO L. REV. 33 (1987); Christopher E. Smith, *Justice Antonin Scalia and the Institutions of American Government*, 25 WAKE FOREST L. REV. 783 (1990). *See also* Richard L. Revesz, *Environmental Regulation, Ideology, and the D.C. Circuit*, 83 VA. L. REV. 1717 (1997) (finding ideology an important, and at times dispositive, influence, though within confined range of decision possibilities defined by external authority); Gregory C. Sisk, Michael Heise & Andrew Morriss, *Charting the Influences on the Judicial Mind: An Empirical Study of Judicial Reasoning*, 73 N.Y.U. L. REV. 1377 (1998) (same).

6. *See* FRANK, *supra* note 1; Karl Llewellyn, *Realistic Jurisprudence, supra* note 1; McNollgast, *Politics and the Courts: A Positive Theory of Judicial Doctrine and the Rule of Law*, 68 S. CAL. L. REV. 1631 (1995); Richard A. Posner, *What Do Judges and Justices Maximize? (The Same Thing Everybody Else Does)*, 3 SUP. CT. ECON. REV. 1 (1995) [hereinafter *Judges*]; Eric Rasmusen, *Judicial Legitimacy as a Repeated Game*, 10 J.L. ECON. & ORG. 163 (1994).

7. Although some authors contend for more radical versions of this approach, better-known works promote judicial freedom within much more modest scope. *See, e.g.*, LON FULLER, THE MORALITY OF LAW 81–87, 228–32 (Yale Univ. Press, rev. ed. 1969); EDWARD H. LEVI, AN INTRODUCTION TO LEGAL REASONING (Univ. of Chicago Press 1949); William N. Eskridge, Jr., *Dynamic Statutory Interpretation*, 135 U. PA. L. REV. 1479 (1987); William N. Eskridge, Jr., & Philip P. Frickey, *Statutory Interpretation as Practical Reasoning*, 42 STAN. L. REV. 321 (1990); Rubin & Feeley, *supra* note 1.

8. *See* ROBERT COVER, JUSTICE ACCUSED: ANTISLAVERY AND THE JUDICIAL PROCESS (Yale

Univ. Press 1975); Tushnet, *supra* note 1. *See also* RICHARD A. POSNER, THE PROBLEMS OF JURISPRUDENCE 220–44 (Harvard Univ. Press 1990) [hereinafter JURISPRUDENCE]; CASS R. SUNSTEIN, THE PARTIAL CONSTITUTION (Harvard Univ. Press 1993) [hereinafter CONSTITUTION]; Paul Brest, *The Misconceived Quest for the Original Understanding,* 60 B.U. L. REV. 204 (1980); Thomas C. Grey, *Do We Have an Unwritten Constitution?* 27 STAN. L. REV. 703 (1975); Michael J. Klarman, *Anti-Fidelity,* 70 S. CAL. L. REV. 381 (1997) [hereinafter *Anti-Fidelity*].

9. *See* J. WOODFORD HOWARD, JR., COURTS OF APPEALS IN THE FEDERAL JUDICIAL SYSTEM: A STUDY OF THE SECOND, FIFTH, AND DISTRICT OF COLUMBIA CIRCUITS 181–86 (Princeton Univ. Press 1981) [hereinafter COURTS]; ROBERT E. KEETON, JUDGING (West Pub. Co. 1990); NEIL MACCORMICK, LEGAL REASONING AND LEGAL THEORY 229–58 (Clarendon Press 1978); Ronald A. Cass, *Judging: Norms and Incentives of Retrospective Decision-Making,* 75 B.U. L. REV. 942 (1995) [hereinafter *Judging*]. *See also* Orley Ashenfelter, Theodore Eisenberg & Stewart Schwab, *Politics and the Judiciary: The Influence of Judicial Background on Case Outcomes,* 24 J. LEGAL STUD. 257 (1995); Frank B. Cross, *Political Science and the New Legal Realism: A Case of Unfortunate Interdisciplinary Ignorance,* 92 NW. U. L. REV. 251 (1997). For a critical review of empirical literature, offering some support for both models, see Sisk, Heise & Morriss, *supra* note 5, at 1385–96.

10. *See* MELVIN A. EISENBERG, THE NATURE OF THE COMMON LAW (Harvard Univ. Press 1988); H. L. A. HART, THE CONCEPT OF LAW 119–32 (Oxford Univ. Press 1961) (especially respecting decisions within the "core" of a legal rule, as distinct from those at the periphery); HENRY M. HART, JR., & ALBERT M. SACKS, THE LEGAL PROCESS: BASIC PROBLEMS IN THE MAKING AND APPLICATION OF LAW (William N. Eskridge, Jr., & Philip P. Frickey eds., Foundation Press 1994); JACK RAKOVE, ORIGINAL MEANINGS: IDEAS IN THE MAKING OF THE CONSTITUTION (Alfred A. Knopf 1996); Ashenfelter, Eisenberg & Schwab, *supra* note 9; Frederick Schauer, *Giving Reasons,* 47 STAN. L. REV. 633 (1995). As noted above, the better writings do not fall at one or another polar position. For example, the Hart & Sacks presentation of judicial decision making suggests an autonomous domain for law but also intimates that decisions may import considerations similar to those Fuller sees embodied in judges' work. Professor Schauer, likewise, sees judges as able to give reasons for decisions that are internal to the argumentation from relevant legal materials, but he recognizes as well the inevitable influence of external factors on the way judges construe those materials.

11. *See* JOHN AUSTIN, THE PROVINCE OF JURISPRUDENCE DETERMINED AND THE USES OF THE STUDY OF JURISPRUDENCE (Noonday Press 1954); HART, *supra* note 10, at 113, 117, 123–28, 132 (norm for "core" decisions); JOSEPH RAZ, THE CONCEPT OF A LEGAL SYSTEM 213–16 (Oxford Univ. Press, 2d ed. 1980) [hereinafter CONCEPT]; Frank H. Easterbrook, *Text, History, and Structure in Statutory Interpretation,* 17 HARV. J.L. & PUB. POL'Y 61 (1994); Antonin Scalia, *Originalism: The Lesser Evil,* 57 U. CIN. L. REV. 849 (1989); Frederick Schauer, *Formalism,* 97 YALE L.J. 509 (1988) [hereinafter *Formalism*]. *See also* RONALD DWORKIN, TAKING RIGHTS SERIOUSLY (Harvard Univ. Press 1977) (ostensibly contending for an interpretive mode in which judges seek right answers, bound, among other things, by prior legal authority); Michael Oakeshott, *The Rule of Law, in* ON HISTORY AND OTHER ESSAYS 119, 157–64 (Barnes & Noble Books 1983) [hereinafter *Rule*].

12. *See* RONALD DWORKIN, FREEDOM'S LAW: THE MORAL INTERPRETATION OF THE AMER-ICAN CONSTITUTION (Harvard Univ. Press 1996) [hereinafter FREEDOM'S LAW]; RONALD DWORKIN, LAW'S EMPIRE 225–27 (Belknap Press 1986) [hereinafter EMPIRE]; 1 FRIEDRICH A. HAYEK, LAW, LEGISLATION, AND LIBERTY 118–22 (Univ. of Chicago Press 1973); Charles Fried, *Perfect Justice, Perfect Freedom,* 78 B.U. L. REV. 717 (1998) [hereinafter *Perfect Justice*]; Charles Fried, *Philosophy Matters,* 111 HARV. L. REV. 1739 (1998); Friedrich A. Hayek, *The Legal and Political Philosophy of David Hume (1711–1776), in* 3 THE COLLECTED WORKS OF F. A. HAYEK: THE TREND OF ECONOMIC THINKING: ESSAYS ON POLITICAL ECONOMISTS AND ECONOMIC HIS-TORY 101–17 (W. W. Bartley III & Stephen Kresge eds., Univ. of Chicago Press 1989; lecture orig. pub. 1963). Again, thoughtful writers take positions closer one to another than assign-ment to polar models will suggest. Though Fuller suggests a role for moral considerations that draw on norms he must supply, he expressly locates the norms as coming from within the legal system, a posture close to that of Dworkin. Dworkin purports to resolve cases by virtue of principles that are located within the legal system, but in fact he supports a more expansive inquiry into philosophical considerations not expressly given by extrinsic legal authority than does Justice Fried, who asserts openness to philosophical considerations not derived from law (though one must query whether *that* openness is to be found more in his jurisprudential writing than in his judicial opinions).

13. *See* Frank H. Easterbrook, *What's So Special about Judges?* 61 COLO. L. REV. 773 (1990). *See also* RAZ, CONCEPT, *supra* note 11; Meir Dan-Cohen, *Decision Rules and Conduct Rules: On Acoustic Separation in Criminal Law,* 97 HARV. L. REV. 625 (1984); Antonin Scalia, *The Rule of Law as a Law of Rules,* 56 U. CHI. L. REV. 1175 (1989).

14. *E.g.,* POSNER, JURISPRUDENCE, *supra* note 8, at 24–26 (tracing back a similar division 2,000 years).

15. Posner, *Judges, supra* note 6.

16. *See, e.g.,* ALEXANDER TABARROK & ERIC HELLAND, COURT POLITICS: THE POLITICAL ECONOMY OF TORT AWARDS (Center for the Study of Amer. Bus. Working Paper 166, Oct. 1997) (evidence that electoral politics explains why elected judges' decisions are skewed in favor of in-state plaintiffs and against nonresident defendants).

17. *See, e.g.,* COLO. CONST., art. 6, § 25; FLA. CONST., art. 5, § 10.

18. *See* ADMINISTRATIVE OFFICE OF THE UNITED STATES COURTS, JUDICIAL BUSINESS OF THE UNITED STATES COURTS: 1996 REPORT OF THE DIRECTOR 14–18 (Govt. Printing Office 1996) [hereinafter UNITED STATES COURTS]; ADMINISTRATIVE OFFICE OF THE UNITED STATES COURTS, JUDICIAL BUSINESS OF THE UNITED STATES COURTS: 1999 REPORT OF THE DIREC-TOR (Govt. Printing Office 1999), *available at* <www.uscourts.gov/judbus1999/index.html> [hereinafter UNITED STATES COURTS, 1999]; BRIAN J. OSTROM & NEAL B. KAUDER, EXAMIN-ING THE WORK OF STATE COURTS, 1995: A NATIONAL PERSPECTIVE FROM THE COURT STATIS-TICS PROJECT 10, 14, 68 (State Justice Inst. 1996) [hereinafter STATE COURTS]; BRIAN J. OSTROM & NEAL B. KAUDER, EXAMINING THE WORK OF STATE COURTS, 1998: A NATIONAL PERSPEC-TIVE FROM THE COURT STATISTICS PROJECT (National Center for State Courts 1999), *avail-able at* <www.ncsc.dni.us> [hereinafter STATE COURTS, 1998]; Thomas C. Goldstein, *Statis-tics for the Supreme Court's October Term 1995,* 65 U.S.L.W. 3029 (July 9, 1996).

19. *See Statistical Recap of Supreme Court's Workload during Last Three Terms,* 66 U.S.L.W. 3136 (Aug. 12, 1997) [hereinafter *Recap*].

20. *See* David G. Savage, *Getting the High Court's Attention,* 83 ABA J. 46, 47 (Nov. 1997).

21. See discussion of the different incentives faced by trial judges and appellate judges, *infra* text accompanying notes 103–4.

22. McNollgast, *supra* note 6.

23. McNollgast, in fact, recognize that judges may have preferences apart from case outcomes, such as a preference for predictable judicial decisions. This preference is treated identically to outcome preferences in their model. *Id.*

24. Cass, *Judging, supra* note 9; Patricia M. Wald, *Some Real-Life Observations about Judging,* 26 IND. L. REV. 173 (1992).

25. *See, e.g.,* Cass, *Judging, supra* note 9.

26. This was, for instance, a major premise for opponents of Judge Robert Bork's nomination to be an associate justice of the Supreme Court. *See, e.g.,* Ronald Dworkin, *The Bork Nomination,* 9 CARDOZO L. REV. 101 (1987); Philip B. Kurland, *Bork: The Transformation of a Conservative Constitutionalist,* 9 CARDOZO L. REV. 127 (1987).

27. In 1998 there were 25,270 trial court judges in the state courts, 946 judges on intermediate state appellate courts, and 357 judges on state courts of last resort.

*See* BUREAU OF JUSTICE STATISTICS, STATE COURT ORGANIZATION 1998 (U.S. Dept. of Justice 1998), *available at* <www.ojp.usdoj.gov/bjs/abstract/sco98.htm>. There were approximately 1,500 more trial judges and 20 fewer appellate judges a few years earlier. *See* STATE COURTS, *supra* note 18, at 14; STATE COURT CASELOAD STATISTICS, 1995: *Supplement to* EXAMINING THE WORK OF STATE COURTS, 1995, at 96 (State Justice Inst. 1996) [hereinafter STATE COURT STATISTICS]. Variation may be due to the increasing use of magistrates (who may not be counted formally as judges) to perform functions traditionally within the province of judges. This trend probably owes more to the interplay between judicial pay and constraints on state funding of courts than to conscious design of state judicial systems.

28. UNITED STATES COURTS, *supra* note 18, at 16; UNITED STATES COURTS, 1999, *supra* note 18.

29. *See* Deborah J. Barrow & Gary Zuk, *An Institutional Analysis of Turnover in the Lower Federal Courts, 1900–1987,* 52 J. POLITICS 457, 460 (1990); James Spriggs & Paul Wahlbeck, *Calling It Quits: Strategic Retirement on the Federal Court of Appeals,* 48 POL. RES. Q. 573, 588 (1995); Emily Van Tassel, *Resignations and Removals: A History of Federal Judicial Service—and Disservice—1789–1992,* 142 U. PA. L. REV. 333, 349 (1993).

30. *E.g.,* Palsgraf v. Long Island R.R. Co., 248 N.Y. 339, 162 N.E. 99, (1928); MacPherson v. Buick Motor Co., 217 N.Y. 382, 111 N.E. 1050 (N.Y. Ct. App. 1916); Vegelahn v. Guntner, 167 Mass. 92, 44 N.E. 1077 (1896). *See* FREDERICK SCHAUER, PLAYING BY THE RULES: A PHILOSOPHICAL EXAMINATION OF RULE-BASED DECISION-MAKING IN LAW AND LIFE 177–78 (Oxford Univ. Press 1991) [hereinafter RULES] ("The common-law judges who receive the most glory, at least from history, are those like Cardozo, for whom the pre-existing rules seem to act more as opportunity for change than as constraint against it"). *See generally,* RICHARD A. POSNER, CARDOZO: A STUDY IN REPUTATION (Univ. of Chicago Press 1990)

[hereinafter CARDOZO]; G. EDWARD WHITE, JUSTICE OLIVER WENDELL HOLMES: LAW AND THE INNER SELF (Oxford Univ. Press 1993).

31. *See, e.g.,* POSNER, CARDOZO *supra* note 30, at 126, 131–34, 142–43 (re Cardozo's judging); *id.* at 139 (re Holmes's performance as a state court judge); WHITE, *supra* note 30, at 481, 487 (suggesting that Holmes's personality and posture of judicial deference, if developed with unmatched clarity, may have accounted for his acceptance by peers). Professor Fred Schauer observes that the opportunity for judges such as Cardozo to break with precedent and at the same time to remain within professional norms is attributable to the fact that Cardozo made his mark as a *common law* judge; unlike most statute law, which consists of mandatory rules, common law rules are, in Schauer's words, both contingent and noncanonical—i.e., they are not conceived as rules in the ordinary sense but rather as presumptive syntheses of the principles and policies that lie behind the rule. SCHAUER, RULES, *supra* note 30, at 174–81. Professor Larry Lessig makes a similar point with respect to constitutional law. *See* Lawrence Lessig, *Understanding Changed Readings: Fidelity and Theory,* 47 STAN. L. REV. 395, 396 (1995). Cardozo himself, though declaring that judges did not merely apply but also *made* law, nonetheless asserted that judicial lawmaking was always in conformity to governing principles of law. *See* BENJAMIN N. CARDOZO, THE NATURE OF THE JUDICIAL PROCESS 111–15, 124–30 (Yale Univ. Press 1921).

32. As noted elsewhere, the question raised by some scholars is not whether the disposition is *predictable* but whether it is *determined* by external authority. *See* Singer, *supra* note 4; discussion *infra,* text accompanying notes 84–102.

33. 347 U.S. 483 (1954).

34. 87 A.2d 862 (Del. Chanc. 1952).

35. 163 U.S. 537 (1896).

36. A highly readable account of the cases leading up to *Brown* is RICHARD KLUGER, SIMPLE JUSTICE (Vintage Books 1977).

37. *See, e.g.,* Alexander Bickel, *The Original Understanding and the Segregation Decision,* 69 HARV. L. REV. 1 (1955); Edmund Cahn, *Jurisprudence,* 30 N.Y.U. L. REV. 150 (1955); Herbert Wechsler, *Toward Neutral Principles in Constitutional Law,* 73 HARV. L. REV. 1, 31–34 (1959). *See also* Michael J. Klarman, *An Interpretive History of Modern Equal Protection,* 90 MICH. L. REV. 213 (1991); Michael J. Klarman, Brown, *Racial Change, and the Civil Rights Movement,* 80 VA. L. REV. 7 (1994); Michael J. Klarman, Brown, *Originalism, and Constitutional Theory: A Response to Professor McConnell,* 81 VA. L. REV. 1881 (1995). Professor Klarman does not debate the *justice* of the decision, but he does debate both its propriety and its effective contribution to evolving constitutional protection for racial justice.

38. *See, e.g.,* HART, *supra* note 10; Oakeshott, *Rule, supra* note 11.

39. *E.g.,* Cahn, *supra* note 37; Ernest van den Haag, *Social Science Testimony in the Desegregation Cases—A Reply to Professor Kenneth Clark,* 6 VILL. L. REV. 69 (1960).

40. *See* Wechsler, *supra* note 37.

41. *See id.*

42. *See* Michael McConnell, *Originalism and the Desegregation Decisions,* 81 VA. L. REV. 947 (1995).

43. It may be possible to square these decisions with an originalist approach to constitutional interpretation that does not value precedent. *See* Gary Lawson, *The Constitutional Case against Precedent,* 17 HARV. J.L. & PUB. POL'Y 3 (1994). But neither *Belton* nor *Brown* makes the case for the decision reached in those terms.

44. *See, e.g.,* McLaurin v. Oklahoma State Regents, 339 U.S. 637 (1950); Sweatt v. Painter, 339 U.S. 629 (1950); Sipuel v. Board of Regents, 332 U.S. 631 (1948); HAROLD W. HOROWITZ & KENNETH L. KARST, LAW, LAWYERS AND SOCIAL CHANGE: CASES AND MATERIALS ON THE ABOLITION OF SLAVERY, RACIAL SEGREGATION, AND INEQUALITY OF EDUCATIONAL OPPORTUNITY 150–85 (Bobbs-Merrill 1969); KLUGER, *supra* note 36. *See also* Shelley v. Kraemer, 334 U.S. 1 (1948).

45. *See* McConnell, *supra* note 42.

46. This claim directly contravenes a major premise of much CLS scholarship. *Compare* Lawrence B. Solum, *On the Indeterminacy Crisis: Critiquing Critical Dogma,* 54 U. CHI. L. REV. 462 (1987), *with* Singer, *supra* note 4.

47. *See* Frederick Schauer, *Prediction and Particularity,* 78 B.U. L. REV. 773 (1998).

48. People v. Rincon-Pineda, 14 Cal.3d 864, 538 P.2d 247, 123 Cal. Rptr. 119 (1975).

49. For a description of this case and its subsequent effects, see Armand Arabian, *The Cautionary Instruction in Sex Cases: A Lingering Insult,* 10 SW N. L. REV. 585 (1978).

50. *Id.* at 615–16.

51. Conversation with Carl McGowan, U.S. Circuit Judge, April 1977.

52. *See* Hugh Baxter, *Managing Legal Change: The Transformation of Establishment Clause Law,* 46 UCLA L. REV. 343 (1998).

53. *See, e.g.,* JOHN W. SALMOND, JURISPRUDENCE 16 (Sweet & Maxwell 1902); Cassius J. Keyser, *On the Study of Legal Science,* 38 YALE L.J. 41 (1929); Christopher Columbus Langdell, *Harvard Celebration Speeches,* 3 L.Q. REV. 123 (1887), *excerpted in* READINGS IN JURISPRUDENCE 645 (Jerome Hall ed., Bobbs-Merrill 1938). *See also* AUSTIN, *supra* note 11; HANS KELSEN, THE PURE THEORY OF LAW (Max Knight trans., 2d ed., Univ. of California Press 1967) (both offering relatively determinate systems of law, but not nearly so mechanical as often depicted today).

54. *See, e.g.,* FRANK, *supra* note 1, at 59, 207, 264–84; Felix S. Cohen, *Transcendental Nonsense and the Functional Approach,* 35 COLUM. L. REV. 809 (1935); Oliver Wendell Holmes, *Law in Science and Science in Law,* 12 HARV. L. REV. 443 (1899); Roscoe Pound, *Mechanical Jurisprudence,* 8 COLUM. L. REV. 605 (1908).

55. *See, e.g.,* Revesz, *supra* note 5; Sisk, Heise & Morriss, *supra* note 5.

56. *See, e.g.,* HOWARD, COURTS, *supra* note 9; Ashenfelter, Eisenberg & Schwab, *supra* note 9.

57. *See, e.g.,* Lucien Arye Bebchuk, *Litigation and Settlement under Imperfect Information,* 15 RAND J. ECON. 404 (1984) [hereinafter *Imperfect Information*]; Keith N. Hylton, *Asymmetric Information and the Selection of Disputes for Litigation,* 22 J. LEGAL STUD. 187 (1993); William M. Landes & Richard A. Posner, *Adjudication as a Private Good,* 8 J. LEGAL STUD. 235 (1979); George L. Priest, *Selective Characteristics of Litigation,* 9 J. LEGAL STUD. 399 (1980); George Priest & Benjamin Klein, *The Selection of Disputes for Litigation,* 13 J. LEGAL STUD. 1 (1984);

Steven Shavell, *Sharing of Information Prior to Settlement or Litigation,* 20 RAND J. ECON. 183 (1989). This presumption should hold, *ceteris paribus,* when the divergence in predicted outcomes is in the direction of optimism for each party (a condition that is commonly met). Although positing risk neutrality facilitates analysis, the statement in text should hold for risk-neutral or risk-averse parties.

58. *See, e.g.,* Robert D. Cooter & Daniel L. Rubinfeld, *Economic Analysis of Legal Disputes and Their Resolution,* 27 J. ECON. LIT. 1067 (1989); Keith N. Hylton, *An Asymmetric Information Model of Litigation,* INT'L REV. L. & ECON. (forthcoming 2001–02) [hereinafter *Asymmetric Information Model*]; Daniel Kessler, Thomas Meites & Geoffrey P. Miller, *Explaining Deviations from the Fifty-Percent Rule: A Multimodal Approach to the Selection of Cases for Litigation,* 25 J. LEGAL STUD. 233 (1996); Geoffrey P. Miller, *An Economic Analysis of Rule 68,* 15 J. LEGAL STUD. 93 (1986); Katherine Spier, *The Dynamics of Pretrial Negotiation,* 59 REV. ECON. STUD. 93 (1992). *See also* Ronald A. Cass, *Principle and Interest in Libel Law after New York Times: An Incentive Analysis, in* THE COST OF LIBEL: ECONOMIC AND POLICY IMPLICATIONS (Everett Dennis & Eli Noam eds., Columbia Univ. Press 1989).

59. *See* Libel Defense Resource Center, *LDRC 1997 Report on Summary Judgment,* 3 LDRC BULL. 1 (1997); Andrew Blum, *Libel Favors the Defense: Study Finds Defendants Win 7 of 10 Dismissals,* NAT'L L. J., May 27, 1996, at A7; *Notebook: Media Defendants' Success Rate,* TV DIGEST, Aug. 18, 1997, at 7.

60. *See* ERIK MOLLER, TRENDS IN CIVIL JURY VERDICTS SINCE 1985, 16–17 (RAND 1996); MARK A. PETERSON, CIVIL JURIES IN THE 1980S: TRENDS IN JURY TRIALS AND VERDICTS IN CALIFORNIA AND COOK COUNTY, ILLINOIS 17–18 (RAND 1987).

61. *See, e.g.,* Lucien Arye Bebchuk, *A New Theory Concerning the Credibility and Success of Threats to Sue,* 25 J. LEGAL STUD. 1 (1996) [hereinafter *Credibility*]; Hylton, *Asymmetric Information Model, supra* note 58. Prediction here encompasses both the expectation of liability and the expected damages or other award. J. Mark Ramseyer & Minoru Nakazato, *The Rational Litigant: Settlement Amounts and Verdict Rates in Japan,* 18 J. LEGAL STUD. 263 (1989). Predictability helps narrow the range of expectations respecting the gain or loss from litigation. Legal predictability, however, is not the sole factor affecting litigation decisions. Different expectations respecting the facts that a decision maker will find plainly affect predictions of litigation success. And the costs associated with litigation also play a role in litigation decisions. Differing predictions of litigation success tend to increase the likelihood of litigation, and those differences increase as unpredictability increases. But the strength of this correlation depends on the significance of the other factors affecting litigation decisions.

62. *See* UNITED STATES COURTS, *supra* note 18, at 14–18; STATE COURTS, *supra* note 18, at 10, 14, 68; Goldstein, *supra* note 18, at 3029.

63. *See* UNITED STATES COURTS, *supra* note 18, at 14–16; STATE COURTS, *supra* note 18, at 68; Goldstein, *supra* note 18, at 3029.

64. *See* STATE COURTS, *supra* note 18, at 17, 71; RICHARD A. POSNER, ECONOMIC ANALYSIS OF LAW 607, § 21.5 n.1 (5th ed., Aspen Law & Bus. 1998); H. LAURENCE ROSS, SETTLED OUT OF COURT: THE SOCIAL PROCESS OF INSURANCE CLAIMS ADJUSTMENT 179, 216 (Aldine-

Atherton, 2d ed. 1980); Patricia M. Danzon & Lee A. Lillard, *Settlement out of Court: The Disposition of Medical Malpractice Claims*, 12 J. LEGAL STUD. 345, 365 (1983).

65. *See, e.g.,* authorities cited *supra* note 57. *See also* John P. Gould, *The Economics of Legal Conflicts*, 2 J. LEGAL STUD. 279 (1973); William M. Landes, *An Economic Analysis of the Courts*, 14 J.L. & ECON. 61 (1971); Richard A. Posner, *An Economic Approach to Legal Procedure and Judicial Administration*, 2 J. LEGAL STUD. 399 (1973).

66. *See* Cooter & Rubinfeld, *supra* note 58, at 1076.

67. *See, e.g.,* FRANK H. EASTERBROOK & DANIEL R. FISCHEL, THE ECONOMIC STRUCTURE OF CORPORATE LAW (Harvard Univ. Press 1991); MARK J. ROE, STRONG MANAGERS, WEAK OWNERS: THE POLITICAL ROOTS OF AMERICAN CORPORATE GOVERNANCE (Princeton Univ. Press 1994); Eugene F. Fama & Michael C. Jensen, *Separation of Ownership and Control*, 26 J.L. & ECON. 301 (1983); Roberta Romano, *A Guide to Takeovers: Theory, Evidence, and Regulation*, 9 YALE J. REG. 119 (1992).

68. Priest & Klein, *supra* note 57.

69. *See* RICHARD A. POSNER, LAW AND LEGAL THEORY IN ENGLAND AND AMERICA 82 n.36 (Clarendon Press 1996) [hereinafter ENGLAND AND AMERICA]; STATE COURTS, *supra* note 18, at 10–11; UNITED STATES COURTS, *supra* note 18, at 14–21.

70. Lon L. Fuller, *The Forms and Limits of Adjudication*, 92 HARV. L. REV. 353, 394–404 (1978) [hereinafter *Forms and Limits*].

71. Cass, *Judging, supra* note 9; Fuller, *Forms and Limits, supra* note 70, at 392.

72. *Id.* I return below to the less common cases, such as constitutional decisions.

73. Even in inquisitorial systems, where judges assume roles played by lawyers in the United States, judges do not exercise significant lawmaking power in ordinary cases. *See, e.g.,* POSNER, ENGLAND AND AMERICA, *supra* note 69, at 33–34.

74. Commentary endeavoring to make the opposite point gravitates to illustrations that diverge sharply from the norm. Consider, for example, Professor Hasnas's argument that law is too imprecise, too contradictory, or otherwise too uncertain to explain judicial decisions. His evidence is the divergence of cases decided almost a century apart, Hasnas, *supra* note 4, at 205, and of cases decided by courts in different jurisdictions, *id.* at 202–3.

Of course, legal rules do change over time, and in some transition periods we may have rules that offer alternative routes to resolve the same issue—and at least arguably differing outcomes depending on which route is chosen. But handy examples of such alternatives lasting for extended periods are hard to come by. The one I know best, the alternative doctrines known as the *right-privilege distinction* and the *unconstitutional conditions doctrine,* involves complex constitutional-law issues, not the matter of ordinary litigation; moreover, the doctrines probably are complements rather than substitutes, so that this would not support the strong indeterminacy hypothesis of Professor Hasnas and others. *See, e.g.,* Seth F. Kreimer, *Allocational Sanctions: The Problem of Negative Rights in a Positive State,* 132 U. PA. L. REV. 1293 (1984); Kathleen Sullivan, *Unconstitutional Conditions,* 102 HARV. L. REV. 1413 (1989); Cass R. Sunstein, *Why the Unconstitutional Conditions Doctrine Is an Anachronism (with Particular Reference to Religion, Speech, and Abortion),* 70 B.U. L. REV. 593 (1990); William W. Van Alstyne, *The Demise of the Right-Privilege Distinction in Constitutional Law,* 81 HARV. L.

Rev. 1439 (1968). *See generally* RICHARD A. EPSTEIN, BARGAINING WITH THE STATE (Princeton Univ. Press 1993).

75. On the incidence of litigation as a consumption good, see Ward Farnsworth, *Do Parties to Nuisance Lawsuits Bargain after Judgment? A Glimpse Inside the Cathedral,* 66 U. CHI. L. REV. 373 (1999).

76. This does not, however, mean that Supreme Court justices behave in radically different fashion than other judges. *See* discussion *infra,* chap. 5, text accompanying notes 55–77.

77. That, of course, is why so much attention is lavished on the means appropriate to constitutional adjudication. *See, e.g.,* ALEXANDER M. BICKEL, THE LEAST DANGEROUS BRANCH: THE SUPREME COURT AT THE BAR OF POLITICS (Bobbs-Merrill 1962); CHARLES L. BLACK, STRUCTURE AND RELATIONSHIP IN CONSTITUTIONAL LAW (Louisiana St. Univ. Press 1969); ROBERT H. BORK, THE TEMPTING OF AMERICA: THE POLITICAL SEDUCTION OF THE LAW (Free Press 1990); DWORKIN, FREEDOM'S LAW, *supra* note 12; JOHN HART ELY, DEMOCRACY AND DISTRUST: A THEORY OF JUDICIAL REVIEW (Harvard Univ. Press 1980); SUNSTEIN, CONSTITUTION, *supra* note 8; Bruce Ackerman, *Discovering the Constitution,* 93 YALE L.J. 1013 (1984); Brest, *supra* note 8; Ronald A. Cass, *Perils of Positive Thinking: Constitutional Interpretation and Negative First Amendment Theory,* 34 UCLA L. REV. 1405 (1987); Klarman, *Anti-Fidelity, supra* note 8; Henry P. Monaghan, *Our Perfect Constitution,* 56 N.Y.U. L. REV. 353 (1981); Frederick Schauer, *An Essay on Constitutional Language,* 29 UCLA L. REV. 797 (1982).

78. *See* William N. Eskridge, Jr., *Overruling Statutory Precedents,* 76 GEO. L.J. 1361 (1990).

79. How important each variable—stakes and uncertainty—is in the appeal calculus depends on assumptions about the precise relationship between parties' stakes and their litigation expenditures and the relationship between expenditures and outcomes. *See, e.g.,* Cooter & Rubinfeld, *supra* note 58, at 1069–82.

80. On the U.S. Court of Appeals, excluding the federal circuit, during the twelve-month period ending September 30, 1999, of the 26,727 cases terminated on the merits after oral hearings or submission on briefs, 78.1% were unpublished opinions. *See* UNITED STATES COURTS, 1999, *supra* note 18, at table S-3. Two decades earlier that figure was about 60%. *See* POSNER, FEDERAL COURTS, *supra* note 2, at 73–74, 173–74.

81. Thomas C. Goldstein, *Statistics for the Supreme Court's October Term 1999,* 69 U.S.L.W. 3076 (July 18, 2000).

82. *Id.*

83. Goldstein, *supra* note 18, at 3029.

84. Posner, *Judges, supra* note 6.

85. Singer, *supra* note 4.

86. Posner, *Judges, supra* note 6.

87. Singer, *supra* note 4, at 19–25.

88. *See, e.g.,* Hasnas, *supra* note 4, at 207–8 ("the normative predispositions of the decisionmakers, rather than the law itself, determine the outcome of cases").

89. Duncan Kennedy, *Legal Formality,* 2 J. LEGAL STUD. 351 (1973); Duncan Kennedy, *The Structure of Blackstone's Commentaries,* 28 BUFF. L. REV. 205 (1979); Duncan Kennedy,

*Form and Substance in Private Law Adjudication,* 89 HARV. L. REV. 1685, 1687–1713 (1976); Singer, *supra* note 4.

90. *See, e.g.,* HOWARD, COURTS, *supra* note 9; Frank B. Cross, *Political Science and the New Legal Realism: A Case of Unfortunate Interdisciplinary Ignorance,* 92 NW. U. L. REV. 251 (1997); Alvin B. Rubin, *Does Law Matter? A Judge's Response to the Critical Legal Studies Movement,* 37 J. LEGAL EDUC. 307 (1987).

91. Cass, *Judging, supra* note 9. *See also* DWORKIN, EMPIRE, *supra* note 12, at 225–66, 353–54, 400–413 (drawing on general sense of judicial constraint in decision making, despite the existence of some unconfined decision space, in opposition to Hartian notion of tightly constrained [rule-bound] core of judicial decision making but largely unconstrained, discretionary periphery).

92. *See, e.g.,* Donald J. Boudreaux & A. C. Pritchard, *Reassessing the Role of the Independent Judiciary in Enforcing Interest-Group Bargains,* 5 CONST. POL. ECON. 1 (1994); Cass, *Judging, supra* note 9; Schauer, *Formalism, supra* note 11.

93. *See* MARY ANN GLENDON, A NATION UNDER LAWYERS: HOW THE CRISIS IN THE LEGAL PROFESSION IS TRANSFORMING AMERICAN SOCIETY (Farrar, Straus & Giroux 1994). The creation of a professional ethos through legal training can be seen as part of a broader process of norm creation, a process sometimes seen as interactive with the enactment of positive law. *See, e.g.,* Lawrence Lessig, *The Regulation of Social Meaning,* 62 U. CHI. L. REV. 943 (1995); Richard H. McAdams, *The Origin, Development, and Regulation of Norms,* 96 MICH. L. REV. 338 (1997); Cass R. Sunstein, *Social Norms and Social Roles,* 96 COLUM. L. REV. 903 (1996).

94. William M. Landes & Richard A. Posner, *The Independent Judiciary from an Interest Group Perspective,* 18 J. LEGAL STUD. 875 (1975) [hereinafter *Independent Judiciary*]. This interest of politicians is not debated, even by those who see its connection to the design of our legal system in very different terms than Professor Landes and Judge Posner. *See* Boudreaux & Pritchard, *supra* note 92.

95. Justice Antonin Scalia views the interaction of judges' behavior and politicians' preferences in a less benign light: he sees judges' departures from textualist approaches to interpretation as encouraging greater willingness by politicians to screen judges for congruence to desired political views. ANTONIN SCALIA, A MATTER OF INTERPRETATION: FEDERAL COURTS AND THE LAW 46–47 (Princeton Univ. Press 1997).

96. *See* Cass, *Judging, supra* note 9; William M. Landes & Richard A. Posner, *Legal Precedent: A Theoretical and Empirical Analysis,* 19 J.L. & ECON. 249 (1976) [hereinafter *Legal Precedent*]; Frederick Schauer, *Precedent,* 39 STAN. L. REV. 571 (1987). The argument here does not require coordinated action in opposition to individual self-interest to arrive at judicial rule-fidelity, a requirement that arguably undermines some other claims about the source of such fidelity. *Compare* Boudreaux & Pritchard, *supra* note 92, *with* Landes & Posner, *Independent Judiciary, supra* note 94.

97. Thurgood Marshall and Ruth Bader Ginsburg—who served on the U.S. Court of Appeals and then on the Supreme Court—may be exemplary in this regard. The basis for appointment of such strong advocates of particular views of justice only to higher appel-

late courts is that such courts are more likely to have cases that are less rule-governed, where judges' intuitions on broader questions of justice are thought to properly affect the principles drawn out of legal authority. Those judgeships both will be more attractive to lawyers with stronger intuitive commitments and will be seen by political leaders as more appropriate positions for such lawyers—so long as the appointee's intuitions are congruent with the politicians' instincts.

98. *See, e.g.,* HART, *supra* note 10; KEETON, *supra* note 9; Cass, *Judging, supra* note 9.

99. Duncan Kennedy, *Freedom and Constraint in Adjudication: A Critical Phenomenology,* 36 J. LEGAL EDUC. 518 (1986). Professor Kennedy does not assert that judges invariably find ways of construing law to fit personal preferences, but he does begin from the proposition that something apart from law informs the judge's "initial sense of how-I-want-to-come-out." *Id.* at 519.

100. *See, e.g.,* SCHAUER, RULES, *supra* note 30, at 173–228.

101. Judge Guido Calabresi of the U.S. Court of Appeals for the Second Circuit has described experiences of this sort, making clear that he seeks a reading of the law that makes a local rule fit with a coherent set of broader legal principles and not merely a bend in doctrine that suits his current intuition.

102. *See* COVER, *supra* note 8 (finding this the right positive description of judges' behavior, even if at times normatively wrong). Although Professor Cover was troubled by judges' failure to stake out the moral high ground when law and morality clashed, the job of judging seems to call for something other than simple fidelity to one's own highest morality. Thus, Adam Smith in his Theory of Moral Sentiments speaks of what the *law's* justice commands as less than what would seem a high morality: "The man who barely abstains from violating either the person or the estate, or the reputation, of his neighbours, has surely very little positive merit. He fulfils, however, all the rules of what is peculiarly called justice." ADAM SMITH, THE THEORY OF MORAL SENTIMENTS 116 (Arlington House 1969; orig. pub. 1759). In Smith's view, a judge's job is to implement a set of mostly negative commands that fall well short of what would make each of us admirable. It is Smith's understanding, not Cover's, that has become both the conventional view of judging and the model that judges believe better describes their job.

103. For an argument that these may be important, see SHEPSLE & BONCHEK, *supra* note 3, at 418.

104. For explication of the role of repeat play in game theory, see, e.g., ROBERT AXELROD, THE EVOLUTION OF COOPERATION (Basic Books 1984); MARTIN J. OSBORNE & ARIEL RUBINSTEIN, A COURSE IN GAME THEORY 133–61 (MIT Press 1994).

## 5. The Weak Agency Model

1. Although not referred to by the name *Weak Agency Model,* the contours of this model (and exposition of its normative attraction) are set out in Ronald A. Cass, *Judging: Norms and Incentives of Retrospective Decision-Making,* 75 B.U. L. REV. 942 (1995) [hereinafter *Judging*].

2. *See, e.g.,* FREDERICK SCHAUER, PLAYING BY THE RULES: A PHILOSOPHICAL EXAMINA-
TION OF RULE-BASED DECISION-MAKING IN LAW AND LIFE 167–96 (Oxford Univ. Press 1991)
[hereinafter RULES]; Isaac Ehrlich & Richard A. Posner, *An Economic Analysis of Legal Rule-
making,* 3 J. LEGAL STUD. 257 (1974); Jerry Mashaw, *Prodelegation: Why Administrators Should
Make Political Decisions,* 1 J.L., ECON. & ORG. 81 (1985). *See also* PHILIP K. HOWARD, THE DEATH
OF COMMON SENSE: HOW LAW IS SUFFOCATING AMERICA 22–31, 50–53 (Random House
1994); Colin S. Diver, *The Optimal Precision of Administrative Rules,* 93 YALE L.J. 65 (1983).

3. *See, e.g.,* Gary Peller, *The Metaphysics of American Law,* 73 CAL. L. REV. 1151 (1985);
Joseph Singer, *The Player and the Cards: Nihilism and Legal Theory,* 94 YALE L.J. 1 (1984); Mark
Tushnet, *Following the Rules Laid Down: A Critique of Interpretivism and Neutral Principles,* 96
HARV. L. REV. 781 (1983).

4. *See, e.g.,* SCHAUER, RULES, *supra* note 2, at 174–81, 188–91, 196–206. For Professor
Schauer's explanation of the terms he employs to capture the relative specificity, conclusiveness, and authoritativeness, see *id.* at 12–14. To the categories of instruction given above,
Ronald Dworkin (following the tradition of Henry Hart and Albert Sacks, Walter Gell-
horn, and other "legal process" scholars) would add another category, *policies,* composed of
consequentialist considerations generally viewed as the realm of political decision makers.
*See* RONALD DWORKIN, TAKING RIGHTS SERIOUSLY 22–28, 90–100 (Harvard Univ. Press 1977)
[hereinafter RIGHTS]; William N. Eskridge, Jr., & Philip P. Frickey, *An Historical and Critical
Introduction to* The Legal Process, *in* HENRY M. HART, JR., & ALBERT M. SACKS, THE LEGAL
PROCESS: BASIC PROBLEMS IN THE MAKING AND APPLICATION OF LAW li, lxxv, cxvii (William
N. Eskridge, Jr., & Philip P. Frickey eds., Foundation Press 1994). Professor Isaac Ehrlich and
Judge Posner note that the line between rules and fuzzier decision guides (standards or principles) blurs when it is recognized that a "rule" can include both regulative instructions and
categorical exceptions to those instructions. Ehrlich & Posner, *supra* note 2. Even so, it is
useful to acknowledge the existence of more and less binding legal constraints, a task to
which the terminology of *rules* and *principles* is frequently assigned. *See* discussion *supra,*
chap. 1, text accompanying notes 39–61.

5. *See, e.g.,* RICHARD A. POSNER, LAW AND LEGAL THEORY IN ENGLAND AND AMERICA
20–37 (Clarendon Press 1996). Commentators often distinguish between common law decision making and statutory interpretation, labeling the former principle-based and the latter rule-based. Though that is a useful heuristic for some purposes, unfortunately, cases do
not neatly fit that division. Some statutory construction (e.g., of the antitrust laws) looks
like classic principle-based decision making. Bodies of precedent in some common law
fields have hardened into rules, and many—most of commercial law and much of contract
law, for example—have been codified in statute law. Although distinctions among bodies
of law are possible, they are not helpful to the discussion in the text.

6. Richard A. Posner, *What Do Judges and Justices Maximize? (The Same Thing Everybody
Else Does),* 3 SUP. CT. ECON. REV. 1 (1995) [hereinafter *Judges*]. *See also* Cass, *Judging, supra*
note 1.

7. Posner, *Judges, supra* note 6.

8. *See, e.g.,* SCHAUER, RULES, *supra* note 2, at 172–73.

9. *See, e.g.,* Tom Stoppard, *Introduction* to ANTON CHEKHOV, THE SEAGULL v–viii (Tom Stoppard trans., Faber & Faber 1997). Stoppard notes the special difficulty of translating a play, which is meant to be spoken and acted. More generally, Stoppard stresses the difficulty of translation and the need for each translator to be guided by a considered answer to the question "What is translation for?"

10. For an explication of the difficulties encountered in one effort at translation, see Walter Kaufmann's comments in HEGEL: TEXTS AND COMMENTARY 1–4 (Walter Kaufmann ed., Anchor Books 1966). *See also* Stoppard, *supra* note 9, at v–xii.

11. *See, e.g.,* Barry Hoberman, *Translating the Bible: Scholars Are Still Laboring to Produce a Contemporary English Version of God's Holy Word,* ATLANTIC MONTHLY, Feb. 1985, at 43–58.

12. Larry Lessig and James Boyd White have also used the heuristic of translation to explore judicial interpretation. *E.g.,* JAMES BOYD WHITE, JUSTICE AS TRANSLATION: AN ESSAY IN CULTURAL AND LEGAL CRITICISM (Univ. of Chicago Press 1990); Lawrence Lessig, *Fidelity as Translation,* 65 FORDHAM L. REV. 1365 (1997) [hereinafter *Fidelity II* ]; Lawrence Lessig, *Understanding Changed Readings: Fidelity and Theory,* 47 STAN. L. REV. 395, 396 (1995) [hereinafter *Changed Readings*]; Lawrence Lessig, *Fidelity in Translation,* 71 TEX. L. REV. 1165 (1993) [hereinafter *Fidelity I* ]. Although there is comfort in other authors' attraction to the same imagery, neither Professor Lessig nor Professor White exactly supports the use of the translation metaphor suggested here. *See* discussion *infra,* notes 32–43 and text accompanying those notes.

13. RONALD DWORKIN, LAW'S EMPIRE 229–31 (Belknap Press 1986).

14. *Id.* at 234–38.

15. *See, e.g.,* BRUCE ACKERMAN, WE THE PEOPLE: FOUNDATIONS (Belknap Press 1991); JOHN HART ELY, DEMOCRACY AND DISTRUST: A THEORY OF JUDICIAL REVIEW (Harvard Univ. Press 1980); Robert Bork, *Neutral Principles and Some First Amendment Problems,* 47 IND. L.J. 1 (1971); Ronald Dworkin, *Hard Cases,* 88 HARV. L. REV. 1057 (1975); Frank I. Michelman, *Law's Republic,* 97 YALE L.J. 1493, 1513–14 (1988) [hereinafter *Republic*]. There is, to be sure, a serious debate over the degree to which a focus on the rare case is the best way to build interpretive theory, but few scholars seem attentive to the issue. For discussion of that question in a particular context, see Vincent Blasi, *The Pathological Perspective and the First Amendment,* 85 COLUM. L. REV. 449 (1985).

16. *See, e.g.,* ACKERMAN, *supra* note 15; Robert H. Bork, THE TEMPTING OF AMERICA: THE POLITICAL SEDUCTION OF THE LAW (Free Press 1990); MICHAEL PERRY, THE COURTS, THE CONSTITUTION, AND HUMAN RIGHTS (Yale Univ. Press 1982); Antonin Scalia, *Originalism: The Lesser Evil,* 57 U. CHI. L. REV. 849 (1989); Frederick Schauer, *Easy Cases,* 58 S. CAL. L. REV. 399 (1986); Frederick Schauer, *The Jurisprudence of Reasons,* 85 MICH. L. REV. 847 (1987) (book review); Tushnet, *supra* note 3.

17. Dworkin's analogy also is deficient as a prescriptive template for judging, because it abstracts away from both limitations on real-world judges and strategic interactions between judges' decisions and actions by other government officials, especially legislators. Elaboration of the concern with Dworkin's work as prescription, however, is beyond the

scope of this book. *Cf.* Cass, *Judging, supra* note 1 (exploring normative derivation of limited role for judges).

18. 40 Mass. App. Ct. (1996).

19. Lumbermens Mutual Cas. Co. v. Malacaria, 40 Mass. App. Ct. 184 (1996); Minasian v. City of Somerville, 40 Mass. App. Ct. 25 (1996).

20. Lumbermens Mutual Cas. Co. v. Malacaria, 40 Mass. App. Ct. 184, 192–94 (1996) (Brown, J., dissenting).

21. Minasian v. City of Somerville, 40 Mass. App. Ct. 25, 28 (1996) (Lenk, J., dissenting).

22. The page count also includes a fair amount of blank space at the end of cases, as each case begins on a separate page.

23. School Comm. of Boston v. Labor Rel'ns Comm'n, 40 Mass. App. Ct. 327 (1996). *See* John Ellemont, *Court Rules Custodian Firings Were Illegal*, BOSTON GLOBE, Apr. 25, 1996, at 31.

24. Ardizioni v. Raymond, 40 Mass. App. Ct. 734 (1996). *See* John Ellemont, *Court Suggests Twins Should Be Reunited*, BOSTON GLOBE, July 19, 1996, at B5.

25. In 1996 Massachusetts was the thirteenth most populous state in the United States, had the third-highest income per capita, and had the third-highest concentration of lawyers. *See* BARBARA CURRAN & CLARA N. CARSON, THE LAWYER STATISTICAL REPORT: THE U.S. LEGAL PROFESSION IN THE 1990S 113 (American Bar Found. 1994); WORLD ALMANAC AND BOOK OF FACTS 1998, at 662–87 (World Almanac Books 1997).

26. Apology for misconstruing Dworkin is probably in order, since almost any position ascribed to Dworkin can be refuted by reference to another Dworkin passage. For that reason, some commentators, when discussing Dworkin's interpretive theories, have begun to refer to Professor Dworkin in the plural. Notably, Dworkin sometimes seems to prefer judges to be very constrained by legal authorities (the approach Professor Mike McConnell refers to as championed by "the Dworkin of Fit") and other times seems to prefer a mode of judging that regards the authorities as minor annoyances along the route to morally satisfying decisions (which McConnell labels "the Dworkin of Right Answers"). *See* Michael W. McConnell, *The Importance of Humility in Judicial Review: A Comment on Dworkin's "Moral Reading" of the Constitution*, 65 FORDHAM L. REV. 1269, 1270–78 (1997).

27. *See* discussion *supra,* chap. 4, text accompanying notes 33–47, 52.

28. *See, e.g.,* Exxon Corp. v. Hunt, 475 U.S. 355, 363 (1986); United States v. Rohm & Haas Co., 2 F.3d 1265, 1270 n.6 (3d Cir. 1993); Ronald A. Cass, *Trade Subsidy Law: Can a Foolish Inconsistency Be Good Enough for Government Work?* 21 L. & POL'Y INT'L BUS. 609 (1990); William N. Eskridge, Jr., *The New Textualism*, 37 UCLA L. REV. 621 (1990); Richard Pierce, *The Role of the Judiciary in Implementing an Agency Theory of Government*, 64 N.Y.U. L. REV. 1239 (1989); Edward Rubin, *Law and Legislation in the Administrative State*, 89 COLUM. L. REV. 309 (1989); W. David Slawson, *Legislative History and the Need to Bring Statutory Interpretation under the Rule of Law*, 44 STAN. L. REV. 383, 388–95 (1992). For evidence that judges see their cases in this light, see Hon. Thomas E. McHugh, *State of the Judiciary Address*, 10 W.VA. LWYR 16 (1996) ("Judges must frequently decide contentious cases through the inter-

pretation of often ambiguous and sometimes conflicting constitutional, statutory, and regulatory provisions").

29. *See, e.g.,* Daniel J. Meador, *Struggling against the Tower of Babel, in* RESTRUCTURING JUSTICE:THE INNOVATIONS OF THE NINTH CIRCUIT AND THE FUTURE OF THE FEDERAL COURTS 195, 200 (Arthur D. Hellman ed., Cornell Univ. Press 1990) (reviewing "areas of the law in which there are multiple precedents pointing in different directions" within a single circuit of the U.S. Court of Appeals); Patricia M. Wald, *Some Thoughts on Judging as Gleaned from One Hundred Years of the Harvard Law Review and Other Great Books,* 100 HARV. L. REV. 887, 904 (1987) ("Escalating caseloads . . . produce inevitable inconsistencies within and among courts").

30. *See, e.g.,* MARY ANN GLENDON,A NATION UNDER LAWYERS: HOW THE CRISIS IN THE LEGAL PROFESSION IS TRANSFORMING AMERICAN SOCIETY 222, 224 (Farrar, Straus & Giroux 1994); SCOTT TUROW, ONE L (Penguin Books 1978).

31. *See, e.g.,* ABNER J. MIKVA & ERIC LANE,AN INTRODUCTION TO STATUTORY INTERPRE-TATION AND THE LEGISLATIVE PROCESS 6 (Aspen Law & Bus. 1997); RICHARD A. POSNER,THE PROBLEMS OF JURISPRUDENCE 265 (Harvard Univ. Press 1990); Frank H. Easterbrook, *Statutes' Domain,* 50 U. CHI. L. REV. 533 (1983); Kenneth W. Starr, *Observations about the Use of Leg-islative History,* 1987 DUKE L.J. 371; Patricia M. Wald, *The Sizzling Sleeper: The Use of Leg-islative History in Construing Statutes in the 1988–89 Term of the Supreme Court,* 39 AM. U. L. REV. 277, 281 (1990).

32. Professor Larry Lessig's use of the metaphor of translation is discussed in the text accompanying notes 33–43 of this chapter. Professor James Boyd White's use of the trans-lation metaphor has captured less attention and is less easily summarized. It is similar to the use here in its attention to the difficulties of capturing the tone, text, and texture of the original in another language, but his basic point is quite different. Professor White argues that translation as commonly conceived is impossible—in law and in everyday life—and that translation is also ubiquitous, as each of us has a personal language: "In the real world all language is idiolect." WHITE, *supra* note 12, at 254. *See id.* at 252–69.

33. *See* Lessig, *Changed Readings, supra* note 12; Lessig, *Fidelity I, supra* note 12; Lessig, *Fidelity II, supra* note 12; Lawrence Lessig, *Translating Federalism:* United States v. Lopez, 1995 SUP. CT. REV. 125.

34. Lessig, *Fidelity II, supra* note 12, at 1399.

35. Lessig, *Changed Readings, supra* note 12, at 410–26; Lessig, *Fidelity II, supra* note 12, at 1365–86.

36. Lessig, *Changed Readings, supra* note 12, at 426–38; Lessig, *Fidelity II, supra* note 12, at 1386–1432.

37. *See, e.g.,* BRUCE ACKERMAN,WE THE PEOPLE:TRANSFORMATIONS (Harvard Univ. Press 1998); GUIDO CALABRESI, A COMMON LAW FOR THE AGE OF STATUTES (Harvard Univ. Press 1982); EDWARD H. LEVI,AN INTRODUCTION TO LEGAL REASONING (Univ. of Chicago Press 1949); MICHAEL PERRY,THE CONSTITUTION IN THE COURTS: LAW OR POLITICS? (Oxford Univ. Press 1993); CASS R. SUNSTEIN,THE PARTIAL CONSTITUTION (Harvard Univ. Press 1993); Bruce Ackerman, *Discovering the Constitution,* 93 YALE L.J. 1013 (1984); William N. Eskridge,

Jr., *Dynamic Statutory Interpretation*, 135 U. PA. L. REV. 1479 (1987); Michelman, *Republic, supra* note 15, at 1493.

38. *See, e.g.,* Vincent Blasi, *The Role of Strategic Reasoning in Constitutional Interpretation*, 1986 DUKE L.J. 696; Henry P. Monaghan, *Our Perfect Constitution*, 56 N.Y.U. L. REV. 353 (1981); Henry P. Monaghan, *Stare Decisis and Constitutional Adjudication*, 88 COLUM. L. REV. 723 (1988); Frederick Schauer, *An Essay on Constitutional Language*, 29 UCLA L. REV. 797 (1982) [hereinafter *Constitutional Language*]; Frederick Schauer, *The Occasions of Constitutional Interpretation*, 72 B.U. L. REV. 729 (1992).

39. Sanford Levinson, *Translation: Who Needs It?* 65 FORDHAM L. REV. 1457, 1461 (1997).

40. *See id.* at 1461–68.

41. RONALD DWORKIN, FREEDOM'S LAW: THE MORAL INTERPRETATION OF THE AMERICAN CONSTITUTION 53 (Harvard Univ. Press 1996).

42. *See* Steven G. Calabresi, *The Tradition of the Written Constitution: A Comment on Professor Lessig's Theory of Translation*, 65 FORDHAM L. REV. 1435 (1997).

43. Abner Greene, *Discounting Accountability*, 65 FORDHAM L. REV. 1489, 1491 (1997).

44. *See, e.g.,* Karl N. Llewellyn, *Remarks on the Theory of Appellate Decision and the Rules or Canons about How Statutes Are to Be Construed*, 3 VAND. L. REV. 395, 399–406 (1950). Justice Antonin Scalia rightly observes that, even if these canons are incomplete guides to interpretation, many commentators—Llewellyn most of all—seriously overstate their deficiencies. *See* ANTONIN SCALIA, A MATTER OF INTERPRETATION: FEDERAL COURTS AND THE LAW 25–27 (Princeton Univ. Press 1997).

45. *See, e.g.,* Armen Alchian & Harold Demsetz, *Production, Information Costs, and Economic Organization*, 62 AMER. ECON. REV. 777 (1972); Kenneth J. Arrow, *The Economics of Agency, in* PRINCIPALS AND AGENTS: THE STRUCTURE OF BUSINESS 37, 49–50 (John W. Pratt & Richard J. Zeckhauser eds., Harvard Bus. School 1985); Michael C. Jensen & William Meckling, *Theory of the Firm: Managerial Behavior, Agency Costs, and Ownership Structure*, 3 J. FIN. ECON. 305 (1976). The same point has been made in specific contexts, such as the liability appropriate for government agents and contractors. *See, e.g.,* Ronald A. Cass, *Damage Suits against Public Officers*, 129 U. PA. L. REV. 1110 (1981); Ronald A. Cass & Clayton P. Gillette, *The Government Contractor Defense: Contractual Allocation of Public Risk*, 77 VA. L. REV. 257 (1991); Jerry Mashaw, *Civil Liability of Government Officers: Property Rights and Official Accountability*, 42 L. & CONTEMP. PROBS. 8 (Winter 1978); Kenneth A. Shepsle, *Official Errors and Official Liability*, 42 L. & CONTEMP. PROBS. 35 (Winter 1978).

46. *See, e.g.,* Jonathan M. Karpov & John R. Lott, *The Reputational Penalty Firms Bear from Committing Criminal Fraud*, 36 J.L. & ECON. 757 (1993); *Symposium: National Conference on Sentencing of the Corporation*, 71 B.U. L. REV. 189 (1991).

47. *See, e.g.,* Albert W. Alschuler, *Ancient Law and the Punishment of Corporations: Of Frankpledge and Deodand*, 71 B.U. L. REV. 307, 308–9 (1991); Ronald A. Cass, *Sentencing Corporations: The Guidelines' White Collar Blues*, 71 B.U. L. REV. 291, 300–305 (1991); Jonathan R. Macey, *Agency Theory and the Criminal Liability of Organizations*, 71 B.U. L. REV. 315, 319, 340 (1991). *See also* authorities cited in note 2 *supra*.

48. *See, e.g.,* UNITED STATES SENTENCING COMM'N, 1996 ANNUAL REPORT 34–35 (Govt.

Printing Office 1997); Paul H. Robinson, *Introduction to Symposium, The Federal Sentencing Guidelines: Ten Years Later,* 91 Nw. U. L. Rev. 1231 (1997); Stephen J. Schulhofer & Ilene H. Nagel, *Plea Negotiations under the Federal Sentencing Guidelines: Guideline Circumvention and Its Dynamics in the Post-*Mistretta *Period,* 91 Nw. U. L. Rev. 1284 (1997); Kate Stith & José A. Cabranes, *Judging under the Federal Sentencing Guidelines,* 91 Nw. U. L. Rev. 1247 (1997); Thomas N. Whiteside, *The Reality of Federal Sentencing: Beyond the Criticism,* 91 Nw. U. L. Rev. 1574 (1997).

49. Frank H. Easterbrook, *Ways of Criticizing the Court,* 95 Harv. L. Rev. 802, 811–31 (1982).

50. *See, e.g.,* Schauer, *Constitutional Language, supra* note 38. Professor Levinson has questioned the use of a translation metaphor for law, given that the language of the original text and of the text application will be the same. Levinson, *supra* note 39, at 1459–60, 1466–68. Given the way legal authorities are written, however, that objection seems misplaced. American economists speak English of a sort, but anyone who has tried to make economic theory accessible to policymakers will understand how much translation the exercise demands and how much this English-English translation looks like German-English (or for some economists, and some public policymakers, Swahili-English). So, too, the translation metaphor seems apt in law.

51. Judicial opinions contain statements of several varieties. In addition to the description of facts, opinions contain a set of arguments and conclusions that are essential to the disposition of the case. Those statements constitute the court's *holding.* All other statements are *dicta* that do not bind later judicial decision makers. The distinction between holding and dictum, however, is often blurry. Moreover, in some cases, nonessential reasoning announced by a court about a legal topic is of greater import—and clearly is understood by the court to be more important—than anything strictly necessary to the decision. Virtually all the significant statements in Marbury v. Madison, 5 U.S. (1 Cranch) 137 (1803), are of this stripe. They are dicta, but it would be a mistake to think of them as throwaway lines that would be of little relevance to future judicial decisions. Understanding what judicial statements have received enough thought and have enough relevance to the case to be considered binding is as much art as science, but it is essential to prediction of judicial decisions. *See* Levi, *supra* note 37.

52. *See, e.g.,* Oliver Wendell Holmes, Jr., *The Path of the Law,* 10 Harv. L. Rev. 457, 457 (1897) ("the object of our study, then, is prediction").

53. *See* U.S. Bureau of the Census, Statistical Abstract of the United States 1999, at 873 (Govt. Printing Office, 119th ed. 1999).

54. *See, e.g.,* Lawrence B. Solum, *On the Indeterminacy Crisis: Critiquing Critical Dogma,* 54 U. Chi. L. Rev. 462 (1987).

55. *See* State Court Caseload Statistics, 1995: *Supplement* to Examining the Work of State Courts, 1995 at 96 (State Justice Inst. 1996); *Statistical Recap of Supreme Court's Workload during Last Three Terms,* 66 U.S.L.W. 3136 (Aug. 12, 1997). *See also* Peter L. Strauss, *One Hundred Fifty Cases per Year: Some Implications of the Supreme Court's Limited Resources for Judicial Review of Agency Action,* 87 Colum. L. Rev. 1093 (1987).

56. President Lyndon Johnson also sought to elevate Associate Justice Abe Fortas to chief justice, but Fortas's nomination was withdrawn before reaching a vote in the Senate. *See* LAURA KALMAN, ABE FORTAS: A BIOGRAPHY 327–56 (Yale Univ. Press 1990).

57. *See* William N. Eskridge, Jr., *Overruling Statutory Precedents,* 76 GEO. L.J. 1361 (1990).

58. Constitutional questions now account for approximately 40% of Supreme Court cases. *See* RICHARD A. POSNER, THE FEDERAL COURTS: CRISIS AND REFORM 83 (Harvard Univ. Press 1985); *The Supreme Court, 1996 Term,* 111 HARV. L. REV. 51, 437–39 (1997). *See also* Seth Kreimer, *Exploring the Dark Matter of Judicial Review: A Constitutional Census of the 1990s,* 5 WM. & MARY BILL OF RTS. J. 427, 434 (1997).

59. Brown v. Allen, 344 U.S. 443, 540 (1953) (Jackson, J., concurring).

60. *See, e.g.,* CHARLES FAIRMAN, HISTORY OF THE SUPREME COURT OF THE UNITED STATES: RECONSTRUCTION AND REUNION, 1864–88, pt. 1, 168–74, 586–88 (Macmillan 1971); CHARLES WARREN, THE SUPREME COURT IN UNITED STATES HISTORY, vol. 1, 222–24, 663–83, vol. 2, 39–42, 418–97 (Little, Brown & Co. 1935).

61. The Religious Freedom Restoration Act of 1993, 107 Stat. 1488, was intended to reverse the Supreme Court's decision in Employment Div., Dept. of Human Resources v. Smith, 494 U.S. 872 (1990). *See* Christopher Eisgruber & Lawrence G. Sager, *Why the Religious Freedom Restoration Act Is Unconstitutional,* 69 N.Y.U.L. REV. 437 (1994).

62. *See* City of Boerne v. Flores, 117 S. Ct. 2157 (1997).

63. The Eleventh, Sixteenth, and Twenty-sixth Amendments reversed, respectively, the Supreme Court's decisions in Chisholm v. Georgia, 2 U.S. (2 Dall.) 419 (1793); Pollack v. Farmers' Loan & Trust Co., 157 U.S. 429 (1895); and Oregon v. Mitchell, 400 U.S. 112 (1975). Each can be seen as a fairly direct response to the particular Supreme Court decision. *See* John J. Gibbons, *The Eleventh Amendment and State Sovereign Immunity: A Reinterpretation,* 83 COLUM. L. REV. 1889, 1894–95 (1983). The Thirteenth Amendment, of considerably more complex provenance, also reversed a Supreme Court decision, specifically the Court's decision in Dred Scott v. Sanford, 60 U.S. (19 How.) 393 (1857). For discussion of *Dred Scott,* its origins, and its aftermath, see, e.g., ROBERT A. BURT, THE CONSTITUTION IN CONFLICT 155–231 (Belknap Press 1992).

64. *See, e.g.,* GLENDON SCHUBERT, THE JUDICIAL MIND: THE ATTITUDES AND IDEOLOGIES OF SUPREME COURT JUSTICES 1946–1963 (Northwestern Univ. Press 1965); JEFFREY A. SEGAL & HAROLD J. SPAETH, THE SUPREME COURT AND THE ATTITUDINAL MODEL (Cambridge Univ. Press 1993).

65. *See* chap. 4, text accompanying notes 16–24, *supra.*

66. *See, e.g.,* ALEXANDER M. BICKEL, THE LEAST DANGEROUS BRANCH: THE SUPREME COURT AT THE BAR OF POLITICS 254–59 (Bobbs-Merrill 1962).

67. THE FEDERALIST Nos. 51 (Hamilton or Madison), 78 (Hamilton); BICKEL, *supra* note 66, at 24–33; Charles L. Black, Jr., *The Supreme Court and Democracy,* 50 YALE L. REV. 188 (1961), *excerpted in* 2 THE CONSTITUTION AND THE SUPREME COURT 418–21 (Louis H. Pollak ed., World Pub. Co. 1966).

68. Thomas G. Goldstein, *Statistics for the Supreme Court's October Term 1995,* 65 U.S.L.W. 3029 (July 9, 1996).

69. Whether those other considerations take on undue weight, or whether considerations at odds with fidelity to extrinsic authority improperly intrude on Supreme Court decision making, is a matter of debate. *See, e.g.,* Thomas W. Merrill, *A Modest Proposal for a Political Court,* 17 HARV. J.L. & PUB. POL'Y 137 (1994) (the Supreme Court in some cases, though professing fidelity to some preexisting legal rule, behaves as though it were invested with authority to render decisions on political grounds rather than being confined to elucidation of principles framed in governing authority). *See also* SCALIA, *supra* note 44, at 16–23, 29–44. A controversial "kiss and tell" account of the Court makes more sweeping contentions regarding the sources and nature of exogenous influence on Supreme Court decisions. EDWARD LAZARUS, CLOSED CHAMBERS (Times Books 1998) (Supreme Court justices are unduly influenced by politically biased law clerks).

70. *See* Hugh Baxter, *Managing Legal Change: The Transformation of Establishment Clause Law,* 46 UCLA L. REV. 343 (1998).

71. *See, e.g.,* ROBERT AXELROD, THE EVOLUTION OF COOPERATION 7–21 (Basic Books 1984); MARTIN J. OSBORNE & ARIEL RUBINSTEIN, A COURSE IN GAME THEORY 16–17, 133–61 (MIT Press 1994); Anatol Rapoport, *Prisoner's Dilemma, in* THE NEW PALGRAVE: GAME THEORY 199 (John Eatwell, Murray Milgate & Peter Newman eds., W. W. Norton 1989).

72. *See* Posner, *Judges, supra* note 6.

73. *See* discussion, *supra,* chap. 4, text accompanying notes 93–95.

74. *See* DANIEL A. FARBER & SUZANNA SHERRY, BEYOND ALL REASON: THE RADICAL ASSAULT ON TRUTH IN AMERICAN LAW (Oxford Univ. Press 1997); GLENDON, *supra* note 30, at 199–253; Ronald A. Cass & Jack M. Beermann, *Throwing Stones at the Mudbank: The Effect of Scholarship on Administrative Law,* 45 AD. L. REV. 1 (1993).

75. *Cf.* GLENDON, *supra* note 30; SOL M. LINOWITZ & MARTIN MAYER, THE BETRAYED PROFESSION: LAWYERING AT THE END OF THE TWENTIETH CENTURY (Chas. Scribner's Sons 1994).

76. The position advanced in the text was certainly the view of many scholars who supported Robert Bork's nomination to the Court, even while voicing skepticism about some of his academic work, and of the scholars who supported Lani Guinier's nomination to the post of assistant attorney general for civil rights. *See, e.g.,* Mary Ann Glendon, *The Probable Significance of the Bork Appointment for Issues of Concern to Women,* 9 CARDOZO L. REV. 95, 99 (1987); Michael W. McConnell, *The First Amendment Jurisprudence of Judge Robert H. Bork,* 9 CARDOZO L. REV. 63 (1987); Daniel D. Polsby, *Analysis of Judge Robert H. Bork's Opinions on Standing,* 9 CARDOZO L. REV. 175 (1987); David Rudenstine, *Foreword—The Bork Nomination: Essays and Reports,* 9 CARDOZO L. REV. 5, 10–11 (1987); Richard B. Stewart, *The Judicial Performance of Robert H. Bork in Administrative and Regulatory Law,* 9 CARDOZO L. REV. 135 (1987); Daniel Klaidman, *Guinier's Backers Play Defense as Confirmation Battle Looms: A War of (and over) Words,* LEGAL TIMES, May 24, 1993, at 1; *The Destruction of Lani Guinier,* CHI. TRIB., Jun. 6, 1993, at C2.

77. *See, e.g.,* WILLIAM H. REHNQUIST, THE SUPREME COURT: HOW IT WAS, HOW IT IS 287–303 (Wm. Morrow & Co. 1987).

78. Bush v. Gore, 121 S. Ct. 525 (2000) (per curiam).

79. *See The Supreme Court Dealt What All Signs Point to as a Mortal Blow to Gore: What's News Worldwide,* WALL ST. J., Dec. 13, 2000, at A1; Yochi Dreazen & Evan Perez, *For Florida Counters, Wait May Be Over: US High Court Overturns State Ruling, Making Hand Count Unlikely,* WALL ST. J., Dec. 13, 2000, at A28; Dan Balz & Charles Lane, *Court Overturns Recounts, Giving Bush the Presidency; Divided Justices Cite Concerns with Timeframe,* WASH. POST, Dec. 13, 2000, at A1; Jeanne Cummings, *Gore Will Call for Unity, but Defend His Actions: Vice President Expected to End Legal Battle,* WALL ST. J. EURO., Dec. 14, 2000, at 1; Charles Lane, *Fla. High Court Says Recount Case Is Over; No New Action Possible after Reversal,* WASH. POST, Dec. 23, 2000 at A6.

80. *See* Jess Bravin, Richard Schmitt & Robert Greenberger, *Supreme Interests: For Some Justices, the Bush-Gore Case Has a Personal Angle,* WALL ST. J., Dec. 12, 2000, at A1; David Roder, *Courts Risk Public Image in Election Case,* WASH. POST, Dec. 12, 2000, at A35; Jeffrey Rosen, *Disgrace,* NEW REPUBLIC, Dec. 25, 2000, at 18; *Rehnquist Hopes Courts Can Avoid Election Fights,* WASH. POST, Jan. 1, 2001, at A2 [hereinafter *Rehnquist Hopes*]; *306 Law Professors Say: By Stopping the Vote Count in Florida, the U.S. Supreme Court Used Its Power to Act as Political Partisans, Not Judges of a Court of Law, available at* <http://www.pfaw.org/news/law_prof .pdf>, visited Jan. 7, 2001 [hereinafter *306 Law Professors*].

81. *See, e.g.,* Touchston v. McDermott, No. 00-15985, 2000 WL 1781942 (11th Cir. Dec. 6, 2000); Seigel v. LePore, No. 00-15981, 2000 WL 1781946 (11th Cir. Dec. 6, 2000); McDermott v. Harris, No. 00-2700, 2000 WL 1693713 (Fla. Cir. Ct. Nov. 14, 2000), *rev'd sub nom.* Palm Beach Canvassing Bd. v. Harris, Nos. SC00-2346, SC00-2348 & SC00-2349, 2000 WL 1725434 (Fla. Nov. 21, 2000); Jacobs v. Seminole County Canvassing Bd., No. 00-2816, 2000 WL 1793429 (Fla. Cir. Ct. Dec. 8, 2000); Gore v. Harris, No. 00-2808, 2000 WL 1770257 (Fla. Cir. Ct. Dec. 4, 2000), *rev'd,* No. SC00-2431, 2000 WL 1800752 (Fla. Dec. 8, 2000).

82. Palm Beach Canvassing Board v. Harris, Nos. SC00-2346, SC00-2348 & SC00-2349, 2000 WL 1725434 (Fla. Nov. 21, 2000); Gore v. Harris, No. SC00-2431, 2000 WL 1800752 (Fla. Dec. 8, 2000).

83. Palm Beach Canvassing Board v. Harris, Nos. SC00-2346, SC00-2348 & SC00-2349, 2000 WL 1725434 (Fla. Nov. 21, 2000).

84. *Id.*

85. Gore v. Harris, No. SC00-2431, 2000 WL 1800752 (Fla. Dec. 8, 2000).

86. *See* discussion *supra,* chap. 1, text accompanying notes 45-61; chap. 5, text accompanying notes 8–47; Cass, *Judging, supra* note 1.

87. *See, e.g.,* Shaw's Supermarkets, Inc., v. NLRB, 884 F.2d 34, 37 (1st Cir. 1989); Adair Standish Corp. v. NLRB, 912 F.2d 854, 865 (6th Cir. 1990); Harold J. Krent, *Reviewing Agency Action for Inconsistency with Prior Rules and Regulations,* 72 CHI.-KENT L. REV. 1187, 1121 (1997).

88. *See generally* chap. 1, *supra.*

89. Bush v. Palm Beach County Canvassing Board, 121 S. Ct. 471 (Dec. 4, 2000) (per curiam).

90. Bush v. Gore, 121 S. Ct. 525, 533 (2000) (per curiam); *id.* at 545 (Souter, J., dissenting); *id.* at 551, 557–58 (Breyer, J., dissenting).

91. *Id.* at 533 (per curiam).

92. *Id.* at 540 (Stevens, J., dissenting); *id.* at 543 (Souter, J., dissenting); *id.* at 550 (Ginsburg, J., dissenting); *id.* at 553 (Breyer, J., dissenting).

93. *Id.* at 545 (Souter, J., dissenting); *id.* at 550 (Ginsburg, J., dissenting); *id.* at 551–52 (Breyer, J., dissenting).

94. *See id.* at 537 (Rehnquist, C. J., concurring).

95. There were at that point several possible scenarios for concluding the election contests apart from the court-supervised recount process: the Florida legislature certifying electors; the U.S. House of Representatives declaring the victor; or certification of two competing sets of Florida electors, followed by congressional selection of the set that would count in the electoral college. Each of these possibilities looked certain to result in a Bush victory. The Florida legislature had a Republican majority and was already moving to certify a slate of electors pledged to George W. Bush. The U.S. House of Representatives, with a Republican majority, would have been predicted to certify a Bush election if the election were thrown into the House. If there were two competing slates of Florida electors, the matter would have gone to the Congress. There would be a Republican majority in the House and an evenly divided Senate (allowing Al Gore, as vice president, to cast the deciding vote in that body). In the event of a split between the House and the Senate over selection of the Florida electors, the selection would have devolved to the governor of Florida. That, of course, was Jeb Bush, George W. Bush's brother. Even if the recount process ultimately had produced a different outcome, all of these other processes, then, were strongly likely to secure a victory for George Bush.

96. *See, e.g.,* Bravin, Schmitt & Greenberger, *supra* note 80; Roder, *supra* note 80; Rosen, *supra* note 80; *Rehnquist Hopes, supra* note 80; *306 Law Professors, supra* note 80.

97. Sanford Levinson, *Return of Legal Realism,* NATION, Jan. 8, 2001, at 8.

98. *306 Law Professors, supra* note 80.

99. Bush v. Gore, 121 S. Ct. 525, 542 (2000) (Stevens, J., dissenting).

## 6. Problems and Progress

1. *See, e.g.,* JAMES A. BUCHANAN & GORDON TULLOCK, THE CALCULUS OF CONSENT: LOGICAL FOUNDATIONS OF CONSTITUTIONAL DEMOCRACY (Univ. of Michigan Press 1962); MANCUR OLSON, THE LOGIC OF COLLECTIVE ACTION (Harvard Univ. Press 1965) [hereinafter LOGIC]; TOWARD A THEORY OF THE RENT-SEEKING SOCIETY (James M. Buchanan, Robert D. Tollison & Gordon Tullock eds., Texas A&M Press 1980) [hereinafter RENT-SEEKING SOCIETY]; George J. Stigler, *Economic Markets and Political Markets,* 13 PUB. CHOICE 91 (1972). For an excellent overview of the literature, see DENNIS E. MUELLER, PUBLIC CHOICE II (Cambridge Univ. Press 1989).

2. *See generally* MUELLER, *supra* note 1; OLSON, LOGIC, *supra* note 1; KENNETH A. SHEPSLE & MARK S. BONCHEK, ANALYZING POLITICS: RATIONALITY, BEHAVIOR, AND INSTITUTIONS (W. W. Norton 1997).

3. *See, e.g.,* BUCHANAN & TULLOCK, *supra* note 1, at 286–89; MANCUR OLSON, THE RISE AND DECLINE OF NATIONS: ECONOMIC GROWTH, STAGFLATION, AND SOCIAL RIGIDITIES

69–73 (Yale Univ. Press 1982) [hereinafter RISE AND DECLINE]. *See generally* RENT-SEEKING SOCIETY, *supra* note 1. A similar view of the positive evidence, though openly skeptical about the value of normative assessments, is SHEPSLE & BONCHEK, *supra* note 2, at 192–94.

4. *See, e.g.,* THOMAS W. HAZLETT & MATTHEW L. SPITZER, PUBLIC POLICY TOWARD CABLE TELEVISION (MIT Press 1997); Richard A. Ippolito & Robert T. Masson, *The Social Cost of Government Regulation of Milk,* 21 J.L. & ECON. 33 (1978); Paul W. MacAvoy, *The Regulation-Induced Shortage of Natural Gas,* 14 J.L. & ECON. 167 (1971); Thomas G. Moore, *The Beneficiaries of Trucking Regulation,* 21 J.L. & ECON. 327 (1978).

5. BRUCE A. ACKERMAN & WILLIAM T. HASSLER, CLEAN COAL/DIRTY AIR (Yale Univ. Press 1981).

6. *See, e.g.,* ALLAN FELDMAN, WELFARE ECONOMICS AND SOCIAL CHOICE THEORY 186–94 (Nijhoff 1980); MUELLER, *supra* note 1, at 376–407, 424–40; AMARTYA K. SEN, CHOICE, WELFARE, AND MEASUREMENT 327–47 (MIT Press 1982); Jules Coleman, *Efficiency, Exchange, and Auction: Philosophic Aspects of the Economic Approach to Law,* 68 CALIF. L. REV. 221 (1980); Duncan Kennedy, *Cost-Benefit Analysis of Entitlement Problems: A Critique,* 33 STAN. L. REV. 387 (1981).

7. *See, e.g.,* RICHARD A. POSNER, THE PROBLEMS OF JURISPRUDENCE 353–92 (Harvard Univ. Press 1990); Ronald A. Cass, *Coping with Life, Law, and Markets: A Comment on Posner and the Law-and-Economics Debate,* 67 B.U. L. REV. 73 (1987); Frank H. Easterbrook, *Developments in the Law—Foreword: The Court and the Economic System,* 98 HARV. L. REV. 4 (1984).

8. *See, e.g.,* Gary S. Becker, *Nobel Lecture: The Economic Way of Looking at Behavior,* 101 J. POL. ECON. 395 (1993).

9. *See, e.g.,* JOHN SILBER, STRAIGHT SHOOTING: WHAT'S WRONG WITH AMERICA AND HOW TO FIX IT 214–41 (Harper & Row 1989).

10. JEFFREY O'CONNELL, THE LAWSUIT LOTTERY (Free Press 1979). *See also* PETER W. HUBER, LIABILITY: THE LEGAL REVOLUTION AND ITS CONSEQUENCES (Basic Books 1988); RICHARD NEELY, THE PRODUCT LIABILITY MESS (Free Press 1988).

11. PHILIP K. HOWARD, THE DEATH OF COMMON SENSE: HOW LAW IS SUFFOCATING AMERICA 6 (Random House 1994) [hereinafter COMMON SENSE].

12. *Id.*

13. *See, e.g.,* Walter Hettich & Stanley Winer, *Economic and Political Foundations of Tax Structure,* 78 AM. ECON. REV. 701 (1988); Julie A. Roin, *United They Stand, Divided They Fall: Public Choice Theory and the Tax Code,* 74 CORNELL L. REV. 62 (1988).

14. Americans with Disabilities Act of 1990, Pub. L. No. 101-336, 104 Stat. 327 (1990), codified as amended at 42 U.S.C. §§ 12101–213 (1994 & Supp. IV 1998).

15. For example, Senator Edward Kennedy, in supporting the passage of the ADA, argued that the legislation represented "an emancipation proclamation" for disabled Americans. 135 Cong. Rec. S10, 789 (daily ed. Sept. 7, 1989), *quoted in* Michael A. Stein, *From Crippled to Disabled: The Legal Empowerment of Americans with Disabilities,* 43 EMORY L.J. 245, 247, & n. 6 (1994). *See also* Justin Dart, Chairman of Taskforce on Rights and Empowerment of Americans with Disabilities, *Hearings before the Committee on Labor and Human Resources and Subcommittee on the Handicapped, S93,* U.S. Senate, 101st Cong., 1st Sess., 252,

438, 500 (May 9, 10 & 16 and June 2, 1989); Nathaniel C. Nash, *Bush and Senate Leaders Support Sweeping Protection for Disabled*, N.Y. TIMES, Aug. 3, 1989, at A1 (pronouncing the act "the most comprehensive civil rights measure in the past two and a half decades").

16. *See* Edward L. Hudgins, *Handicapping Freedom: The Americans with Disabilities Act*, 18 REGULATION 67 (No. 2, 1995); Robert P. O'Quinn, The Americans with Disabilities Act: Time for Amendments, Cato Inst. Pol'y Analysis No. 158 (Aug. 9, 1991); William Raspberry, *Claims against Common Sense*, WASH. POST, Nov. 16, 1998, at A25.

17. *See, e.g.,* HOWARD, COMMON SENSE, *supra* note 11, at 151; *Hearings on S.933 before the Senate Comm. on Labor and Human Resources and the Subcomm. on the Handicapped*, 101st Cong., 1st Sess. (May 9, 1989); Michael J. Norton, *The ADA: A Trap for the Unwary Building Owner*, 23 COLO. LAW. 1293 (1994).

18. *See, e.g.,* HOWARD, COMMON SENSE, *supra* note 11, at 113–15.

19. *See, e.g.,* Hudgins, *supra* note 16; Raspberry, *supra* note 16.

20. *See, e.g.,* J. Freedley Hunsicker, *Accommodation of Writing Disorders in Law School: A Lawyer's View*, 27 J. LEGAL ED. 621, 622–23 (1998). *See generally* Laura F. Rothstein, *Higher Education and Disabilities: Trends and Developments*, 27 STETSON L. REV. 119 (1997).

21. Hunsicker, *supra* note 20, at 622.

22. *See, e.g.,* Phyllis Coleman, Robert Jarvis & Ronald Shellow, *Law Students and the Disorder of Written Expression*, 26 J. LEGAL ED. 1 (1997).

23. HOWARD, COMMON SENSE, *supra* note 11, at 151.

24. *See, e.g.,* GUIDO CALABRESI, A COMMON LAW FOR THE AGE OF STATUTES (Harvard Univ. Press 1982).

25. *See, e.g.,* Babbitt v. Sweet Home Chapter of Communities for a Great Oregon, 515, U.S. 687 (1995); Pension Benefit Guaranty Corp. v. LTV Corp., 496 U.S. 633 (1990); Chevron U.S.A., Inc. v. Natural Resources Defense Council, 467 U.S. 837 (1984).

26. *See, e.g.,* HOWARD, COMMON SENSE, *supra* note 11; authorities cited *supra* notes 1–5.

27. The legal system, indeed, is designed to give deference to administrative decisions. *See* Chevron U.S.A., Inc. v. Natural Resources Defense Council, 467 U.S. 837 (1984).

28. *See* discussion *infra*, text accompanying notes 75–86.

29. Ronald H. Coase, *The Problem of Social Cost*, 3 J.L. & ECON. 1 (1960).

30. ROBERT ELLICKSON, ORDER WITHOUT LAW: HOW NEIGHBORS SETTLE DISPUTES (Harvard Univ. Press 1991); Lisa Bernstein, *Opting Out of the Legal System: Extralegal Contractual Relations in the Diamond Industry*, 22 J. LEGAL STUD. 115 (1992). *See also* Lawrence Lessig, *The Regulation of Social Meaning*, 62 U. CHI. L. REV. 943 (1995); Richard H. McAdams, *The Origin, Development, and Regulation of Norms*, 96 MICH. L. REV. 338 (1997); Cass R. Sunstein, *Social Norms and Social Roles*, 96 COLUM. L. REV. 903 (1996).

31. *See, e.g.,* William M. Landes & Richard A. Posner, *The Private Enforcement of Law*, 18 J.L. & ECON. 875 (1975).

32. HOWARD, COMMON SENSE, *supra* note 11, at 31–38.

33. *See* discussion *supra*, chap. 5, text accompanying notes 46–47.

34. *See, e.g.,* MUELLER, *supra* note 1; GLEN O. ROBINSON, AMERICAN BUREAUCRACY: PUBLIC CHOICE AND PUBLIC LAW (Univ. of Michigan Press 1991); JAMES Q. WILSON, BUREAU-

CRACY: WHAT GOVERNMENT AGENCIES DO AND WHY THEY DO IT (Basic Books 1989). For a brief, cogent explanation of the difficulty of changing this fact, see *id.* at 315–45.

35. *See, e.g.,* WILSON, *supra* note 34, at 325–45.

36. Pub. L. No. 91-596, 84 Stat. 1590, *codified at* 29 U.S.C. §§ 651–78 (1994).

37. 29 U.S.C. § 652 (8) (1994).

38. 29 U.S.C. § 655 (b) (5) (1994).

39. *See* Industrial Union Dept., AFL-CIO v. American Petroleum Institute, 448 U.S. 607 (1981) (*The Benzene Case*).

40. *Id.* at 671 (Rehnquist, J., concurring); American Textile Mftrs. v. Donovan, 452 U.S. 490, 543 (1981) (Rehnquist, J. & Burger, C. J., dissenting).

41. *See* discussion *infra,* text accompanying notes 94–144.

42. JOSEPH A. SCHUMPETER, CAPITALISM, SOCIALISM, AND DEMOCRACY (Harper & Row 1975) (1942).

43. OLSON, RISE AND DECLINE, *supra* note 3.

44. BUCHANAN & TULLOCK, *supra* note 1, at 96–116.

45. *See* Kenneth A. Shepsle, *The Strategy of Ambiguity: Uncertainty and Electoral Competition,* 66 AM. POL. SCI. REV. 555 (1972).

46. *See, e.g.,* Ronald A. Cass & Warren F. Schwartz, *Causality and Coherence in Administration of International Trade Laws, in* FAIR EXCHANGE: REFORMING TRADE REMEDY LAWS 24–90 (Michael Trebilcock & Robert York eds., C. D. Howe Inst. 1990).

47. *See, e.g.,* Ronald A. Cass & Michael S. Knoll, *The Economics of "Injury" in Antidumping and Countervailing Duty Cases: A Reply to Professor Sykes, in* ECONOMIC DIMENSIONS IN INTERNATIONAL LAW: COMPARATIVE AND EMPIRICAL PERSPECTIVES 126–65 (Jagdeep Bhandari & Alan O. Sykes eds., Cambridge Univ. Press 1997).

48. Indeed, ambiguity may often reflect differing bets by well-placed groups on what the nature of that ongoing relationship will be. Each group may believe that it will control interpretation of the ambiguous language, or at least will control interpretation in instances of greatest importance to the particular group. *See* Cass & Knoll, *supra* note 47.

49. The word *general* is intended to exclude private bills, pleas for special relief directed at specified individuals.

50. *See, e.g.,* RICHARD A. EPSTEIN, SIMPLE RULES FOR A COMPLEX WORLD 6–7 (Harvard Univ. Press 1995).

51. *See, e.g.,* EPSTEIN, *supra* note 50, at 7.

52. Mark Seidenfeld, *A Table of Requirements for Federal Administrative Rulemaking,* 27 FLA. ST. U. L. REV. 533 (2000).

53. *Id.*

54. *See, e.g.,* Thomas O. McGarity, *Some Thoughts on Deossifying the RulemakingProcess,* 41 DUKE L.J. 1426 (1992).

55. *Id.*

56. ROBERT H. BORK, SLOUCHING TOWARD GOMORRAH: MODERN LIBERALISM AND AMERICAN DECLINE (HarperCollins 1996); ROBERT H. BORK, THE TEMPTING OF AMERICA: THE POLITICAL SEDUCTION OF THE LAW (Free Press 1990).

57. THOMAS SOWELL, KNOWLEDGE & DECISIONS 229–340 (Basic Books 1980).

58. EPSTEIN, *supra* note 50.

59. *See, e.g.,* PAUL F. CAMPOS, JURISMANIA: THE MADNESS OF AMERICAN LAW (Oxford Univ. Press 1998); WALTER K. OLSON, THE LITIGATION EXPLOSION: WHAT HAPPENED WHEN AMERICA UNLEASHED THE LAWSUIT 152–219 (Dutton 1991) [hereinafter EXPLOSION].

60. SOWELL, *supra* note 57, at 300 (footnotes omitted).

61. *Id.* at 300–301.

62. EPSTEIN, *supra* note 50.

63. *Id.* at 37–39.

64. *Id.* at 30–36, 39–49, 307.

65. *See, e.g.,* PETER H. SCHUCK, SUING GOVERNMENT: CITIZEN REMEDIES FOR OFFICIAL WRONGS (Yale Univ. Press 1983); Ronald A. Cass, *Official Liability in America: Actors and Incentives, in* GOVERNMENT LIABILITY: A COMPARATIVE STUDY 110–44 (John Bell & Anthony Bradley eds., British Inst. Int'l Law 1991).

66. *See, e.g.,* Ronald A. Cass, *Damage Suits against Public Officers,* 129 U. PA. L. REV. 1110 (1981) [hereinafter *Officers*]. *See also* Harold J. Krent, *Preserving Discretion without Sacrificing Deterrence: Federal Governmental Liability in Tort,* 38 UCLA L. REV. 871 (1991).

67. Gregoire v. Biddle, 177 F.2d 579, 581 (2d Cir. 1949), *cert. denied,* 339 U.S. 949 (1950). *See* Cass, *Officers, supra* note 66, at 1123–25 (arguing that *Gregoire* relied on arguments that previously had been deployed in favor of immunity for one class of officials but extended the immunity to officials of a different class).

68. Complaints about lawyers' costs include claims that, beyond a certain level, lawyers' redistributive exertions impose a net cost on the economy. *See, e.g.,* William A. Brock & Stephen P. Magee, *The Invisible Foot and the Waste of Nations: Lawyers vs. the US Economy, in* NEOCLASSICAL POLITICAL ECONOMY: THE ANALYSIS OF RENT-SEEKING AND DUP ACTIVITIES 177 (David C. Collander ed., Ballinger 1984).

69. DANIEL A. FARBER & SUZANNA SHERRY, BEYOND ALL REASON: THE RADICAL ASSAULT ON TRUTH IN AMERICAN LAW (Oxford Univ. Press 1997).

70. Clayton P. Gillette, *The Path-Dependence of the Law, in* THE PATH OF THE LAW AND ITS INFLUENCE 245–71 (Steven Burton ed., Cambridge Univ. Press 2000) [hereinafter *Path Dependence*]; Clayton P. Gillette, *Lock-In Effects in Law and Norms,* 78 B.U. L. REV. 813 (1998) [hereinafter *Lock-In*]. *See also* OLIVER WENDELL HOLMES, JR., THE COMMON LAW 35–37 (Little, Brown & Co. 1881).

71. *See, e.g.,* FREDERICK SCHAUER, PLAYING BY THE RULES: A PHILOSOPHICAL EXAMINATION OF RULE-BASED DECISION-MAKING IN LAW AND LIFE 174–81, 218–28 (Oxford Univ. Press 1991).

72. For explanations of the basis for reliance on prior decisions, see EDWARD H. LEVI, AN INTRODUCTION TO LEGAL REASONING (Univ. of Chicago Press 1949); Larry Alexander, *Constrained by Precedent,* 63 S. CAL. L. REV. 1 (1989); Ronald A. Cass, *Perils of Positive Thinking: Constitutional Interpretation and Negative First Amendment Theory,* 34 UCLA L. REV. 1405 (1987); William M. Landes & Richard A. Posner, *Legal Precedent: A Theoretical and Empirical*

*Analysis,* 19 J.L. & ECON. 249 (1976); Frederick Schauer, *Precedent,* 39 STAN. L. REV. 571 (1987).

73. Gillette, *Lock-In, supra* note 70; Gillette, *Path Dependence, supra* note 70. *See also* Alexander, *supra* note 72; Schauer, *Precedent, supra* note 72.

74. In economic terms, the initial principle may describe a local optimum whereas the divergent decision moves away from a local optimum toward a global optimum. Over some domain, however, the movement will involve increased social costs (or decreased social benefits). Professor Bob Cooter sharpened this point during a colloquium at Boston University School of Law celebrating the 100th anniversary of Holmes's *Path of the Law* address (which was delivered at the dedication of a new building for the school). For exposition of these concepts, and their limitations, in other contexts, see Stanley M. Besen & Garth Saloner, *The Economics of Telecommunications Standards,* in CHANGING THE RULES: TECHNO-LOGICAL CHANGE, INTERNATIONAL COMPETITION, AND REGULATION IN COMMUNICATIONS 177 (Robert W. Crandall & Kenneth Flamm eds., Brookings 1989); Joseph Farrell & Garth Saloner, *Standardization, Compatibility, and Innovation,* 16 RAND J. ECON. 70 (1985); Stan J. Leibowitz & Stephen E. Margolis, *Path Dependence, Lock-ins, and History,* 11 J.L. ECON. & ORG. 205 (1995).

75. *See, e.g.,* Alex Kozinski, *The Case of Punitive Damages v. Democracy,* WALL ST. J., Jan. 19, 1995, at A18.

76. *See* Liebeck v. McDonald's Restaurants, P.T.S. Inc., No. CV-93-02419, 1995 WL 360309 (D.N.M. Aug. 18, 1994); Andrea Gerlin, *A Matter of Degree: How a Jury Decided That One Coffee Spill Is Worth $2.9 Million,* WALL ST. J. EUROPE, Sept. 2, 1994, *available in* 1994 WL-WSJE 2037634.

77. *See, e.g.,* Gerlin, *supra* note 76; Kozinski, *supra* note 75; Aric Press, Ginny Carroll & Steven Waldman, *Are Lawyers Burning America?* NEWSWEEK, Mar. 20, 1995, at 32; Rick Steel-hammer, *Warning: Don't Read the Labels,* CHARLESTON GAZETTE, Sept. 10, 1995, at C1.

78. *See, e.g.,* John L. Mitchell & Jeff Leeds, *Half of Americans Disagree with Verdict,* L.A. TIMES, Oct. 4, 1995, at A1; Laura Mansnerus, *Under Fire, Jury System Faces Overhaul,* N.Y. TIMES, Nov. 4, 1995, at 9; Sally Ann Stewart & Debbie Howlett, *Verdict: Not Guilty—"It's Not Fair, It's Not Right,"* ATLANTA J. & CONST., Apr. 30, 1992, at 1A; Howard Witt, *Simpson Aftershocks Are Still Rumbling in L.A.,* CHICAGO TRIB., Nov. 20, 1995, at 11.

79. *See, e.g.,* Fred Bayles, *Judge Sets Au Pair Free; Ruling Sparks Anger, Relief in Two Nations,* USA TODAY, Nov. 11, 1997, at 1A; Doreen I. Vigue, *Au Pair's Shriek Set the Tone for Public's Outcry,* BOSTON GLOBE, Nov. 11, 1997, at B6; *Neither Side Is Happy,* NEWSWEEK, Nov. 24, 1997, at 6.

80. Gore v. Bayerische Motoren Werke A.G., CV-90-9658 (Jefferson Cir. Ct., Dec. 17, 1990).

81. *See* Richard Severo, *Man Who Tried to Commit Suicide Wins Settlement,* N.Y. TIMES, Dec. 22, 1983, at B3. For a partial justification of this outcome, see Glen O. Robinson, *Probabilistic Causation and Compensation for Tortious Risk,* 14 J. LEGAL STUD. 779 (1985).

82. *See, e.g.,* HOWARD, COMMON SENSE, *supra* note 11.

83. A highly readable account is Brockton Lockwood & Harlan H. Mendenhall, Operation Greylord: Brockton Lockwood's Story (So. Illinois Univ. Press 1989).

84. *See, e.g.,* Amos Tversky & Daniel Kahneman, *Judgment under Uncertainty: Heuristics and Biases, in* Judgment under Uncertainty: Heuristics and Biases chap. 1 (Daniel Kahneman, Paul Slovic & Amos Tversky eds., Cambridge Univ. Press 1982) (discussing the "availability heuristic" and related biases in individuals' assessments of events' probabilities).

85. Gary A. Hengstler, *Vox Populi,* ABA J., Sept. 1993, at 60, 62.

86. *See, e.g.,* Paul Rubin, John Calfee & Mark Grady, BMW v. Gore: *Mitigating the Punitive Economics of Punitive Damages,* 1997 Sup. Ct. Econ. Rev. 179. For a review of both complaints about the civil jury and efforts to correct for perceived distortions created by civil jury practice, see *Developments in the Law—The Civil Jury,* 110 Harv. L. Rev. 1408 (1997).

87. *Compare* Olson, Explosion, *supra* note 59, *with* James A. Henderson, Jr., & Theodore Eisenberg, *The Quiet Revolution in Products Liability: An Empirical Study of Legal Change,* 37 UCLA L. Rev. 479 (1990).

88. The litigation is described in Marcia Angell, Science on Trial: The Case of Medical Evidence and the Law in the Breast Implant Case (W. W. Norton 1996).

89. *See* David Bernstein, *The Breast Implant Fiasco,* 87 Calif. L. Rev. 457, 472–70 (1999).

90. *See* Angell, *supra* note 88; Bernstein, *supra* note 89.

91. *See* David Schadke, Cass R. Sunstein & Daniel Kahneman, Are Juries Less Erratic Than Individuals? Deliberation, Polarization, and Punitive Damages (Univ. of Chicago Law School, John D. Olin Law & Econ. Working Paper No. 81, Sept. 1999).

92. *See* Daubert v. Merrill-Dow Pharmaceuticals, 509 U.S. 579 (1993).

93. *See* Bernstein, *supra* note 89, at 461.

94. *See, e.g.,* Kenneth J. Arrow, Social Choice and Individual Values (Yale Univ. Press, 2d ed. 1963).

95. *But see* Herbert A. Simon, Reason in Human Affairs 84–87 (Stanford Univ. Press 1983); James G. March, *Bounded Rationality, Ambiguity, and the Engineering of Choice,* 9 Bell J. Econ. 587 (1978).

96. The best-known exposition of this point is in Arrow, *supra* note 94. For a cogent discussion, see Mueller, *supra* note 1, at 388–92.

97. *See, e.g.,* Kenneth W. Simons, *Equality as a Comparative Right,* 65 B.U. L. Rev. 387 (1985).

98. *See, e.g.,* Hans Kelsen, General Theory of Law and State 401–4 (Anders Wedberg, trans., Harvard Univ. Press 1945).

99. Lon Fuller, The Morality of Law 111–13 (Yale Univ. Press, rev. ed. 1969).

100. *See* discussion *supra,* chap. 1, text accompanying notes 39–61. *See also* Ronald A. Cass, *Judging: Norms and Incentives of Retrospective Decision-Making,* 75 B.U. L. Rev. 942 (1995).

101. Fuller, *supra* note 99, at 90–93, 210–11. *See also* Joseph Raz, The Concept of a Legal System 210, 232–34 (Oxford Univ. Press, 2d ed. 1980).

102. *See, e.g.,* Adam Clymer, *Even When Blind, Justice Feels the Political Winds,* N.Y. Times, Nov. 26, 2000, at 4-1, 4-4.

103. *See, e.g.,* MARTIN MAYER, THE GREATEST-EVER BANK ROBBERY: THE COLLAPSE OF THE SAVINGS AND LOAN INDUSTRY 188–225 (Chas. Scribner's Sons 1990) (criticizing lax enforcement of rules against Charles Keating, whose wealth allowed influence with politicians and regulators); ROBERT SHERRILL, THE LAST KENNEDY 207–11 (Dial Press 1976) (asserting impropriety of decision respecting Sen. Edward Kennedy's responsibility for death of Mary Jo Kopechne from accident at Chappaquiddick); Clifford Krauss, *State Department Concedes Flaws in Investigation of Envoy,* N.Y. TIMES, Dec. 13, 1997, at A16 (reporting criticism of burial of nonveteran, wealthy campaign contributor and fund-raiser Larry Lawrence in Arlington National Cemetery); Donald J. Newman, *The Agnew Plea Bargain,* 10 CRIM. L. BULL. 85 (1974) (impropriety of Vice President Spiro Agnew's plea agreement following charges that he received bribes).

104. *See* Don Phillips, *Top Wright Aide Quits over Criminal Record; Mack Brutally Attacked Woman in 1973,* WASH. POST, May 12, 1989, at A1. For the underlying story, see Ken Ringle, *Memory and Anger: A Victim's Story; Watching As the Man Who Tried to Kill Her Rose to Power,* WASH. POST, May 4, 1989, at B1.

105. *See, e.g.,* Marc Fisher, *The Simpson Legacy: Transformed Attitudes toward Justice System,* WASH. POST, Oct. 6, 1995, at A1; Robert Scheer, *Justice for the Rich Isn't Justice for All; Simpson Won Acquittal Because He Played the Money Card, Not the Race Card,* L.A. TIMES, Oct. 8, 1995, at M5; Stuart Taylor, *Judicious Jury Reform,* AM. LAWYER, Jan./Feb. 1996, at 42.

106. *See* Richard McAdams, *Cooperation and Conflict: The Economics of Group Status Production and Race Discrimination,* 108 HARV. L. REV. 1003 (1995); Richard McAdams, *Relative Preferences,* 102 YALE L.J. 1 (1992).

107. *See, e.g.,* PATRICK S. ATIYAH & ROBERT S. SUMMERS, FORM AND SUBSTANCE IN ANGLO-AMERICAN LAW: A COMPARATIVE STUDY OF LEGAL REASONING, LEGAL THEORY, AND LEGAL INSTITUTIONS 169–75 (Oxford Univ. Press 1987); *Developments in the Law—The Civil Jury,* 110 HARV. L. REV. 1408 (1997) [hereinafter *Developments—Jury*].

108. ATIYAH & SUMMERS, *supra* note 107, at 175–77.

109. *See, e.g,* ROBINSON, *supra* note 34, at 130–36, 144–49; WILSON, *supra* note 34, at 74–89.

110. *See* FULLER, *supra* note 99, at 65–70. The same difficulty of identifying the relevant variables and the effects of slight (perhaps unobservable) differences in those variables explains the appearance of chaos in other complex systems. *See* JAMES GLEICK, CHAOS: MAKING A NEW SCIENCE 18–30 (Penguin Books 1987).

111. *See* FULLER, *supra* note 99, at 81–91; LEVI, *supra* note 72.

112. RICHARD A. POSNER, LAW AND LEGAL THEORY IN ENGLAND AND AMERICA 80 (Clarendon Press 1996) [hereinafter ENGLAND AND AMERICA].

113. *Id.*

114. RICHARD A. POSNER, THE FEDERAL COURTS: CRISIS AND REFORM 58–59 (Harvard Univ. Press 1985).

115. *Id.*

116. *See id.* at 64; ADMINISTRATIVE OFFICE OF THE UNITED STATES COURTS, JUDICIAL

BUSINESS OF THE UNITED STATES COURTS: 1999 REPORT OF THE DIRECTOR (Govt. Printing Office 1999), *available at* <www.uscourts.gov-/judbus1999/index.html>.

117. *See* Yates v. BMW of North America, 642 So.2d 937 (Ala. Civ. App. 1993) (award of compensatory damages of $4,000).

118. BMW of North America v. Gore, 646 So.2d 619, 627 (Ala. 1994). Fourteen of these vehicles were sold in Alabama. *See id.*

119. O'CONNELL, *supra* note 10.

120. This seemingly obvious observation turns out, like much about litigation, to be considerably more complicated. The effects of inconsistency on litigation of weak cases depend, among other things, on the precise definition of "weak cases." These can be conceived as cases that in a world of perfect information would fail, as cases that have a high probability of failure but nonetheless sufficiently high stakes if successful that litigation is a rational bet, or as cases that are poor litigation bets (because their expected litigation cost exceeds their expected payout independent of any settlement prospects). *See* Robert G. Bone, *Modeling Frivolous Suits*, 145 U. PA. L. REV. 519 (1997).

121. *See, e.g.*, Lucien Arye Bebchuk, *A New Theory Concerning the Credibility and Success of Threats to Sue*, 25 J. LEGAL STUD. 1 (1996); Bone, *supra* note 120; Robert D. Cooter & Daniel L. Rubinfeld, *Economic Analysis of Legal Disputes and Their Resolution*, 27 J. ECON. LIT. 1067 (1989); Keith N. Hylton, *Asymmetric Information and the Selection of Disputes for Litigation*, 22 J. LEGAL STUD. 187 (1993); Steven Shavell, *Sharing of Information Prior to Settlement or Litigation*, 20 RAND J. ECON. 183 (1989).

122. *See* Bone, *supra* note 120, at 389–93; Cooter & Rubinfeld, *supra* note 121.

123. *See, e.g.*, WALTER K. OLSON, THE EXCUSE FACTORY: HOW EMPLOYMENT LAW IS PARALYZING THE AMERICAN WORKPLACE (Free Press 1997); OLSON, EXPLOSION, *supra* note 59. *See also* STEVEN SHAVELL, ECONOMIC ANALYSIS OF ACCIDENT LAW 80–83 (Harvard Univ. Press 1987).

124. *See, e.g.*, OLSON, EXPLOSION, *supra* note 59; SILBER, *supra* note 9, at 235.

125. For one example of a setting where that is *not* the case, see Cass, *Officers, supra* note 66.

126. *See generally* VERDICT: ASSESSING THE CIVIL JURY SYSTEM (Robert E. Litan ed., Brookings 1993) (arguments for reexamination of the civil jury, for retention of the present civil jury system, and for various modest reforms) [hereinafter LITAN, VERDICT]. *See also* Samuel R. Gross & Kent Syverud, *Don't Try: Civil Jury Verdicts in a System Geared to Settlement*, 44 UCLA L. REV. 1 (1996).

127. *See, e.g.*, CONTRACT WITH AMERICA: THE BOLD PLAN BY REP. NEWT GINGRICH, REP. DICK ARMEY, AND THE HOUSE REPUBLICANS TO CHANGE THE NATION 11, 145–46, 150–52 (Times Books 1994) [hereinafter CONTRACT WITH AMERICA]; SILBER, *supra* note 9, at 232–35; Dan Quayle, *Civil Justice Reform*, 41 AM. U.L. REV. 559, 567–68 (1992); Walter Olson & David Bernstein, *Loser Pays: Where Next?* 55 MD. L. REV. 1161 (1996); Dick Thornburgh, *America's Civil Justice Dilemma: The Prospects for Reform*, 55 MD. L. REV. 1074, 1086–87 (1996).

128. *See, e.g,* CONTRACT WITH AMERICA, *supra* note 127, at 143, 147, 153–54; Dorsey D. Ellis, Jr., *Punitive Damages, Due Process, and the Jury*, 40 ALA. L. REV. 975 (1989); Peter Huber,

*No Fault Punishment,* 40 ALA. L. REV. 1037 (1989); Marcel Kahan & Bruce Tuckman, *Special Levies on Punitive Damages: Decoupling Agency Problems and Litigation Expenditures,* 15 INT'L REV. L. & ECON. 175 (1995); Rubin, Calfee & Grady, *supra* note 86; Thornburgh, *supra* note 127, at 1085–86.

129. *See, e.g.,* Arthur J. Francel & Stevens Point, *Tobacco Verdict: Smokers Shouldn't Be Rewarded,* MILWAUKEE J. SENTINEL, July 26, 2000, at 10A; Thomas P. Houston, *Big Tobacco Should Pay Price,* CHI. TRIBUNE, July 24, 2000, at N14; R. C. Longworth, *This Verdict's Not Just Smoke: The Jury May Not Have Hurt Big Tobacco's Business with Its Huge Award, but Don't Discount the Importance of a Good Roar of Moral Outrage,* CHI. TRIBUNE, July 23, 2000, at C1; Scott Robinson, *Big Tobacco, Big Settlement: Suffocating Award Fitting for Industry Whose Products Kill Millions,* DENVER ROCKY MTN. NEWS, July 23, 2000, at 1B.

130. *See* Leonard H. Glantz, *Suing Tobacco Companies: Impact of a Landmark Case,* ENCYCLOPEDIA BRITANNICA: MEDICAL AND HEALTH ANNUAL (Encyclopedia Britannica 1994); Rick Bragg & Sarah Kershaw, *Juror Says a "Sense of Mission" Led to Huge Tobacco Damages,* N.Y. TIMES, July 16, 2000, at A1.

131. *See* Barry Meier, *Jury Finds That Cigarettes Caused Smokers' Diseases,* N.Y. TIMES Apr. 8, 2000, at A7.

132. *See* UNITED NATIONS MONTHLY BULLETIN OF STATISTICS (Aug. 2000), *available at* <http://www.un.org/Depts/unsd/sd_economic.htm> (1998 data). *See also* CIA WORLD FACT BOOK (1999) (listing 157 of 194 nations with 1998 GDP below $145 billion, figures that would place annual gross domestic product for 80% of the world's nations below the punitive-damage award in Florida).

133. *See, e.g.,* Kozinski, *supra* note 75. The cases are, in truth, more complicated than the first impression suggests. That does not mean that they are decided rightly, only that there is more justification than the capsule description accessible to the public admits. *See* discussion *infra,* text accompanying note 174.

134. *See, e.g.,* POSNER, ENGLAND AND AMERICA, *supra* note 112, at 72–76, 89–94, 106–10; Bone, *supra* note 120.

135. *See, e.g.,* John Hause, *Indemnity, Settlement, and Litigation, or, I'll Be Suing You,* 18 J. LEGAL STUD. 157 (1989); Avery Katz, *Measuring the Demand for Litigation: Is the English Rule Really Cheaper?* 3 J.L. ECON. & ORG. 127 (1987); Edward Snyder & James W. Hughes, *The English Rule for Allocating Legal Costs: Evidence Confronts Theory,* 6 J.L., ECON. & ORG. 345 (1990).

136. *See* A. Mitchell Polinsky & Daniel L. Rubinfeld, *Economic Analysis of Legal Disputes and Their Resolution,* 27 J. ECON. LIT. 1067 (1989).

137. *See, e.g.,* Dorsey D. Ellis, Jr., *Fairness and Efficiency in the Law of Punitive Damages,* 56 S. CAL. L. REV. 1, 73–76 (1982). *But see* Tom Baker, *Reconsidering Insurance for Punitive Damages,* 1998 WIS. L. REV. 101 (1998).

138. *See, e.g.,* W. Kip Viscusi, *The Social Costs of Punitive Damages against Corporations in Environmental and Safety Torts,* 87 GEO. L.J. 285 (1998).

139. *Developments in the Law—The Paths of Civil Litigation,* 113 HARV. L. REV. 1752, 1784 (2000) [hereinafter, *Developments—Civil Litigation*]. The authors also note that juries, lack-

ing a coherent theory for assessing punitives, "sometimes award more than a plaintiff claims, and judges today adjust the size of jury verdicts more routinely than in the past." *Id.* at 1784 (footnote omitted). *See also* Cass R. Sunstein, Daniel Kahneman & David Schadke, *Assessing Punitive Damages (with Notes on Cognition and Valuation in Law)*, 107 YALE L.J. 2071 (1998).

140. *See* A. Mitchell Polinsky, *Are Punitive Damages Really Insignificant, Predictable, and Rational? A Comment on Eisenberg et al.*, 26 J. LEGAL STUD. 663 (1997). *But see* Theodore Eisenberg, John Goerdt, Brian Ostrom, David Rottman & Martin Wells, *The Predictability of Punitive Damages*, 26 J. LEGAL STUD. 623 (1997).

141. *See, e.g.*, Robert D. Cooter, *Punitive Damages for Deterrence: When and How Much?* 40 ALA. L. REV. 1143 (1989); A. Mitchell Polinsky & Steven Shavell, *Punitive Damages: An Economic Assessment*, 111 HARV. L. REV. 869, 874–75 (1998).

142. *See* Cooter, *supra* note 141; Polinsky & Shavell, *supra* note 141.

143. *See* discussion *supra*, chap. 4, text accompanying notes 33–47, 52.

144. *See* Bone, *supra* note 120; J. Robert S. Prichard, *A Systemic Approach to Comparative Law: The Effect of Cost, Fee, and Financing Rules on the Development of the Substantive Law*, 17 J. LEGAL STUD. 451, 465–66 (1988).

145. *See, e.g.*, Peter H. Schuck, *Mapping the Debate on Jury Reform*, in LITAN, VERDICT, *supra* note 126, at 306–18; *Developments—Jury*, *supra* note 107.

146. *See, e.g.*, MARK A. DOMBROFF, DISCOVERY 4–6 (1986); JACK FRIEDENTHAL, MARY KAY KANE & ARTHUR R. MILLER, CIVIL PROCEDURE 386–91 (3d ed., West 1999); Bruce L. Hay, *Civil Discovery: Its Effects and Optimal Scope*, 23 J. LEGAL STUD. 481 (1994).

147. *See, e.g.*, DOMBROFF, *supra* note 146, at 6–8; JOSEPH L. EBERSOLE & BARLOW BURKS, DISCOVERY PROBLEMS IN CIVIL CASES 18–29 (Fed. Judicial Ctr. 1980).

148. *Compare* Chardon v. Fumero Soto, 462 U.S. 650, 659 (1983); American Pipe & Const. Co. v. Utah, 414 U.S. 538, 553–54 (1974), *with* Castano v. American Tobacco Co., 84 F.3d 734, 736 (5th Cir. 1996); Peter H. Schuck, *Mass Torts: An Institutional Evolutionist Perspective*, 80 CORNELL L. REV. 941, 958 (1995). *See Developments—Civil Litigation*, *supra* note 139, at 1810–11.

149. *See* DOMBROFF, *supra* note 146, at 66–69; Robert Ehrenbard, *Cutting Discovery Costs through Interrogatories and Document Requests*, in ADVOCACY SKILLS: DISCOVERY (U.S. Dept. of Justice 1984).

150. *See, e.g.*, Bone, *supra* note 120.

151. *See, e.g.*, Peter A. Diamond, *Search Theory*, in THE NEW PALGRAVE: ALLOCATION, INFORMATION, AND MARKETS 271, 272–73 (John Eatwell, Murray Milgate & Peter Newman eds., W. W. Norton 1989). *See also* Bone, *supra* note 120.

152. See, e.g., FRIEDENTHAL ET AL., *supra* note 146, at 428–31; Bone, *supra* note 120.

153. *See, e.g.*, Ronald A. Cass & Keith N. Hylton, *Antitrust Intent*, 74 S. CAL. L. REV. 657 (2001).

154. Reduced information and retraining requirements yield similar benefits in numerous settings. *See, e.g.*, Stanley M. Besen & Garth Saloner, *The Economics of Telecommunications Standards*, in CHANGING THE RULES: TECHNOLOGICAL CHANGE, INTERNATIONAL COMPETITION, AND REGULATION IN COMMUNICATIONS 177 (Robert W. Crandall & Kenneth Flamm eds.,

Brookings Inst. 1989); Ronald A. Cass, *Copyright, Licensing, and the "First Screen,"* U. MICH. J. TELECOMM. & TECH. 35, 59–61 (1999); Joseph Farrell & Garth Saloner, *Standardization, Compatibility, and Innovation,* 16 RAND J. ECON. 70 (1985).

155. JAMES S. KAKALIK, ET AL., JUST, SPEEDY, AND INEXPENSIVE? AN EVALUATION OF JUDICIAL CASE MANAGEMENT UNDER THE CIVIL JUSTICE REFORM ACT 16, 26–27 (RAND 1996).

156. *See, e.g.,* Robert H. Transgurd, *Mass Trials in Mass Tort Cases: A Dissent,* 1989 U. ILL. L. REV. 69, 79 (arguing that "the asserted efficiency of mass trials . . . rests on a most unsteady foundation").

157. *See* In Re A.H. Robins, Co., 880 F. 2d 709, 732 (4th Cir. 1989); Arthur R. Miller, *Of Frankenstein Monsters and Shining Knights: Myth, Reality, and the "Class Action Problem,"* 92 HARV. L. REV. 664, 666 (1979); *Developments—Civil Litigation, supra* note 139, at 1810.

158. *See* discussion *supra,* text accompanying notes 88–93.

159. *See, e.g.,* John C. Coffee, Jr., *Rethinking the Class Action: A Policy Primer on Reform,* 62 IND. L.J. 625 (1987); Vikramaditya S. Khanna, *Corporate Criminal Liability: What Purpose Does It Serve?* 109 HARV. L. REV. 1477 (1996); John R. Lott, Jr., *An Attempt at Measuring the Total Monetary Penalty from Convictions: The Importance of an Individual's Reputation,* 21 J. LEGAL STUD. 159 (1992).

160. *See* Castano v. American Tobacco Co., 84 F.3d 734, 746 (5th Cir. 1996) (noting the extraordinary risks associated with class-action verdicts that all defendants face). One-way preclusion is not automatic, instead resting on considerations relevant to the likelihood that the decision represents a finding that would be arrived at if the issue were relitigated. Because we cannot know how likely that is if the issue has not been litigated repeatedly, there is a substantial risk to defendants whenever there is a prospect for follow-on litigation. One loss after many repeated victories may not spell disaster; but an early loss might, and repeated victories do not invariably preclude later losses.

161. *See, e.g., Developments—Civil Litigation, supra* note 139, at 1797–98.

162. *See, e.g.,* Polinsky, *supra* note 140.

163. *See* Eisenberg et al., *supra* note 140.

164. *See, e.g., Reductions: Verdicts Reduced after Trial,* NAT'L. L.J., Feb. 22, 1999, at C16; *Developments—Civil Litigation, supra* note 139, at 1783.

165. *See, e.g.,* Susan Koniak & George M. Cohen, *Under Cloak of Settlement,* 82 VA. L. REV. 1051 (1996).

166. *See, e.g.,* STEPHEN GOLDBERG, FRANK E. A. SANDER & NANCY ROGERS, DISPUTE RESOLUTION: NEGOTIATION, MEDIATION, AND OTHER PROCESSES (3d ed., Aspen Law & Bus. 1999); Martin C. Karamon, *ADR on the Internet,* 11 OHIO ST. J. DISP. RESOL. 537 (1996); Jack M. Sabatino, *ADR as "Litigation Lite": Procedural and Evidentiary Norms Embedded within Alternative Dispute Resolution,* 47 EMORY L.J. 1289 (1998); David B. Lipsky & Ronald L. Seeber, *Patterns of ADR Use in Corporate Disputes,* DISP. RESOL. J., Feb. 1999, at 66, 66–71.

167. *See* Jeffrey W. Stempel, *Recent Case Developments,* 6 CONN. INS. L.J. 539, 541 (2000); Katherine Van Wezel Stone, *Mandatory Arbitration of Individual Employment Rights: The Yellow Dog Contract of the 1990s,* 73 DENVER U. L. REV. 1017, 1039 (1996). The courts have, how-

ever, upheld the legality of arbitral awards of punitive damages where consistent with an arbitration accord. *See* Mastrobuono v. Shearson Lehman Hutton, Inc., 514 U.S. 52 (1995).

168. *See* Frances McGovern, *Beyond Efficiency: A Bevy of ADR Justifications (An Unfootnoted Summary)*, DISP. RESOL. MAG., Summer 1997, at 12, 13; Frank E. A. Sander & Stephen Goldberg, *Fitting the Forum to the Fuss: A User-Friendly Guide to Selecting an ADR Procedure*, 10 NEGOTIATION J. 49 (1994).

169. *See* KAKALIK ET AL., *supra* note 155; *Developments—Civil Litigation, supra* note 139, at 1858–59.

170. BMW of North America, Inc. v. Gore, 517 U.S. 599 (1996); Liebeck v. McDonald's Restaurants, P.T.S. Inc., No. CV-93-02419, 1995 WL 360309 (D.N.M. Aug. 18, 1994).

171. BMW of North America, Inc. v. Gore, 701 So.2d 507, 515 (Ala. 1997).

172. *See* Reynolds Holding, *Legal Cases Are Often Less Absurd Than They Seem*, S.F. CHRON., May 27, 1996, at E2.

173. *See* Sally Ann Stewart & Haya El Nasser, *King Case Sparks Outrage; 2 Killed and 72 Injured*, USA TODAY, Apr. 30, 1992, at 1A; Sheryl Stolberg, *L.A. Riots Weigh Heavily on Scales of Justice System, Courts*, L.A. TIMES, May 14, 1992, at A1; Isabel Wilkerson, *Riots in Los Angeles; Around the Nation, Acquittal in Beating Raises Fears over Race Relations*, N.Y. TIMES, May 1, 1992, at A23; Witt, *supra* note 78.

174. *See* Liebeck v. McDonald's Restaurants, P.T.S. Inc., No. CV-93-02419, 1995 WL 360309 (D.N.M. Aug. 18, 1994).

175. DEBORAH HENSLER ET AL., TRENDS IN TORT LITIGATION: THE STORY BEHIND THE STATISTICS 32–33 (RAND 1987); Theodore Eisenberg & Stewart Schwab, *The Reality of Constitutional Tort Litigation*, 72 CORNELL L. REV. 641 (1987); Henderson & Eisenberg, *supra* note 87.

176. *See* TROYEN BRENNAN, JUST DOCTORING: MEDICAL ETHICS IN THE LIBERAL STATE 135–59 (Univ. of California Press 1991); OFFICE OF TECHNOLOGY ASSESSMENT, DEFENSIVE MEDICINE AND MEDICAL MALPRACTICE 74 (Govt. Printing Office 1994); Patricia Danzon, *An Economic Analysis of the Medical Malpractice System*, 1 J. BEHAV. STUD. & L. 39 (1983); Patricia Danzon, *The Frequency and Severity of Malpractice Claims: New Evidence*, 49 L. & CONTEMP. PROBS. 57 (Spring 1986); Kenneth Jost, *Warring over Medical Malpractice*, ABA J. 68, 71 (May 1993); Glen O. Robinson, *The Medical Malpractice Crisis of the 1970s: A Retrospective*, 49 L. & CONTEMP. PROBS. 5 (Spring 1986). *See also* Frances H. Miller, *Medical Discipline in the Twenty-First Century: Are Purchasers the Answer?* 60 L. & CONTEMP. PROBS. 31 (Winter 1997) (observing role played by decisions on discipline of health care providers). But note that insurance rules to which medical practitioners respond are derivative of liability, even if not a straight-line derivation. *See* W. Kip Viscusi & Patricia Born, *Medical Malpractice Insurance in the Wake of Liability Reform*, 24 J. LEGAL STUD. 463 (1995).

177. POSNER, ENGLAND AND AMERICA, *supra* note 112, at 78.

178. *See, e.g.*, Marc Galanter, *Reading the Landscape of Disputes: What We Know and Don't Know (And Think We Know) about Our Allegedly Contentious and Litigious Society*, 31 UCLA L. REV. 4 (1983); Marc Galanter, *Real World Torts: An Antidote to Anecdote*, 55 MD. L. REV. 1093

(1996). *See also* Michael J. Saks, *Do We Really Know Anything about the Behavior of the Tort Litigation System—And Why Not,* 140 U. PA. L. REV. 1147 (1992).

179. *See, e.g.,* Robert C. Clark, *Why So Many Lawyers? Are They Good or Bad?* 61 FORDHAM L. REV. 275 (1992); J. Mark Ramseyer, *Lawyers, Foreign Lawyers, and Lawyer-Substitutes: The Market for Regulation in Japan,* 27 HARV. INT'L L.J. 498 (1986).

180. *See Developments—Civil Litigation, supra* note 139, at 1783; Margaret Cronin Fisk, *Now You See It, Now You Don't!* NAT'L L.J., Sept. 28, 1998, at C1.

181. *See* POSNER, ENGLAND AND AMERICA, *supra* note 112, at 72–74, 98–111.

182. *See, e.g.,* MARY ANN GLENDON, A NATION UNDER LAWYERS: HOW THE CRISIS IN THE LEGAL PROFESSION IS TRANSFORMING AMERICAN SOCIETY 37–59, 288–91 (Farrar, Straus & Giroux 1994); SILBER, *supra* note 9, at 213–19.

183. *See* GLENDON, *supra* note 182, at 1–52, 271–381.

184. ANTHONY T. KRONMAN, THE LOST LAWYER: FALLING IDEALS OF THE LEGAL PROFESSION (Belknap Press 1993).

185. SOL M. LINOWITZ & MARTIN MAYER, THE BETRAYED PROFESSION: LAWYERING AT THE END OF THE TWENTIETH CENTURY (Chas. Scribner's Sons 1994).

186. *See, e.g.,* Koniak & Cohen, *supra* note 165.

187. SILBER, *supra* note 9.

188. LINOWITZ & MAYER, *supra* note 185, at 2–3.

189. *Id.* at 2–4.

190. KRONMAN, *supra* note 184, at 109–62, 271–314.

191. The most accessible discussions of agency costs typically have been in the literature on corporate organization. *See, e.g.,* Armen Alchian & Harold Demsetz, *Production, Information Costs, and Economic Organization,* 62 AMER. ECON. REV. 777 (1972); Kenneth J. Arrow, *The Economics of Agency, in* PRINCIPALS AND AGENTS: THE STRUCTURE OF BUSINESS 37, 49–50 (John W. Pratt & Richard J. Zeckhauser eds., Harvard Bus. School 1985); William J. Carney, *Controlling Management Opportunism in the Market for Corporate Control: An Agency Cost Model,* 1988 WIS. L. REV. 385; Frank H. Easterbrook & Daniel R. Fischel, *Close Corporations and Agency Costs,* 38 STAN. L. REV. 271 (1986); Michael C. Jensen & William Meckling, *Theory of the Firm: Managerial Behavior, Agency Costs, and Ownership Structure,* 3 J. FIN. ECON. 305 (1976).

192. This point is also made in GLENDON, *supra* note 182, at 81–82.

193. *Compare* SILBER, *supra* note 9, at 231–41; OLSON, EXPLOSION, *supra* note 59, at 45–48, *with* OLSON, LOGIC, *supra* note 1 (explaining basis for laws' divergence from cost-minimizing ideal); Arrow, *The Economics of Agency,* 37, 43–48 (explaining basis for compensation of lawyers and other agents); Milton Harris & Artur Raviv, *Some Results of Incentive Contracts with Applications to Education and Employment, Health Insurance, and Law Enforcement,* 68 AM. ECON. REV. 20 (1978).

194. *See, e.g.,* Koniak & Cohen, *supra* note 165; John C. Coffee, Jr., & Susan P. Koniak, *The Latest Class Action Scam,* WALL ST. J., Dec. 27, 1995, at 11.

195. *E.g.,* MILTON FRIEDMAN, CAPITALISM AND FREEDOM (Univ. of Chicago Press 1962); Walter Gellhorn, *The Abuse of Occupational Licensing,* 44 U. CHI. L. REV. 6 (1976); Frederick

McChesney, *Commercial Speech in the Professions: The Supreme Court's Unanswered Questions and Questionable Answers*, 134 U. PA. L. REV. 45 (1985); Jonathan Rose, *Occupational Licensing: A Framework for Analysis*, 1979 ARIZ. ST. L.J. 189.

## Conclusion

1. STEPHEN J. BREYER, BREAKING THE VICIOUS CIRCLE: TOWARD EFFECTIVE RISK REGULATION 10–29 (Harvard Univ. Press 1993); W. KIP VISCUSI, FATAL TRADEOFFS: PUBLIC AND PRIVATE RESPONSIBILITIES FOR RISK 248–92 (Oxford Univ. Press 1992); Thomas D. Hopkins, *The Costs of Federal Regulation*, 2 J. REG. & SOC. COSTS 5, 23–24 (1994).

2. *See, e.g.*, Sam Peltzman, *An Evaluation of Consumer Protection Legislation: The 1962 Drug Amendments*, 81 J. POL. ECON. 1049 (1973).

3. *See, e.g.*, WALTER K. OLSON, THE EXCUSE FACTORY: HOW EMPLOYMENT LAW IS PARALYZING THE AMERICAN WORKPLACE (Free Press 1997).

4. *See, e.g.*, William J. Stuntz, *The Uneasy Relationship between Criminal Procedure and Criminal Justice*, 107 YALE L.J. 1, 8–9 (1997) (after examining budget data, declares it "highly unlikely that either police or prosecutors' offices have kept pace with the huge rise in crime since the early 1960s").

5. 18 U.S.C., pt. I (1964).

6. 18 U.S.C., pt. I (1994), Supp. I (1995), Supp. II (1996), Supp. III (1997).

7. *See, e.g.*, JEFFREY H. REIMAN, THE RICH GET RICHER AND THE POOR GET PRISON: IDEOLOGY, CLASS, AND CRIMINAL JUSTICE 101–48 (Allyn & Bacon, 5th ed. 1998).

8. *See, e.g.*, Richard A. Posner, *The Behavior of Administrative Agencies*, 1 J. LEGAL STUD. 305, 311–13 (1972) (explaining rationality of enforcement strategy based on prosecuting weaker defendants).

9. *See, e.g.*, GUIDO CALABRESI, THE COSTS OF ACCIDENTS: A LEGAL AND ECONOMIC ANALYSIS 164–65 (Yale Univ. Press 1970); William M. Landes & Richard A. Posner, *A Positive Economic Analysis of Products Liability*, 14 J. LEGAL STUD. 529 (1985). *But see* George L. Priest, *The Invention of Enterprise Liability: A Critical History of the Intellectual Foundations of Modern Tort Law*, 14 J. LEGAL STUD. 461 (1985). Sometimes courts also have improved the law by deciding that prior decisions had tilted too far in one direction. *See, e.g.*, James A. Henderson & Aaron D. Twerski, *Closing the American Products Liability Frontier: The Rejection of Liability without Defect*, 66 N.Y.U. L. REV. 1263 (1991).

10. *See, e.g.*, George Priest, *The Current Insurance Crisis and Modern Tort Law*, 96 YALE L. J. 1521, 1534–39 (1987).

11. *See, e.g.*, Theodore Eisenberg & James A. Henderson, Jr., *Inside the Quiet Revolution in Products Liability*, 39 UCLA L. REV. 731, 794–95 (1992); Henderson & Twerski, *supra* note 9.

12. *See, e.g.*, Ronald A. Cass, *Damage Suits against Public Officers*, 129 U. PA. L. REV. 1110 (1981); Ronald A. Cass, *Official Liability in America: Actors and Incentives*, in GOVERNMENT LIABILITY: A COMPARATIVE STUDY 110–44 (John Bell & Anthony Bradley eds., British Inst. Int'l Law 1991); Theodore Eisenberg & Stewart Schwab, *The Reality of Constitutional Tort*

*Litigation,* 72 CORNELL L. REV. 641 (1987). *See also* PETER SCHUCK, SUING GOVERNMENT: CITIZEN REMEDIES FOR OFFICIAL WRONGS (Yale Univ. Press 1983); Harold J. Krent, *Preserving Discretion without Sacrificing Deterrence: Federal Governmental Liability in Tort,* 38 UCLA L. REV. 871 (1991).

13. The Alabama court system has come in for particular criticism. Critics note that Alabama judges are elected and their campaigns for judgeships are funded largely by litigants and lawyers. Alabama judges' decisions in tort cases, which critics observe tilting dramatically in favor of plaintiffs, have, in the words of one commentator, made Alabama "the poster child for tort reform." Roger Parloff, *Is This Any Way to Run a Court? Politics and Power at the Alabama Supreme Court,* AM. LWYR, May 1997, at 50, 51. *See also* Dick Thornburgh, *High Noon for Civil Justice Reform,* METROPOLITAN CORP. COUNSEL, Feb. 1996, at 1, *available in* LEXIS, Legnew Lib., Curnws File ("From 1987 to 1993, Alabama courts awarded more than $100 million in punitive damage awards. . . . Such money has recirculated through the political system in Alabama, corrupting both the political and the judicial process. For example, in Alabama, judges routinely accept campaign contributions from lawyers who practice in their courts. Alabama Supreme Court justices have even accepted contributions from lawyers with cases before the court.").

14. *See, e.g.,* FRANKLIN STRIER, RECONSTRUCTING JUSTICE: AN AGENDA FOR TRIAL REFORM 115 (Quorum Books 1994); Peter H. Schuck, *Mapping the Debate on Jury Reform, in* VERDICT: ASSESSING THE CIVIL JURY SYSTEM 306, 311–12 (Robert E. Litan ed., Brookings 1993).

# Index

57–59, 65–71, 72, 150–51; legitimacy and,
18–19; predictability and, 17–18, 65–69;
Supreme Court and, 63–64, 87–88. *See also*
Weak Agency Model of judging

fair certainty of rules, 10–11
Farber, Daniel, 114
Federal Register, 107–8, 109
fidelity: definition of, 4, 5, 158n. 25; to rules,
4–6
*Fitzgerald* case, 43
Fletcher, George, 1
Florida Supreme Court, 91–93, 95
free speech doctrine, 28, 30
Fried, Charles, 175n. 12
Fuller, Lon: on Hart, 4; on inconsistency, 120,
122, 123; on legal system, 10–11, 157–58n.
24; on norms, 175n. 12

generality, 9–10
general welfare: as goal for government
action, 20–22; meaning of, 164n. 100
Gillette, Clayton, 115
Ginsburg, Ruth Bader, 95, 182–83n. 97
Glendon, Mary Ann, 98, 142, 143–44
Gorbachev, Mikhail, 27
Gore, Ira, case: costs of, 126; description of,
116, 124, 139–40; inconsistency and, 129–
30; reaction to, 127, 128
*Gore v. Harris,* 95
Greene, Abner, 82
Gunther, Gerald, 42

Hamilton, Alexander, 88
Hand, Learned, 112–13
hard inconsistency, 120–22
Hart, H. L. A., 4, 12–13
Hassler, William, 100
Hayek, Friedrich, 3, 7, 10–11, 159n. 41
Hitler's rule, 16
Hobbes, Thomas, 20, 157n. 22
holding, 189n. 51
Holmes, Oliver Wendell, Jr., 46, 52–53, 87,
145
Howard, Philip, 100, 102, 104–5
Hughes, Charles Evans, 86
Hugo, Victor, 74–75
Hume, David, 2–3, 7

immunity, official, 39–40, 43–44, 112–13
impeachment: of Clinton, xii–xiii; Constitution and, 44; of Nixon, 35, 36
incentives: for administrators, 104–5, 122; for
judges, 47–48, 49–53, 65–69, 86–87, 89–90;
for jurors, 121–22; for lawyers, 143–44
inconsistency: costs of, 126–30, 149; hard
type, 120–22; in legal interpretation, 84;
overview of, 119; soft type, 122–26
indeterminacy, problem of, 73, 180–81n. 74
individual activities, rules controlling, 159n. 41
inquisitorial systems, 180n. 73
insurance against punitive damages, 128–29,
141
interest group influence, 100
interpretation of legal authority: *Bush v. Gore
(Bush II),* 91–93; chain-novel metaphor,
76–80; common law decision making,
184n. 5; hard cases *vs.* ordinary cases, 77–
80; implications of, 82–85; judgment and,
72–74, 82–83; translation analogy, 74–76;
translation *vs.* composition, 76–77, 80–82
Italy, 30

Japan, 141
Jaworski, Leon, 35
Jefferson, Thomas, 171n. 13
Jim Crow legislation, 25
judges: career advancement of, 51–53; decisions of, 53–59; efforts to influence, 83–84;
incentives for, 47–48, 49–53, 65–69, 86–87,
89–90; inconsistency among, 84; interpretive room, 72–74; as legislators in robes, 47;
limitations on, xiv, 41, 48; misconduct by,
117; official discretion and, 34–35; output
and domain of, 62–65; personal preferences of, 65–66, 89, 91, 95–96; politics and,
47–48, 150; principles followed by, 110–15;
reversal aversion, 50–51; selection and
motivation of, 49, 65–69; as translators of
law, 74–82; trial compared to appellate, 69–
71; visibility of, 52–53
judging: academic theorists and, 150–51;
chain-novel metaphor of, 76–77; models
of, xv–xvi, 46–49; rule-bound conception
of, 68–69, 83, 150–51. *See also* Agency
Model of judging; Partnership Model of
judging; Weak Agency Model of judging